Garden Design Recipes

Design Without the Designer

A Recipe Book for the Garden
With Installation Instructions

Presented by

harden's gardens designs

HardensGardens.com

Written by

April Harden

ISBN 978-1-7342600-0-7

ver 191216

Acknowledgements

*For the one who always "thinks I can" and never gives
up on me even when I do*

Table of Contents

Introduction

The reality of gardening is even a novice can be a successful gardener. Mother Nature has a way of surviving despite our best efforts to thwart her intentions. To improve the odds of success, the key is knowledge. The problem is--as with any subject as broad as horticulture--there is a ton of information. So much, in fact, the internet is full of both information and disinformation. There are videos of supposed experts planting with poor techniques, bad practices and yet still having limited success. There are text books with too much information to filter through to quickly get started. There are also a myriad of specific gardening books on every subject from how to grow a specific plant to how to design an entire landscape. But there doesn't seem to be anything in the middle of these – a quick start guide which provides the information if needed, but not required to plant beautifully designed beds.

Hopefully, this will serve as the medium to the lack of useful information versus an overload of information. Use the reference chapters to learn professional tricks or simply use the recipes to build great gardens. Either way, my hope is to cultivate a love for gardening in this generation and the next and a love for all things outdoors. Happy planting and remember, Green Side Up!

WITI...why is this important?

When it comes to planting and plants, there is a lot of latitude in how you can put it together, however some things are more important than others and those will be highlighted with WITI explanations. These are things which should absolutely be done or not done with particular plants or when planting. Perhaps "absolutely" isn't the proper term. More accurately, these are "best practices" and "for best results".

How to Use This Text

Jump straight to the designs. Peruse the plant index. Read it cover to cover. Reference it while planting. However you use it is the right way to use it. The world is full of people who can and do. It's full of people who can't and want to. It's full of folks who can and don't want to. This book is for everyone except those last folks. If you want to and can't, it's for you too. Gardening is grounding. It's peaceful. It's creation at its finest. Let this text take the stress out of planning your landscape. Follow the directions just like you would when baking a cake. Don't take short cuts or you won't get the desired results. If your budget can't handle a full design, use the design as a master plan and install it as your plant budget permits. If your budget permits labor to install the plants for you, use the designs to get it installed properly.

Chapter 1 A Little Background

My obsession with dirt started when I was but a wee child and 50 years later, the love affair continues. My mother has told a multitude of stories which started with me in Sunday go-to-meeting clothes and ended with dirt in my mouth. In my youth, I spent summers at my grandmother's house. I consumed more than my share of mud pies. I have memories of grandma bent over in the garden pulling weeds, sowing seeds or harvesting vegetables. I watched countless bean sprouts grow in her kitchen window in glass jars of nothing but water. I personally witnessed her rooting a stick. It was then I knew I was hooked on plants. It would be another 20 years before I rooted my first stick and the awe and joy were just as great.

One particular late summer when I was 5 or 6 years old, I vividly remember a day spent with adults canning the garden harvest while chickens (which had just chased me off the swing set last week) were being boiled over an open fire in a giant black kettle in the yard. Grandma snatched them up, yanked their necks and "snap"...yard bird to pot in one smooth motion. I'm sure there was more to it than that, but from my young perspective, that's what it was.

It was our unfortunate job as kids to pluck the feathers away from the slimy, headless carcass of the unlucky chickens. I'd always imagined it to be a better lot to pick, clean, and can vegetables rather than picking and cleaning nasty chicken feathers.

Over the years, I watched grandma manually hoe as well as use a giant tiller to gently coax her bounty from the ground. I could only imagine at the time, a day when I would be able to do that for myself. Ironically, I have had green houses, I have grown flowers, I have grown miscellaneous vegetables in large pots, and I have designed hundreds of gardens of vegetables and flowers for clients, but I have still to this day to have a full spread vegetable garden of my own. Then again, I'm only 50. Counting back the years from when I was a child watching my grandmother in the garden, she was probably around 50 then herself, though in some ways, she was ageless from my childish viewpoint.

From a very young age, I loved being outside. I recall as a preteen hating the way my dad mowed the grass down to the dirt until nothing was left. He wasn't a fan of mowing but somehow, despite his obvious disdain, I found a love for the lawn and how beautifully it could outline tree beds and gardens, how it felt beneath my hair as we watched stars lying in the grass at night, and how it felt beneath my feet as we ran around at dusk collecting lightning bugs.

My mother wasn't an avid gardener either, but grew old-fashioned roses right in the middle of our front yard. Through these roses, I developed my own disdain for their thorns and yet a sense of awe at the delicately formed blooms. I do recall thinking it seemed like an awful lot of work for such a small reward of those few rose blooms she got every summer. Neither of my parents were particularly gifted in the art or craft of gardening when I was younger, but they have taken to it in their retirement. It doesn't change the fact I'm a lifer and, in some ways, feel the hobby chose me instead of me choosing to garden.

Gardening, landscaping, yard work, chores. I've called it all those things. Regardless, when I don my old yard clothes, lace up my muddy boots and asphyxiate myself with bug repellant and sunscreen for a day in the yard, I'm never happier. Although it is work, it's also exercise for the body and meditation for the mind. Mowing grass is mindless and the straight lines in turf heal the soul of the week's stress. Pruning shrubs is artful and peaceful. Planting annuals on hands and dirty knees is cathartic. Finishing my garden tasks and being so dirty I have to disrobe in the garage is my definition of a nearly perfect day.

Today, it is my life's work to help others create beautiful and functional outdoor spaces with interest, color, texture and functionality, but I didn't develop gardening as a hobby until I owned my own house. I did dabble with the occasional summer seeds like beanstalks, watermelons, pumpkins and morning glories. There is something incredibly satisfying about growing a plant from nothing more than seed, soil and water. It's a special kind of nurturing to watch it grow day after day and know you did your part. Then, no matter how small or misshapen, that was the best vegetable I'd ever eaten. It was mine. It is also arrogant to believe much of anything I did to help it along wasn't already in the grand design of the seed itself to survive and grow. There is a lesson in this realization to release control over those things which are out of one's control.

I tried to instill this love for gardening into my own children because forcing beliefs on our children is a hallmark of parenting, no matter how unintentional. Gardening does tend to be a lot of work and although I have had many major milestones (good and bad) in my life including marriage, giving birth to three children, divorce, death, moving, taxes, cancer and survival, there's nothing quite as satisfying and soothing as admiring the handiwork at the end of a long day of yard work. Gardening has always been there for me and I find solace in the change of seasons, the cultivated landscape and the reliability of plants. Gardening is a lot like raising children. It requires care and nurturing, experimenting to get it right, acceptance with set-backs and joy when they flourish. The advantages over child rearing is plants don't talk back, roll their eyes or need to be coaxed to bed every night. They are similar, however, in that every person you meet will tell you how they did it, what they read about it, or how it must be done. The moral of the story is this: find your own way.

Gardening is supposed to be enjoyable. If it's not, it's time to find a new hobby. The second lesson to learn is no matter how many books you read, the solution to your landscaping problem or temperamental plant may not be in the book--any book. Experiment if you must. Find information to help you on your journey and get out there and get digging.

Chapter 2 Where to Start

Outside. If you want to be a gardener, it's best to start outside. A walkabout in the yard is the best place to start. Take notes. Take pictures. Figure out what's there, what's a keeper and what needs to go. On a smaller scale, look at individual planting areas or existing beds. Again, take notes and pictures. Measure the bed length by width. If it's not a perfect square, don't worry. Break the area up into rectangles and measure those, then put the measurements together to get an accurate square footage of the area. Length and width measurements also come in handy when deciding if a plant or grouping will fit in a pre-defined bed.

Think Like a Designer

There is no real right or wrong when designing a new landscape or garden. If it's appealing to the gardener, it's right. However, being armed with a bit of inside information can make the difference between a hodge-podge garden and a professional looking landscape.

The first question I ask as a designer is "What do you want to do with this space?" I could be referring to an entire landscape, a patio area, pool area, or just a flower garden. Without purpose, there's no purpose. Perhaps I don't want to DO anything in particular with the space. Perhaps I just want it clean and neat or nice color or a point of interest. Maybe I want to eat the tomatoes, smell the Jasmine or use the herbs. Or, just want to look out a certain window and see color or texture. I can shade one area while opening up another to bright sunshine. Screen out an unsightly shed or neighbor's mess. Provide some privacy or provoke feelings of well-being and serenity. Ornamental plants, flowers, hardscapes, trees, patios, ponds and lighting can do all these things and so much more.

Outside design is similar to inside design. Good design incorporates colors, textures, openness, coziness, ambiance, lighting, and a functional use of the space. If the plan is to overhaul the entire landscape, it's a good idea to actually have a plan, a design. If the plan is to piddle and add pieces to the landscape a little at a time as money and time allows, it also wouldn't hurt to have some sort of general plan to keep it all simpatico. What follows are a few things which might be considered when creating a new garden or full landscape.

Mind Games

Designers learn tricks of the trade to take a space to the next level. Combinations of textures and colors can highlight areas, create focal points or cover blemishes.

A taller, skinner plant can make a narrow space appear wider. (Figure 1)

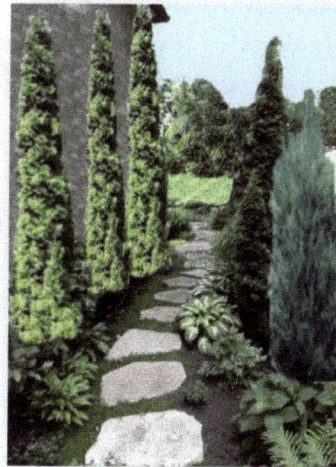

Figure 1

Planting in odd numbers, instead of even numbers (three camellias instead of two or four), creates a grouping by the brain to bring cohesion to an area.

Setting plants and shrubs on an angle to the main focal point leads the brain to group them together, almost as a single large plant to give an area cohesion.

Repeating themes throughout the landscape binds it all together professionally. If there is a red knockout rose in the bed at the mailbox, having more as groupings or focal points in other beds around the landscape tie all the beds together.

Raising an annual bed 12"-18" with soil can make it stand out in the landscape. (Figure 2)

Figure 2

Combining colors, such as red and yellow, in several beds (even if the plants are different), can also tie a full landscape together. If there is a bed to the left of red encore azaleas with yellow reblooming day lily in front, a bed to the right featuring a red-blooming crape myrtle with dapples of yellow Black-Eyed Susan's could provide a similar color palette without repeating the same plants.

Using natural elements instead of man-made elements can make urban areas feel more natural. For example, replace a bench with a garden boulder for seating. (Figure 3)

Figure 3

Adding plants against harsh fences can make the fences disappear into the landscaping.

Painting fences and other harsh, non-natural fixtures black and planting in front of and around the items can make them disappear into the background.

Large groupings of single plants (mass plantings) can create a stunning visual show, especially during bloom season.

A single plant, as a focal point, can make a statement. Placement of these single plants is key. (Figure 4) A stunning single plant such as a specimen Japanese Maple will pull the viewer's eye to this location.

Small plants in a large area can make it look bare. In large,

Figure 4

expansive areas, vary the height of the plants, always placing the taller in the back and tapering down to the smaller plants in the front. This gives the area a relative size for the brain to interpret. By starting tall and moving forward with smaller plants, the brain reduces the size of the area.

Curve lines of shrubs to lead the viewer's eye where it needs to go in the landscape. Nothing in nature is a straight line. Even though fences and property lines tend to be straight lines, create scalloped beds to soften the hard lines.

Soften structures such as houses, sheds and buildings by placing plants on the corners (Figure 5). This is a repetitive theme in home landscaping because it works. Buildings are harsh in nature. Softening the corners with small ornamental trees such as Crape Myrtles or conical evergreens like Emerald Green Arborvitae can blend a house into the landscaping instead of setting it apart as a hard, cold structure.

Always create the beds before adding the plants. Don't plant a bed then attempt to sculpt a bed around it. The results are often undesirable.

Figure 5

If guests usually enter at a side door instead of using the front door, use colorful plants leading to the desired door to pull the eye toward this entrance and make it as welcoming as the front door.

Don't add design elements to undesirable features. A garage door is rarely the desired entrance. Don't add arbors, bright plants, blooming vines or other vibrant plants around or near places which don't need to be highlighted.

If an area is too shady, it's not necessary to remove the trees. Simply thin out the trees in the area by removing lower hanging branches and every third or fourth branch inside the tree to allow more light to penetrate the area. Pruning trees is a job best left to professionals and is money well-spent to open up new planting areas.

Figure 6

Areas without irrigation or too far from a home to be watered by hand can be planted with succulents and highly drought-tolerant plants. (Figure 6)

Remove the confines of a small space such as a deck or small patio by adding narrower plants to corners. This softens the corners and the eye tells the brain the area is not confined.

A grouping of potted plants in a difficult planting area (such as a rocky area) can add texture, color and interest. Choose pots made with different materials, and different shapes and sizes for the most interest.

Chapter 3 Basic Information

Bed Measuring

To get a proper square footage calculation, measure the length of the bed and the width of the bed. Multiply these two numbers and voila, the square footage of the bed. (Figure 7)

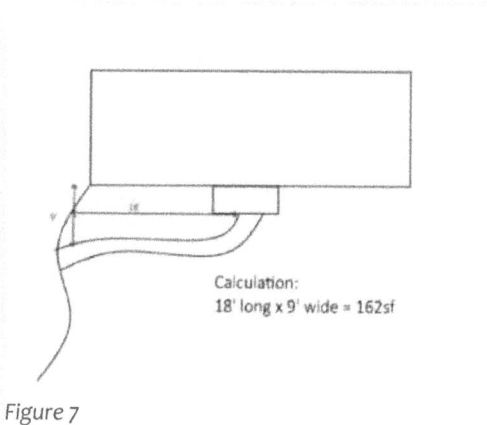

Calculation:
18' long x 9' wide = 162sf

Figure 7

Helpful Calculators

There are a plethora of plant calculators online which can be easily located with the power of the almighty search engine. As a reference and if the old school method is preferred, these calculations will help when calculating bulk materials (soil, mulch, etc.) or plants (flowers, trees, shrubs, etc.)

WITI

Having an accurate measurement of square footage can help calculate plants and bedding materials needed such as annual flowers, pine straw, mulch, turf or additional soil.

Pine Straw Calculation

Pine straw is measured/delivered/sold by the bale. To get an accurate count of what is needed, measure the area, length x width to obtain the square footage. Divide the square footage by 42 for an accurate pine straw count.

Example:
The bed is 10' x 15'. This is 150sf. Divide this number by 42 = 3.57. The bed needs approximately 4 bales of pine straw.

Mulch Calculation

Mulch is typically measured/delivered/sold by the cubic yard (3'x3'x3'). To get an accurate count of what is needed, measure the area, length x width to obtain the square footage. Most mulch is laid at about 2" deep so this shortcut calculation assumes a 2" depth. (If you want a deeper or shallower depth of mulch, use the soil calculation method below). Divide the square footage by 162. This is the number of cubic yards of mulch needed.

Example:
The bed is 10'x15'. This is 150sf. Divide this number by 162 = .92 cubic yards (cuyds). The bed needs roughly 1 cuyds of mulch. If purchasing in bagged mulch, each cubic yard equals about 13 bags. 1 cuyds x 13 bags = 13 bags of mulch.

Soil Calculation

There are 27 cubic feet in a cubic yard (3'x3'x3'). Cubic yards are the common measurement for soil and mulch. Measure the length and width of the bed as in the above examples. This time, you'll need a depth measurement as well. Convert all dimensions into feet by dividing each number by 12 (12 inches). Multiply the length times the width times the depth to get a cubic feet measurement. Divide this result by 27 (the 3'x3'x3' mentioned above) for the final cubic yard result.

Example:

The bed is 10'x15'. The depth is 6". Convert all measurements to feet (6"/12" = 0.5'). Multiply the length x width x depth = 10' x 15' x 0.5' = 75 cubic feet (cuft). Divide 75cuft/27 = 2.8 cubic yards (cuyds). Therefore, you'll need about 3 cuyds of soil for the bed.

Round Planting Bed Calculation

Circles can be challenging to calculate in the landscape. The calculation requires a little geometry. (Figure 8)

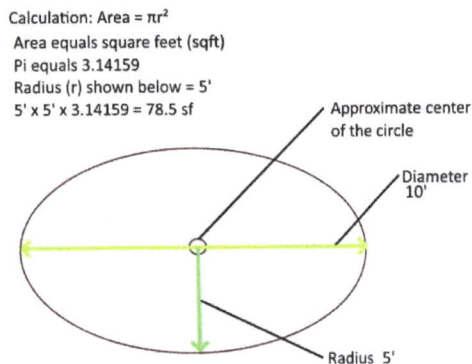

Calculation: Area = πr²
Area equals square feet (sqft)
Pi equals 3.14159
Radius (r) shown below = 5'
5' x 5' x 3.14159 = 78.5 sf

Approximate center of the circle

Diameter 10'

Radius 5'

Figure 8

Find the approximate center of the bed. It's ok if there is a tree or other plant in the center. The measurement from the center to the outer edge is the radius. The measurement all the way across the bed is the diameter. Our calculation only requires radius. However, if it's not possible to get the partial measurement, it is sometimes easier to measure the entire bed and divide by 2.

The formula for the calculation is Area = πr^2. In our example below, the bed is a 10' circle. The radius is then 5'. Pi equals 3.14159 (rounded, of course). The "area" will be the square footage because the two numbers we are multiplying (the radius squared) are both foot measurements. In this case, 5' x 5' = 25sf. Then multiply by 3.14159 = 78.5sf.

Flower Planting Bed Calculations

Planting annuals or perennials professionally requires only basic information. Homeowner's tend to plant the flowers in rows, too far spaced apart. Most Plant Tags for flowers will provide the appropriate distance between plants (typically 8" or 12" between plants). As a professional, we use the term "on center" or OC for short. This means, the distance between plants (whether flowers, shrubs, trees, perennials, etc.) is measured from the center of one plant to the center of the next. The measurement need not be exact, but it can add a professional touch to planting beds if this is followed closely.

Plant on the diagonal, evenly spaced from the center of one plant to the center of the next. The diagonals should line up in both directions, as illustrated by the red arrows and blue arrows.

Figure 9

Flowers should be planted off-set from one another, not in straight rows. (Figure 9)

To calculate the number of flowers, there are charts which can make the activity much simpler.

Table 1

SF of Bed	Plant Spacing – On Center						
	6"	8"	10"	12"	18"	24"	36"
50	200	113	73	50	22	13	6
100	400	225	145	100	44	25	11
150	600	338	218	150	66	38	17
200	800	450	290	200	88	50	22
250	1000	563	362	250	110	63	28
300	1200	675	435	300	132	75	33

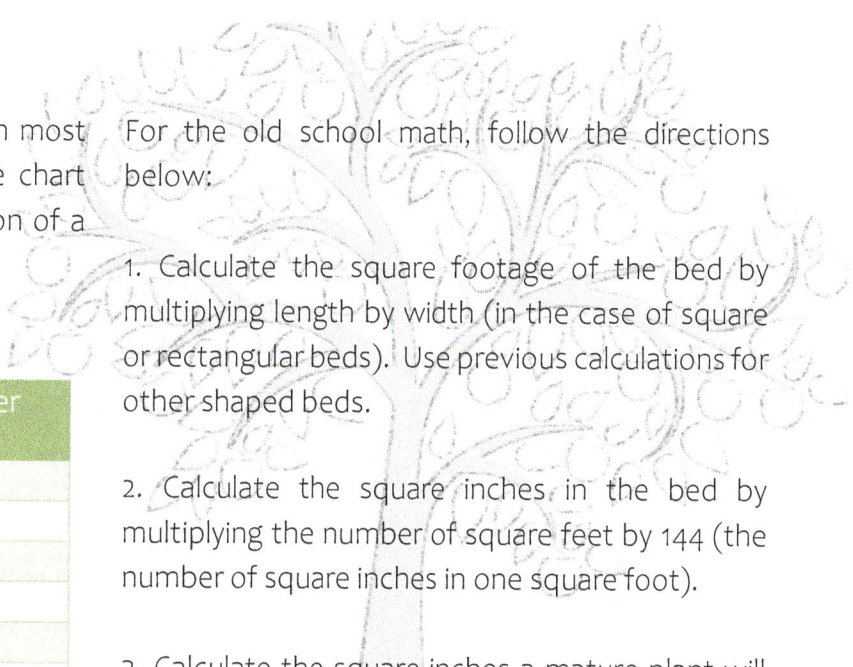

Because the chart isn't always perfect with most exact bed dimensions, there is a separate chart which allows for the simplified multiplication of a multiplier based on plant spacing.

Table 2

Plant Spacing On Centers	Spacing Multiplier (Plants per SF)
6"	4.00
7"	2.94
8"	2.25
9"	1.78
10"	1.45
11"	1.19
12"	1.00
15"	0.64
18"	0.44
24"	0.25
30"	0.16
36"	0.11

To use the charts, first calculate the square footage of the bed by multiplying length times width. Using the information provided with the plant, determine the number of inches the plants should be spaced apart (most annual flower beds are 6", 8" or 12"). If the bed is a nice round number, such as 50sf, Table 1 provides an easy answer. At 6" OC, use 200 plants. At 8", use 113 plants, etc.

If the bed is not a nice round number provided on Table 1, use Table 2 to calculate the number of plants needed.

Example:
The planting bed is 75sf. The plants will be spaced 10" apart.
Multiply 75sf x 1.45 = 108.75
When the result is not an even number, always round up to the next whole plant, in this case, 109 plants.

For the old school math, follow the directions below:

1. Calculate the square footage of the bed by multiplying length by width (in the case of square or rectangular beds). Use previous calculations for other shaped beds.

2. Calculate the square inches in the bed by multiplying the number of square feet by 144 (the number of square inches in one square foot).

3. Calculate the square inches a mature plant will cover by multiplying the number of inches of suggested spacing between plants by itself. If the suggested spacing is 6", multiply 6"x6" = 36"

4. Divide the number of square inches in the bed by the number of square inches required for one plant. This result is the total number of plants needed for that plot.

Example:
The bed is 48sf.
48sf x 144 square inches = 6,912 square inches
The suggested spacing for the flower is 8".
At 8-inch centers, 8 inches x 8 inches = 64 square inches for each plant.
At 8-inch centers, 6,912 square inches ÷ 64 square inches = 108 plants.

To say the least, the two tables provided are a much easier way to quickly calculate the number of plants needed.

Plant Tags

Plant Tags are the fastest and easiest way to get the information you need to successfully plant a particular plant. Yes, the internet is a great resource but reality says, there are many different **cultivars** of the same plant being sold and growing in your area.

With the Plant Tag, you know the exact plant you're dealing with and have the basic information to get it in the ground quickly and successfully. (Figure 10)

The Plant Tag can vary based on the nursery where it was grown, but the basic information is usually about the same:

Plant Name
(Common Name)
Scientific Name
'Cultivar Name in Single Quotes'
Plant Photograph
Brief Description
Plant needs and characteristics

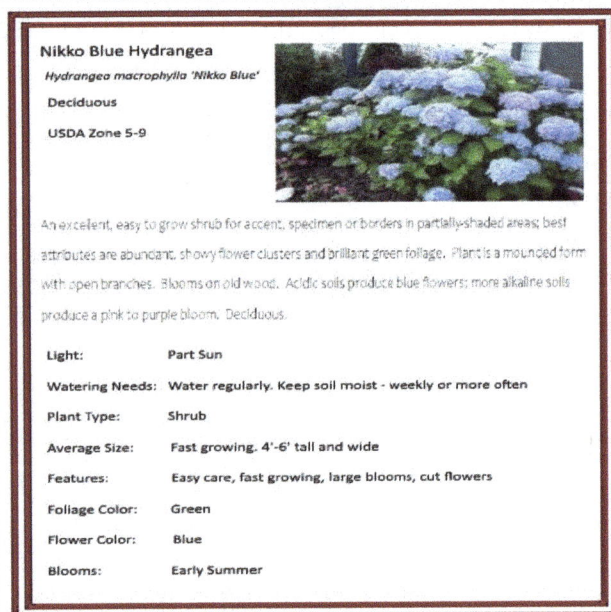

Nikko Blue Hydrangea
Hydrangea macrophylla 'Nikko Blue'
Deciduous
USDA Zone 5-9

An excellent, easy to grow shrub for accent, specimen or borders in partially-shaded areas; best attributes are abundant, showy flower clusters and brilliant green foliage. Plant is a mounded form with open branches. Blooms on old wood. Acidic soils produce blue flowers; more alkaline soils produce a pink to purple bloom. Deciduous.

Light:	Part Sun
Watering Needs:	Water regularly. Keep soil moist - weekly or more often
Plant Type:	Shrub
Average Size:	Fast growing. 4'-6' tall and wide
Features:	Easy care, fast growing, large blooms, cut flowers
Foliage Color:	Green
Flower Color:	Blue
Blooms:	Early Summer

Figure 10

WITI

Cultivars are different varieties of the same plant, an abnormality which was then cultivated or an intentional cultivation of a different set of specifications (such as color or shape or height) for a particular plant. As an example, Encore Azaleas come in many cultivars such as 'Autumn Princess' and 'Autumn Coral'. Although the basic shape and size are the same, the colors are different. Crape Myrtles come in cultivars like 'Tonto' which is a dwarf Crape Myrtle, meaning it only grows to about 15' instead of the taller cultivars which can grow to 35' or taller. If the cultivar of the plant isn't known, it can be a challenge to properly place and plant. However, if you don't have a tag to help you, you can always search the basic plant (such as Crape Myrtle) and use the characteristics you can see (like bloom color) to help narrow it down.

Based on the information on the tag, this plant needs shade, moist soil and can grow to 6' tall and wide. With this small amount of information, placement in the landscape is easy and the plant has an excellent chance of survival.

Soil Test

A soil test is a scientific test in which the contents of the soil are analyzed for the purpose of adding the proper amendments to create an ideal planting area. Simply stated, not all soil is created equal. A soil's pH and nutrient level can determine how well plants or turf will grow or if they will grow. Scientifically, pH is a measure of the alkalinity of the soil. Soil can be corrected to be more acidic or less acidic by the addition of potash or lime, depending on what the soil test shows. Basic nutrient deficiencies can also be corrected based on the results of the soil test with all purpose or selective fertilizers.

Most garden centers sell do-it-yourself soil test kits. However, the easiest way to test the soil, by far, is to dig up about 2 cups of soil, put it in a clean paper bag and take it to the local extension office. The almighty search engine can find the closest extension office to your location. The test takes a week or two and the extension office will mail out the results. It is an easy-to-read form, but some of the terminology may be puzzling. Once the soil test is in hand, any reputable garden center can read the results and recommend the best course of action for amending the soil.

Budgeting

Plants cost money. Bed mulching costs money. Install labor costs money. Do-it-yourself also costs money, in the form of your time and ability. Make a plan, with budget in mind, for what you are able and willing to do versus what you'll need to pay to have done. Another part of budgeting is to make sure the plant fits the space. Although some nurseries accept returns for deceased plants, digging out failed plants, returning and exchanging them and planting the new one all takes time, and in another sense, money. It's always best to prevent your plants from failing. This not only saves your budget, it saves time, effort and sanity.

Drainage

Drainage is one of the most important aspects of any landscaping plan. It's a simple concept, but few builders and fewer homeowners ever plan for the diversion and capturing of run off and rain water until there is an issue. The basics of drainage are to look for evidence of water which is not being diverted away from the foundation, standing water, eroded areas from running water, divots under gutters (indicating gutter spill over), AC condensate build up (soggy soil or turf), negative slope at the foundation (soil slopes back towards house), or drainage fields which have become eroded and ineffective. Most of these items are easily correctable. "Easily" is a relative term, because most of the solutions require digging deep trenches, laying pipe and exiting water to

WITI

It's best to get a sample of soil from different locations in the landscape. Just because one bed is heavy on nitrogen, another may be deficient. Don't combine samples. Soil testing is relatively inexpensive. Test several areas to get an accurate picture of the soil in your landscape. Also note for the examiner what the bed will be used for (flowers, turf, trees, etc.).

specified areas without causing further problems for neighbors, drainage easements, or your own property. This might be a good time to call a professional and have your property evaluated for drainage issues. The advantage to tackling drainage first is you (or a contractor) won't have to dig up your plants or beds after you've installed them to rectify drainage issues.

Dirt matters

Basically, clay soils are hard to wet with very fine particles, but once clay is wet, it holds moisture for a long period. Sandy soils have large particles and water tends to run through these soils quickly and therefore hold very little water for future use (Figure 11).

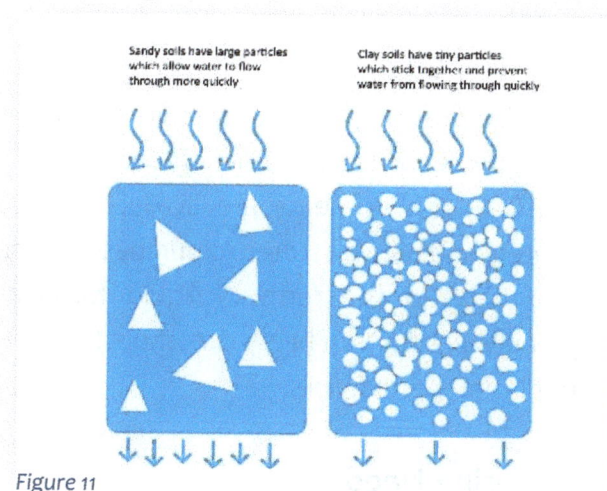

Sandy soils have large particles which allow water to flow through more quickly

Clay soils have tiny particles which stick together and prevent water from flowing through quickly

Figure 11

Different plants have different needs related to soil. The Plant Tag is the place to start when deciding where to place a plant. The soil test is the next line of defense as it can explain the type of soil which exists in the bed.

If the soil in the desired planting bed has no nutrients, is incompatible with a desired planting, is full of roots or rocks or is otherwise undesirable, it is wise to amend the soil. However, it is a best practice to amend the entire planting bed, not just the individual hole.

To amend an entire planting beds involves tilling the soil currently in the bed then shoveling out the entire area to a depth of 6". Keep in mind, based on the size of the bed, this could be a very large amount of soil which needs to go somewhere else. It is also time consuming to amend entire planting bed with new soil. Unless there are no other options available for a particular plant or garden bed, it's best to choose plants which thrive in the soil which is already located in the bed.

It is also possible to use the results of the soil test to add the corrective amendments to the bed. Most lacking nutrients are available at garden centers and big box stores to purchase and spread into beds in the form of liquid formulations, granular products or bagged, composted materials to till into existing soils.

> **WITI**
>
> It is not necessary to amend the soil with new soil when planting, unless a soil test has otherwise advised. This hole is the plant's new home. If there is delicious, nutritious soil only in the hole, the roots will stay in the hole. A healthy plant needs to spread its roots beyond the hole and into the surrounding soil.

Watering Needs

Watering seems to be the most confusing aspect of gardening.

Basically, all plants need water. How they get the water is from irrigation, rain or hand watering. How much water a particular plant needs depends on the plant and specific plant information is located on the Plant Tag.

Most established landscape plantings require very little extra watering above and beyond rain. If uncertainty arises as to whether a plant has enough water, there is an elaborate test to figure it out: stick a finger in the soil and see how moist it is. There are some tell-tale signs of wilting when a plant needs water. There are also signs when a plant has had too much water (such as yellowing or dropping leaves).

Knowing a plant's watering needs can save more than a plant's life. Irrigation water is expensive, so over watering wastes both money and water.

A good watering is one where a plant has been watered gently for a long period to allow water to soak deep into the roots. Hand-watering with a watering can or hose is the most controlled method of watering. Unfortunately, most home irrigation systems aren't set up to water different types of plants at a different rate. The turf usually receives just as much water as the annual beds. A good rule of thumb is one inch of water per week. Turf and grasses require less water. Annuals and perennials may require more water. New plantings require more water more frequently than established plantings.

> **WITI**
>
> An established plant is one which has been growing in a landscape for at least one season (a full summer, a full spring, etc.). The watering needs of these plants is less than those of plants recently planted.

To measure for an inch of water, set an empty tuna can near the bed being watered and begin watering. When the can is full, one inch of water has been achieved. When using a hose and watering by hand, be sure to use a spray head. Don't apply water directly from the hose. This method applies too much water at once and most of the water will be wasted to run off. Different soils have the ability to absorb and hold water at different rates. The soil test can advise regarding soil types.

Dig an 18" deep and wide hole.
Fill hole with water.
Note how long it takes for water to drain from the hole.

Figure 12

As with watering, water drainage is important. Even if a plant only receives one inch of water a week, if the soil will not drain the water, the plant's roots will be prone to rotting in the wet hole. If the soil drains too quickly, the plant may not be able to access the water before it drains away. (Figure 12). Clay soils are composed of very fine particles which hold tightly together therefore letting very little water between the particles. Compacted clay has been further compressed and the fine particles stick together to a point of not allowing water to pass through.

When compacted clay soils are tilled, air gets up between the particles and allows water to pass. However, the particles will once again become compacted over time. The best solution is to amend the soil with a sandy mix. Sandy soils have large particles which leave air gaps between them. By mixing the small and large particles, the soil will not be as likely to compact.

One way to tell if a particular soil is draining too quickly or not draining at all is to dig a hole. Dig down about 18" deep and 18" wide. Pour water inside the hole with a bucket or hose, filling the hole to the top. If the hole is free from standing water in a matter of a few minutes, the soil is sandy and is draining quickly. If an hour has passed and very little (or no) water has left the hole, the soil is compacted clay and will not drain. The best solution to either problem is to dig out the bed and amend the soil with the opposite. If it is too sandy, add clay and blend the two soils together with a tiller, thus having to only remove about half the soil from the bed. If it has too much clay (or is compacted), remove soil and add a sandy soil and till together to blend.

The watering system chosen for an area is usually based on time, money and motivation. Underground irrigation systems are costly to install and maintain but save valuable time when watering (as most have automatic timers). Hand watering is cumbersome and requires hoses, spray heads and copious amounts of time to stand in the garden and water, not to mention the motivation to get out there and do it. However, it is the most efficient and saves money by not overwatering plants or watering areas (such as driveways) with over spray from irrigation systems.

The water source should also be considered. Most homeowners water from a hose or irrigation system tied to the home's water supply. Unfortunately, city water is quite costly.

Another option is to have a separate irrigation meter installed which only feeds the irrigation system or outside spigots. This too is elaborately expensive and requires a master plumber for the connections.

Well water is also utilized and if a well is already present, it is an excellent water source for the landscape as it hasn't been filtered of nutrients like City water. However, having a well installed is quite cost prohibitive for the average landscape use.

Lastly, recaptured rain water is an economical way to water but does require a tank system to hold the water and a pump system to utilize the stored water. Rain barrels at the end of

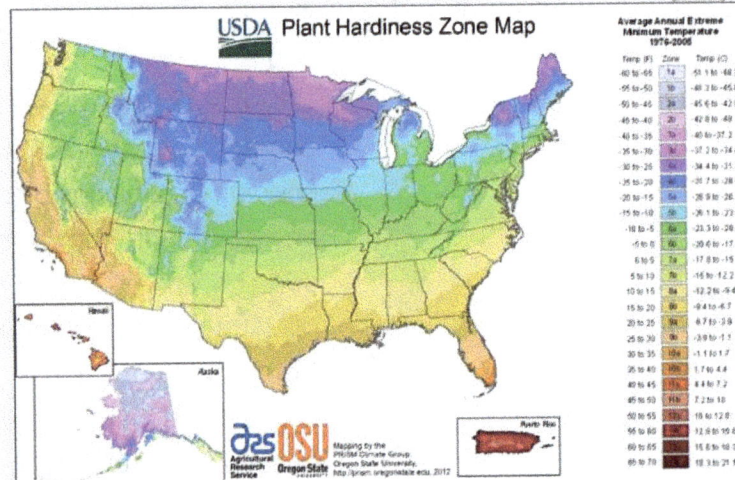

Figure 13

downspouts can economically capture water and can be tapped at the base to force water out to a hose. The user is limited by the distance from the barrel which can be watered before there isn't enough pressure in the hose, and the standing water can breed mosquitos.

Sun or Shade

Light plays a critical role in the development and health of a plant. Placement in too much sun or shade is a primary mistake gardeners make. It is also imperative to understand whether a plant can tolerate afternoon sun or if it's required. Pay attention to how much sun different parts of the desired planting area receives throughout the day before planting. Make note of where the sun rises and sets and where the shady and sunny spots are at different times of the day. The geographically challenged, as I am, can download a map app to show which way is north. The sun then rises in the east and sets in the west. Make note of which side is the north side and which is the south. These notations could not only help with knowing where to plant a plant, but also how much water it will need.

Know the Zone

Planting zones have been developed to help determine which plants will grow in which areas.

According to the USDA website, the "USDA Plant Hardiness Zone Map is the standard by which gardeners and growers can determine which plants are most likely to thrive at a location. The map is based on the average annual minimum winter temperature, divided into 10-degree F zones." (Figure 13)

If there is a question regarding a particular area, the website has an interactive feature which allows the user to enter their specific zip code to obtain the accurate zone.

Typically, the Plant Tag will identify a zone range a particular plant will grow within without suffering or loss during winter months. Plant nurseries and garden centers do not always only carry plants for a particular zone where located. Most tropical plants are not suited to zone 7 yet they are sold in zone 7. The reasoning is the plants can be brought inside in the winter or used as annuals and a new plant replanted in subsequent years. If the intention is to plant directly to the ground and keep the plant for many years, the USDA Zone Map is critical information.

Plan for Eventual Plant Size

Plants always start small and grow. The eventual size is usually classified on the Plant Tag. It's important to realize a plant which is 2' tall and wide when purchased may grow to be 6' tall and wide at maturity and therefore outgrow the area for which it was intended. In this case, the plant will either have to be removed or constantly pruned and nurtured to keep it at the desired size. To avoid unnecessary maintenance and disappointment, and possibly having to remove and discard the plant, always measure and select plants based on their mature dimensions. It is perfectly acceptable to buy a plant larger than the space allotted as long as the knowledge and expectation exists it will need to be contained and controlled as long as it exists in the garden space.

Measuring for plant height and width is an easy proposition and requires only a tape measure. As an example, a hedgerow needs to be installed at the foundation bed against the house. Using a tape measure, measure from the soil to the maximum height desired. This is usually determined by the bottom of the window sill. Typically, homeowners do not like the plants to cover more than the bottom third of the window at the front of the house. This isn't a hard and fast rule, only a guideline.

The measurement is for a maximum height of 4' and five shrubs are desired on either side of the door. Each side of the door is 30'. Divide the number of shrubs desired by the measurement, which is 30' ÷ 5 = 6' maximum width. The shrubs would need to expand to 6' wide in order to accommodate five plants in a 30' space.

Assuming the measurement is 30' but the number of plants isn't known, the height of the plant can be used as a guide to finding the proper shrub. Most plants which would serve as a proper hedge grow as wide as tall. A 4' tall shrub would likely be about 4' wide also. There are plenty of exceptions, but this is a good rule of thumb. The calculation would be 30' ÷ 4' = 7.5, which is the number of plants needed. It is better for the eye to plant in odd numbers, so the row needs 7 plants spaced 4.25' apart (30' ÷ 7 = 4.28').

Know the eventual mature size for best results, less maintenance and overall homeowner and plant simpatico.

Use of Space

It is a common misconception that every square inch of a landscape should have a planting. Open space can provide its own sense of serenity as well. Natural areas can provide room for natural walking paths or doggie business zones. Keeping the natural underbrush under control (weeds, briars, volunteer saplings) can make a natural area neat, clean and inviting. There are many liquid forms of weed and underbrush control available for use at local garden centers. Open turf areas provide run and play areas for children and pets. Open recreation and entertaining areas, free of plants, can allow free movement in the landscape for guests at parties and gatherings.

Planted beds can range from all perennial, all evergreen shrubs, all annuals and combinations of the three to infinity. Consideration for what a bed will look like during all four seasons can make a difference in the landscape. Planting all deciduous or perennial plants in the beds can leave them bare in the winter, without interest or color for a good part of the year. Conversely, choosing all evergreens and conifers for the bed could leave it without color throughout the spring and summer.

When deciding on the use for a particular space, keep in mind the time of year it is most likely to be used. Fire pits aren't much fun in the boiling heat of summer so ideally, the plantings in this area should focus on spring and fall bloomers and winter color and texture. A swimming pool isn't typically used in the late fall through mid-spring. Use plantings around this area which focus on spring bloomers and summer color. Parking and walking areas need to be unhindered by plants with thorns or stickers to avoid the scratching of vehicles or snagging of people or clothing. This theory also applies to play areas. Keep kids safe by avoiding plants which poke around trampolines, play sets, sand boxes or other play areas. Using plants as natural barriers instead of fences often opens up an area to make it feel less confined. Densely packed shrubs like hollies or Ligustrum can prevent wayward balls from getting away down steep hills.

When placing ornamental trees, consider the full mature height of the tree and the area which it over-hangs. Plants which readily discard seeds, sap, fruit, sticks and leaves should be avoided over outdoor kitchens and swimming pools to avoid unnecessary maintenance. Conifers should be kept far away from fire pits to avoid accidental ignition of their needles. The sap from many conifers is also highly flammable.

Maintenance

The one part of the plan most homeowners seem to forget is the maintenance. To maintain a garden, there is a price to pay in terms of free time, exertion and motivation to spend time cleaning, pruning, mowing and weeding. Fewer plants in a larger area allows for the use of chemical weed treatments without fear of harming plants. Densely packed plantings require manual weeding (by hand) to avoid damage to plant and tree roots. Turf areas require mowing on at least a bi-weekly basis. With a little planning, and a lot of mulch, maintenance and weeding needs can be reduced. Using low maintenance plants and placing the right plant in the right place at the right size can also reduce the need for excessive pruning and maintenance.

Picking Plants

The garden center can be a daunting place without foreknowledge of what type of plant is needed. There is no cause to be so rigid about a particular plant that no other cultivar could substitute in the absence of the desired plant. Growers change cultivars and variety regularly to keep gardeners coming back for the latest and greatest version of their plants. Unfortunately, the internet nor printed resources can keep up with the many changes as they happen and some plants just may not be available to purchase.

The most important characteristics of a plant are the right sun/shade, the right water, the right size and the correct zone. Color, texture and shape can be mitigated by having several choices for the bed when headed out to the nursery or garden center.

Annual versus Perennial

Annuals are plants which don't survive the winter season in the area you're growing them. Perennial plants come back again after the winter season and remain dormant during winter. These terms relate to flowers and flowering shrubs.

Deciduous versus Evergreen

A deciduous shrub is one which loses its leaves over the winter months and sits dormant until the ground temperature has risen to support new growth. This could include trees or shrubs. An evergreen is a plant which retains its leaves and color throughout the winter season in a state of dormancy, although there are plants which thrive in cold weather and even bloom during the winter months. Most hardwood trees are deciduous. Christmas trees (fir, spruce, cedar) are evergreen conifers. To convolute the distinction, some plants are semi-deciduous like Abelia and a few azaleas. They retain some of their leaves during the winter but do shed leaves and go dormant during the cooler months.

Shade, Part Shade, Mostly Sun, Full Sun

Two things I learned in school when becoming a horticulturist: "green side up", and "right plant, right place". The distinction between how much sun a plant can take is very convoluted. Sometimes a plant can take full sun but not in the afternoon. Sometimes a plant needs the full blast of the afternoon sun. Some plants can't take any sun, but that's not 100% accurate either because plants need light to produce food. In the case of plant placement for the correct amount of sunlight, it's best to consult the Plant Tag or invoke the power of the almighty search engine.

Mulching

Mulching is the simplest and best way to protect a landscape investment. Mulch protects plants roots during winter, retains water during summer heat and deters weed growth throughout the year. Leaving bare soil in a landscape is the biggest mistake a gardener can make. Every time rain or watering occurs across bare soil, a tiny amount of that soil is carried away with the water. Over time, the top soil is depleted, rocky soil is exposed and underlying beds become inert and unable to support plant or turf growth. Bare soil is also an invitation to weeds and mosses to thrive.

Different parts of the country use different mediums as mulch.

Shredded Hardwood Mulch

Hardwood mulches are an exceptionally effective mulching product. (Figure 14) These are typically hard wood which has been shredded then dyed red, black or brown or left natural.

Hardwood mulch packs tightly on the ground to deter weed development and is more difficult to blow away when maintaining the yard with a leaf

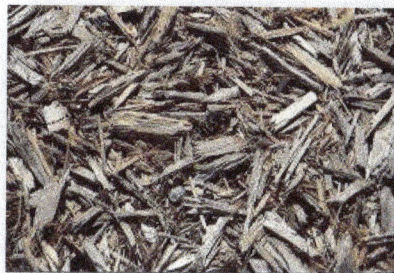

Figure 14

blower. These mulches are attractive and neat in landscaping beds and decompose at a slow rate. The rate of coverage should be 4" thick for best results and reapplied annually. The down side to hardwood mulch is it decomposes to soil, which can raise a bed over several seasons which may need to be dug out to prevent smothering tree or plant roots.

Pine Mulch

Many tree companies offer free mulch delivered to homeowners. This mulch is a combination of pine and hardwood with miscellaneous debris mixed in. (Figure 15) It is typically not dyed and will cover large areas economically. It also packs tightly to deter weed development and is less likely to be blown away with a leaf blower. The down side to pine/miscellaneous mulch is it is not very attractive in cultivated beds, contains spores

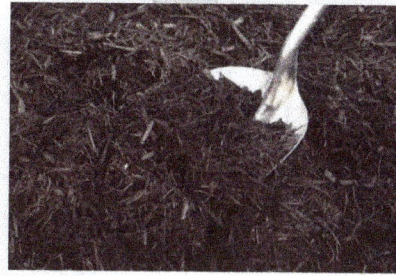

Figure 15

which germinate into oddly shaped fungi and contains a lot of debris. Use of this mulch is also recommended at a depth of 4" and should also be reapplied annually. The best use for this mulch is natural paths and woodland gardens.

Pine Bark

Pine bark is an effective mulch for plants and flower beds (Figure 16). Use "mini" nuggets for smaller plants and "large" nuggets for larger beds. Pine bark is very light weight and prone to floating away during heavy rain fall. It is also very easy to blow away when maintaining an area with a leaf blower. The cost is equivalent to shredded hard wood mulches and needs the same 4" depth for most effective weed deterring. Pine bark decomposes at a faster rate than hardwood mulches so reapplication is required two times per year.

Figure 16

Pine Straw

Figure 17

Pine straw is an attractive and effective mulch for plants and flower beds. (Figure 17) It is relatively inexpensive compared to hardwood mulches but decomposes faster and requires reapplication two times per year. The benefits of pine straw to protect roots and prevent weeds is equivalent to that of hardwood mulch, but it is easier to blow away with maintenance using a leaf blower.

Egg Rock, Pea Gravel or Volcanic Rock

Figure 18

Figure 19

Rock is an effective mulch for plants and flower beds. (Figures 18, 19) It is expensive to purchase and install compared to organic mulches but requires only one application at a 3"-5" depth. Rock doesn't decompose but will become discolored with soil, algae or moss over time. A low chlorine solution bath from a low-pressure hose can mitigate some of the discoloration. Use caution when using chlorine solutions around plant roots.

Smaller rocks have a tendency to migrate from planting beds, causing a hazard to windows when mowing. A 2"–4" size egg rock is the most effective rock bed covering to provide protection against erosion and a lower likelihood of being accidentally blown out of a bed by a leaf blower when maintaining the area.

No Turf? No Problem

All grass is full sun grass, despite what seed and turf companies say. Afterall, they are selling seed and turf. There are varieties of seed and turf which are more shade tolerant than others, but generally, turf areas are for sunny areas. The lowest tolerance level for certain Bermuda, Zoysia and Fescue turfs is 4-5 hours and this only applies to specific varieties of the different turfs. As a general rule, an area should have a minimum of 6-8 hours of full sun for thick, luscious turf.

Shady yards are one of the most difficult design challenges for landscapers and homeowners. For those who don't want to remove trees to reveal more sun, the obvious answer is artificial turf. It is both beautiful and durable but for the average homeowner, restrictively expensive. Artificial turf is a basic 10:1 cost ratio over live turf. For example, if a Bermuda turf installation is $1,000, the same in artificial turf would cost $10,000. Although this isn't a perfect calculation for all situations, it is a good estimate for most installations of turf.

If the area is too shady for turf, there are alternatives to a grassy area. An open area relative to a turf area can still be incorporated into a design and different mulching or groundcover mediums can be used to emulate the lawn. The best type of plant to emulate lawn is dwarf Mondo grass. It is a very low ground cover which stays very low and is walkable without harm to the plant. It grows well in shade and after established, requires little additional watering. The downside is Mondo grass grows very slowly so it would require quite a few plants and take time for the mounded clumps to grow together to form a lawn.

Other ideas could be to emulate the lawn with mulch, stone, pine straw, rubber mulches or other aggregates. The outer beds can be covered with one medium (i.e., pine straw) and the turf areas can be defined with a different medium (i.e., brown shredded mulch). Although not turf, it still provides an open area for play, entertaining or other recreational activities.

Design Elements

Design elements are focal points, interesting finds, yard art, tin, sculptures or other elements which are not plants or hardscapes. (Figure 20) These elements add interest to the garden. Pink Flamingos qualify as do flying pigs. Design elements are a touch of whimsy in between good design. These items let the world know this little patch of dirt is spoken for and has been infused with personality.

Figure 20

Where design elements are concerned, usually less is more. Too much stuff tends to be too much. Strategically placing design elements can bring interest to an existing garden or be the lynch pin to create a new one.

When creating whimsical, themed gardens or beds, consider incorporating bird houses or baths, solar gazing balls, sun dials, whirly gigs, posts or columns, fountains or bubbler pots.

Design elements can also work outside the lines of traditional design. Short sections of fence set inside a garden can provide a back drop. A "gate to nowhere" can provide a focal point in an otherwise bland area. Strategically placed boulders can provide height and interest to beds without plants or ground covers. A lighted decorative column can not only illuminate a dark area, but also provide interest and ambiance to the landscape.

Design Don'ts

Once the rules of design are known, the rules can be broken. There are thousands of creative ways to design planting beds, add design elements and think outside the box when it comes to gardening and landscaping. However, there are some hard and fast rules which should be minded for best results:

Don't water in the mid-day heat. It isn't good for the water bill or the plant.

Don't murder Crape Myrtles by "knuckling" or excessive pruning each year (Figure 21). Home gardeners will prune their Crape Myrtles every year because they see others do it and assume it is correct. Crape Myrtles are trees. Unless there is a reason the tree must remain smaller (growing into power lines or interfering with a roof-line or gutters, etc.), the tree should be allowed to grow into a tree.

Don't top evergreen conifers or cut back past green growth. Conifers such as arborvitaes, spruces, cryptomeria or juniper don't grow in the same manner as hardwood trees such as maples, poplars or redbuds. If the tree is topped, it will not grow back. If the limb is cut back past the green growth, it will also not grow back.

Never use weed cloth. Don't do it. It doesn't prevent weeds, it's expensive and it is a pain to remove later when it hasn't controlled the weeds.

Don't plant trees in rings which constrict the tree's root growth to a small area.

Don't add tree rings which sit on an existing tree's root system. This damages the existing root system and promotes the piling

Improper Pruning   Proper Crape Myrtle
"Crape Murder"   In Tree Form

Figure 21

up of mulch too far up the trunk of the tree (which smothers the tree).

Never create mulch volcanoes around trees. (Figure 22, 23) Always keep the mulch to a

Never pile mulch up the trunk of a tree.

Figure 22

Tapered portion of base of tree should be visible above mulch

Mulch should not exceed 6" and never be piled up base of tree

Figure 23

maximum of 6" and never pile it up around the trunk of the tree. This will slowly smother the tree.

Don't plant too close to houses, AC units, fences, power lines, etc. Plants grow. If they interfere with the gutters, power lines or other house systems, the plant will have to be endlessly pruned or eventually removed.

Don't plant on top of irrigation or utility lines. Plant roots can interfere with the normal operation of irrigation systems, water lines, cable lines, etc. and can lead to costly future repairs.

Don't plant trees with invasive roots next to driveways, sidewalks and foundations (i.e., Maples). Tree roots penetrate slowly but can raise and damage streets, driveways and walks as well as house foundations.

Don't plant deciduous trees or shrubs next to ponds or pools. These are trees and shrubs which lose their leaves in the fall. This is a big don't. Tree leaves not only fill pool filters and ponds with decaying debris, they can also damage the filtration systems and this leads to endless maintenance to prevent damage.

Don't plant turf in the shade. Grass is a full sun plant. At a minimum, plant with 6 hours of full sun per day.

Chapter 4 Planting 101

I love hard-luck plants. By hard-luck, I mean the one at the big box nursery which didn't get the TLC it needed and it's now on clearance, barely clinging to life, at 75% off retail. To heck with what it is, it is in need and I'm on a budget. I dare say this is how many of my favorite gardens got their start in my own landscape.

> **WITI**
>
> *This is the part where there is too much information. Plant science is vast. A literal ton of text books provide any information wanted regarding the exact way photosynthesis works, how roots absorb water and nutrients, transpiration, respiration and an entire discipline of how plants grow. However, the goal here is to provide pertinent information to get started quickly and reference as needed. Consult the power of the almighty search engine for more in-depth information into the world of plant science.*

Many plants are most resilient. Given the proper nutrients, sunlight and water, even hard-luck plants can recover and thrive in the landscape. Giving a plant the right start, in the right place is of monumental importance.

Plants need three things to be successful: sunlight, water, nutrients. Plants are resilient and even if neglected, can be recovered when the proper ingredients are provided. Where a plant is placed is the most important factor in its eventual success. Too much sun burns. Too little starves. If the area is too wet for a particular plant, it will be drowned. If it's too dry, it will thirst to death. If the soil has no nutrients (the most important being nitrogen, phosphorous and potassium), no matter how much love you give it, it will not survive.

Every plant has different nutrient needs and the only way a plant can use those nutrients is if they are present in the soil and there is sufficient water so the plant can take up the nutrients through the root system.

Always place plants based on the information on the Plant Tag. Just because a bed isn't sunny, it doesn't mean it can't be beautiful with a different set of plants. Forcing sun plants into shade areas always disappoints. The rule of thumb is "Right Plant, Right Place" for the most success in the landscape.

Professional landscapers use a set of "best practices" to not only place plants in the proper place, but also to ensure the plant has the best chance of survival. Properly digging the hole, providing the right nutrients and placing plants properly are the best way to ensure success.

Digging A Hole

"Any fool can dig a hole." These were the famous last words of a previous landscaping crew member. Yes. Any fool can dig a hole if you want a hole dug like a fool. I prefer a proper hole. In life, there are also plenty of holes we've dug. Asking that sales clerk when the baby is due…never a good idea. The best way to get out of those holes is to, of course, stop digging. In gardening, as with life, there is a time to stop digging.

The most common mistake folks make when digging a hole is digging it too deep and not wide enough. Plants need room to spread their roots and grow. If the hole is too tight, this just promotes the roots to continue growing in a circle resembling the container from which it started.

A "proper" hole is simple. Without a lot of fluff, it is basically a hole which is twice as wide as the root ball and as deep as the root ball. (Figure 24)

As the hole is dug, turn over the soil with the shovel while it is still in the hole and chop up any large clumps with the shovel. After the soil is mostly free of clumps, remove it from the hole and set it aside and take out the next shovel full of soil. It is much easier to manipulate the soil while it's in the hole than it is to try and chop it up after it's out of the hole. This method saves the soil and creates much less mess to clean up after planting.

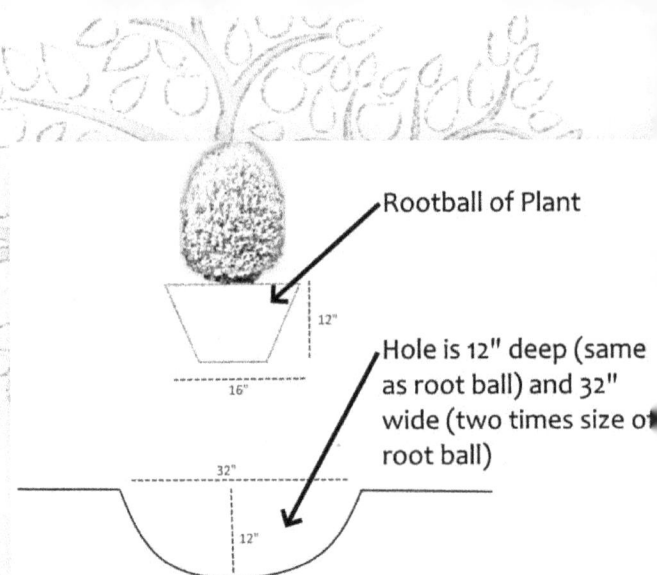

Figure 24

The Moment of Truth

Once all the soil needed is removed from the hole, it's time for the piece de resistance, planting the plant. Again, not difficult, but with a little care, the plant will root, thrive, bloom, repeat, year after glorious year.

When planting, add a little all-purpose fertilizer to the finished hole, place the plant gently, making sure it's straight, then replace the soil which was removed. Tamp the soil with the shovel, a booted foot or gloved hands to create a snug fit with the soil. Always water gently after planting to help remove any trapped air inside the soil. Roots only grow in soil, not in air so getting rid of air pockets can make a difference in how well the plant roots and ultimately thrives.

All Things Considered

We all have things in our life, over time, we wish we'd handled differently. I've had some amazing opportunities in my life as I'm sure we all have. For those who can't see they've had amazing opportunities, here's some insight I've learned from gardening: it's cliché, but you have to bloom where you're planted. Spread your roots wherever you happen to be. It's ok to want for a different place, a different circumstance, a better life, but until the opportunity or ability to change your current situation comes along, grow and thrive where you've been placed. This is exactly what we want for our plants.

Chapter 5 Garden Design Recipes

Sometimes, the hardest part about starting any new project is the information the world thinks you need to know before doing it yourself. I'll be honest, if I want to replace a toilet, I don't necessarily want to know how it works, how plumbing works or how the sewage system works. Just tell me, step by step, how to get the old one out and the new one installed. Period. No plumbing lessons. The design recipes in this chapter follow this mentality. The photo and plant information are included if needed, after each recipe. The design is scaled so measuring and installing is a snap. The previous chapters have explanations with more in-depth information as a reference. Only the information needed for each specific garden is included in each recipe for a quick and easy way to create a beautiful garden and landscape.

Before You Begin

Always, always, always have the utilities in your planting area marked before digging, no matter how small a plant or project.

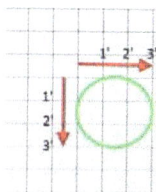

How to Use the Recipe Plans

When using the diagrams and designs, plant substitutions are ok. Many plants come in a variety of different bloom colors to suit every gardener. Check the plant description to see if other cultivars exist to substitute or talk to your local garden professional.

Smaller plans can be enlarged for larger areas by repeating a planting pattern.

Portions of large designs can be omitted or moved to match existing conditions or pulled out of larger designs to plant in smaller spaces.

For larger designs, install in phases for smaller budgets.

No two yards, hardscapes, houses or hills are identical. Therefore, all these variables have been intentionally omitted from the diagrams.

Boulder sizes vary. Those shown in the diagrams are for illustration only and don't represent boulders available to be purchased locally.

The size of each diagram may vary to fit the format, but the scale for each design is 1' x 1' based on the

This plant is 3' x 3'. This is measured by counting the lines or boxes. Each box represents 1' wide by 1' tall.

grid shown. Use this scale to calculate where to dig holes for your plants.

As stated in an earlier chapter, all holes are twice as wide as the root ball and dug as deep as the root ball. Use a measuring tape and measure the top of the root ball from one side to the other. Double this number for hole width. Measure the root ball from the top of the soil to the bottom of the soil. This is the depth of the hole. Any exceptions will be noted at the bottom of each recipe.

When measuring placement of plants based on the diagrams, the bushiness of plants varies, so always measure from the approximate center of the plant. Measure from the center of one plant to the center of the next when placing. Mark the centers with a stick or preferably, spray paint, to know where to start digging the center of the hole. Don't be afraid to remeasure after digging has begun. Measure twice, dig once.

Plants in renderings and diagrams are shown at their mature size. When purchased, new plants are much smaller and do not appear to need as much space as shown. Plants will grow and if plant spacing is altered when plants are young, gardens will become overgrown and crowded. This will lead to plant loss and frustration.

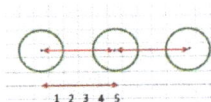

The diagrams are straight forward, easy to read and easy to use.

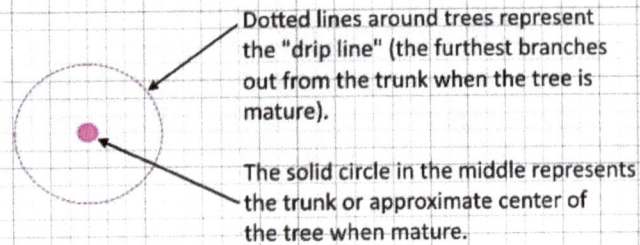

Dotted lines around trees represent the "drip line" (the furthest branches out from the trunk when the tree is mature).

The solid circle in the middle represents the trunk or approximate center of the tree when mature.

The assembly instructions give all the information needed to install the entire garden. Again, if only part of a garden is wanted, by all means, only plant part of it. The scaled diagram makes it easy to pick and choose the plan which best fits your needs.

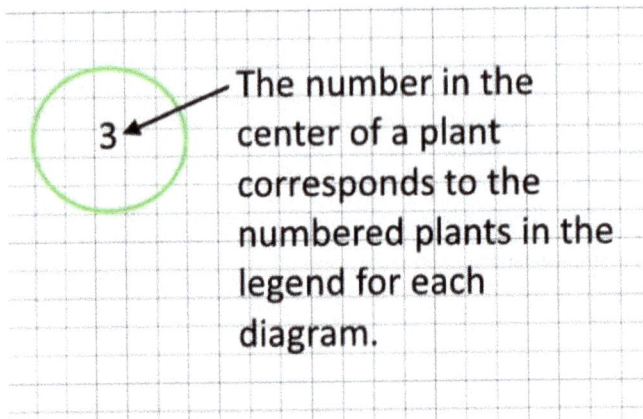

The number in the center of a plant corresponds to the numbered plants in the legend for each diagram.

Within each recipe, there is general information regarding the garden, as a whole.

Garden Size (Approximate): This is the general length and width of the garden. Do not use this for purposes of calculating mulch, pine straw or other bedding materials. This just gives a general overall idea of size.

Pruning Category: Pruning takes up a lot of time in the landscape.

Each full garden is graded with a 1 (least amount of time spent pruning) to 5 (most amount of time spent pruning).

This can help when deciding which garden plan to install based on individual needs and desires for pruning and maintenance.

The dot represents the center of the plant
Measure from the center of one plant to the next
The dots are in the center of a box, not on a line.
The center between two lines represents half of 1 foot (6 inches). From the middle of one line to the middle of the next line is 1' (6" + 6")
Therefore, these plants are 3' x 3' but the centers are 5' apart
This is because, as shown on the diagram, the approximate space between mature plants will be 2', but unless planting mature plants, this method of calculating spacing will not work out. The plants will be much smaller when purchased.

1 2 3 4 5

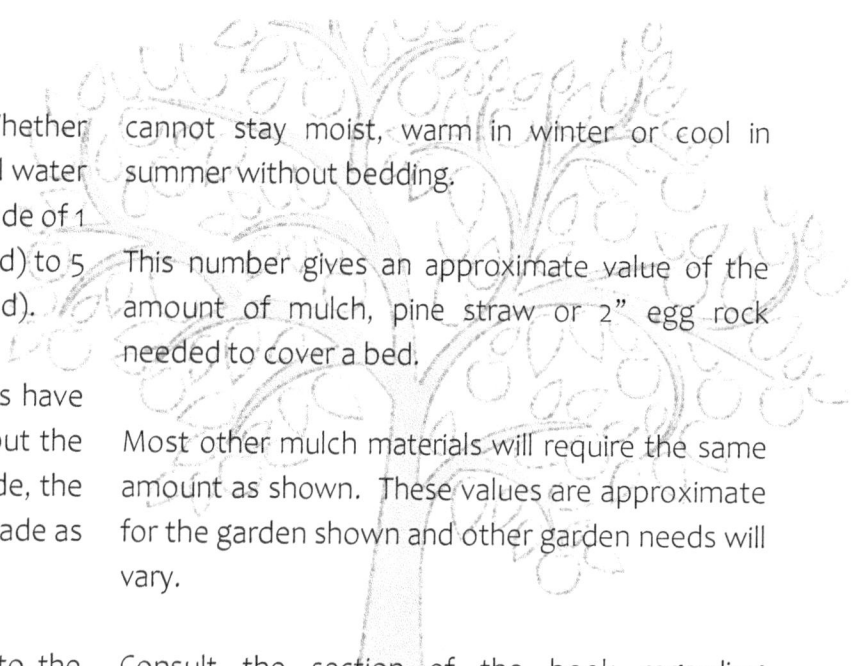

Watering Needs: All gardens need water. Whether it's just rain water or if regular supplemental water is necessary, this system gives an overall grade of 1 (least amount of additional watering needed) to 5 (most amount of additional watering needed).

Sun Requirements: In general, the gardens have plants grouped together which require about the same amount of sun. If a plant is part shade, the remainder of the plants can tolerate part shade as well.

This rating system gives a number value to the amount of sun required with 1 being the least amount of sun and 5 being the most.

Plant Zones: This is a range of the zones for the overall garden. Individual zone requirements are listed for each plant in the companion section.

The first number is the lowest zone. The second is the highest zone.

Bloom Range: This range is for the overall garden. If something is blooming throughout the year, then the indication will be four seasons.

This is a compilation of all plants in the specific garden plan. Individual plant bloom times and colors are available in the companion section of plants for each recipe.

The renderings are shown with all the plants in bloom, typically. Please take note that all plants in all beds don't necessarily bloom at the same time of the year. The renderings are for illustrative purposes.

Approximate Bedding: It's a major mistake to plant, till, amend and build a garden then not provide a mulch or bedding on top of the ground. This causes erosion and the roots of the plants cannot stay moist, warm in winter or cool in summer without bedding.

This number gives an approximate value of the amount of mulch, pine straw or 2" egg rock needed to cover a bed.

Most other mulch materials will require the same amount as shown. These values are approximate for the garden shown and other garden needs will vary.

Consult the section of the book regarding measuring for bedding materials to calculate your specific needs.

Average Time to Install Plants: This number assumes an average homeowner, with average skills, proper tools and a blank landscape.

It does not include time to remove any existing plants, bedding material, stumps, etc. This is just an average and actual results will vary.

There are 75 designs in 15 categories. Each category represents 5 original designs which can be altered to fit any garden shape and size.

When working on your garden, take your recipe to the garden center for assistance picking plants.

Specific plant information is included as a companion to each recipe for reference.

The appendix contains a comprehensive list of all plants used in these recipes.

Tools of the Trade

Every recipe has a section for "Special Needs". If you need a special tool or a plant requires planting a certain way, this is where you'll find that information. Every plan has a set of recommended basic tools you'll need to get it installed. To avoid being redundant on every plan, those are shown in the table below.

A wheel barrow or wagon comes in handy to keep tools contained and transport plants or debris.

Always follow safety procedures for tools and chemical use. Long sleeves and long pants are recommended to protect otherwise exposed skin from scrapes and scratches from plants or tools. Wear a hat to protect from the sun as well as sun screen and bug spray when working outside. Stay hydrated and take breaks as needed.

Protective shoes or boots		Protective eye wear	
Gardening gloves		Measuring tape	
Pick axe (to get through roots)		Marking paint	
Starter fertilizer for plants		Hand pruners to remove tags or unwanted leaves or branches	
Pointed shovel		Hard rake	

Garden Designs

Accent Gardens

Look At My Bloomers

Just The Facts, Ma'am

Come Sit A Spell

Shady Corners, Not Shady Neighbors

Cheeky Garden

Birds, Bees and Butterflies

Flirty Fences

Bursting at the Seams

Sassy and Sunny

Style for Miles

Serenity At Last

Color Palette

Sunny Disposition

Moonlight Serenade

The New Black

Rhymes with Emu

Always a Bride's Maid

Combinations

Magic Balls and Broomsticks

Heavenly Hedge

Buffed, Puffed and Fluffed

Beauty Queen

Prom Date

Curb Appeal

Spring Fling

Nook, Nook – Who's There?

Eye Candy

Encore Performance

Business in the Front, Party in the Back

Design Elements

Rock and Roll

Comfy Cozy

Exit Stage Left

Common Scents

Pot Garden

Dry Areas

Zen Vogue

Afternoon Tea

Size Matters

Rain, No Rain... Whatever

Southwest, But With Color

Edible Gardens

The Bee's Knees

Tootie Fruity – Hold The Fruit

Play With Your Food

Down to Earth

Granny's Pantry

Garden Designs

Evergreen

Tall Tales

Brand New Do

Enticing Entrances

Business Casual

Home Sweet Home

Foundation

Executive Privilege

That's Amore

Fabuloso

Jacket and Tie

Gravitas

Hillside Gardens

Rocky Top Retreat

Easy Peesy

Jack and Jill

Frankly My Dear

Beer Thirty

Mailbox Gardens

Silver Linings

Fall Festival

Season's Greetings

De-Vine-Ly Simple

Easy Like Sunday Morning

Perennial Gardens

Homecoming Queen

No Apologies

Old Friends

Southern Belle

Sugar Daddy

Privacy

No Peeking

Spectacular Debut

Belle of the Ball

Height of Excellence

Raising the Bar

Woodland Gardens

La Tee Da

Easy Street

Prince Charming

Counting Sheep

Stealing Kisses

Look At My Bloomers

Description

A year-round corner or side garden to attract birds, butterflies and attention. The simple design and no prune lifestyle makes it easy to both install and maintain. The crape myrtle is a dwarf variety so no need to trim each year.

Ingredients

(4) Autumn Embers Encore Azalea
(4) Kaleidoscope Abelia
(1) Natchez Crape Myrtle
(2) Garden Boulders

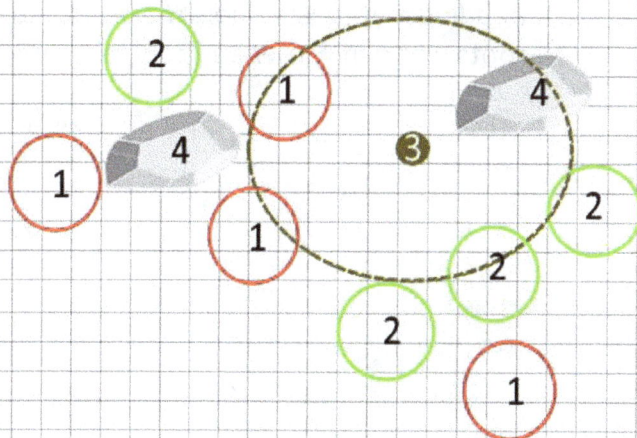

1 - Autumn Embers Encore Azalea
2 - Kaleidoscope Abelia
3 - Natchez Crape Myrtle
4 - Garden Boulders

1 block = 1' x 1' (1 square foot)

Assembly Instructions

Garden Size (Approximate):	21'Lx15'W
Pruning Category:	1
Watering Needs:	2
Sun Requirements:	4
Plant Zones:	7-11
Bloom Colors:	Red, Pink, White
Bloom Time Range:	Spring-Fall
Average Time to Install:	8 hours
Approximate Bedding:	315sf
Mulch:	2 cuyds
Pine Straw:	8 bales
Rock:	4 tons at 3" thick
Other Cultivars Available to Sub:	Yes
Special Needs:	This cultivar of crape myrtle is considered dwarf. There is no need to cut back every year (also called "knuckling").

Till garden and amend soil with composted material such as mulched leaves or shredded pine.

Using the planting diagram, set boulders by digging into the soil several inches to create a foundation slightly below the grade of the garden. Set the boulder on to the foundation then spread the removed soil around the boulders to bring the soil height back up to grade level.

Measure for plant placement and sit each plant in its proper place. Adjust placement based on the shape of the actual bed.

Dig each hole twice as wide as the root ball. Sprinkle in starter fertilizer to the bottom of the hole (follow directions on package for proper application). Set plant in hole. Push soil back around plant, tamping in tight with the handle end of the shovel to remove all air pockets. Tamp soil tight at top of root ball.

Repeat for each plant.

Water in all plants thoroughly.

Top beds with mulch, pine straw or other bedding materials to hold moisture and keep roots warm in winter and cool in summer.

Look At My Bloomers

Accent Gardens

Common Name	Autumn Embers Encore Azalea
Scientific Name	Rhododendron 'Conleb'
Status	Evergreen
Mature Size (H x W)	4x4.5
Pruning Category (1-5)	2
Watering Category (1-5)	3
Sun Category (1-5)	4
USDA Hardiness Zone:	7-10
Bloom Season	Spring, Fall

Common Name	Kaleidoscope Abelia
Scientific Name	Abelia x grandiflora 'Kaleidoscope'
Status	Semi Deciduous
Mature Size (H x W)	3x3
Pruning Category (1-5)	1
Watering Category (1-5)	2
Sun Category (1-5)	4
USDA Hardiness Zone:	6-9
Bloom Season	Fall

Common Name	Natchez Crape Myrtle
Scientific Name	Lagerstroemia indica x fauriei 'Natchez'
Status	Deciduous
Mature Size (H x W)	30x10
Pruning Category (1-5)	1
Watering Category (1-5)	2
Sun Category (1-5)	4
USDA Hardiness Zone:	6-11
Bloom Season	Summer

Description

A great garden for a slight slope between yards, at the back for a focal point or up front at the street. Planted properly, pruning is at a minimum with maximum color and texture. The varying colors provide year-round interest.

Ingredients

(1) Kousa Dogwood
(3) Gold Mop Cypress
(1) Hinoki Cypress
(3) False Holly
(5) Crimson Fire Loropetalum

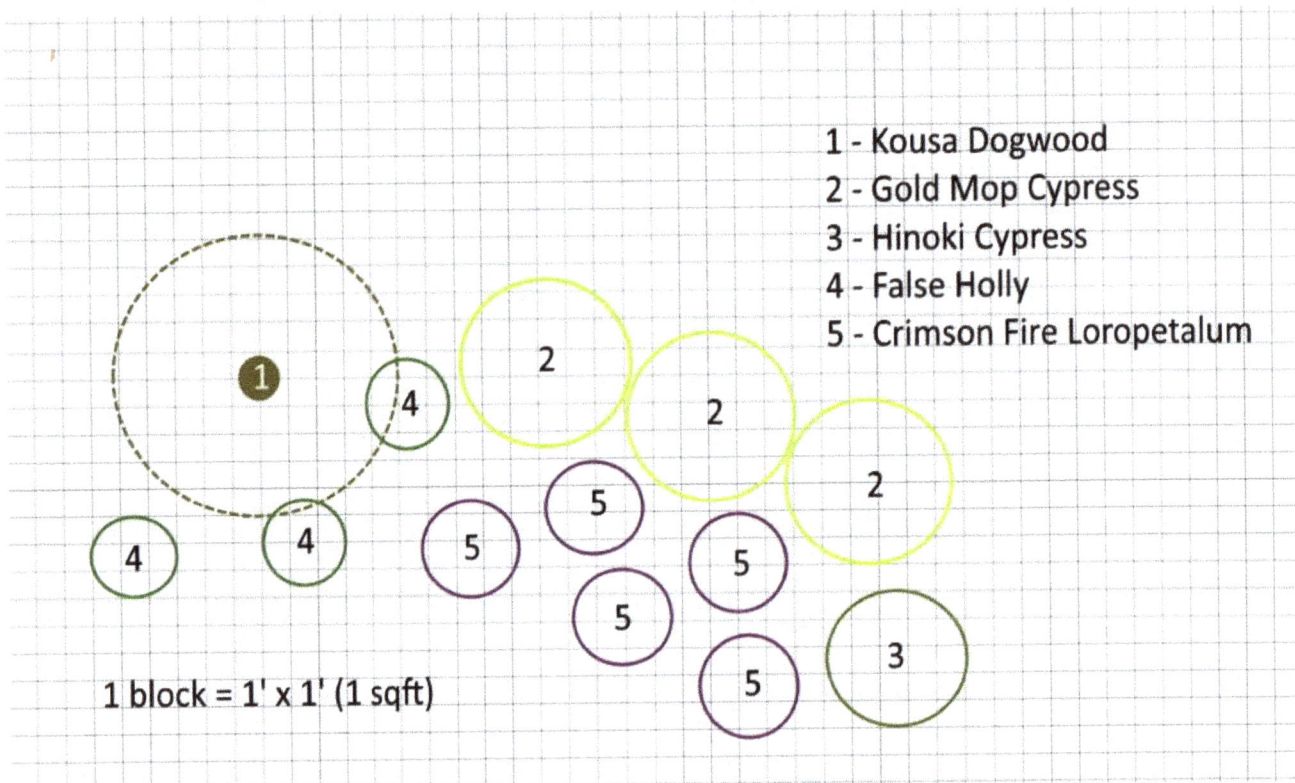

1 - Kousa Dogwood
2 - Gold Mop Cypress
3 - Hinoki Cypress
4 - False Holly
5 - Crimson Fire Loropetalum

1 block = 1' x 1' (1 sqft)

Just The Facts, Ma'am

Assembly Instructions

Garden Size (Approximate):	31'Lx19'W
Pruning Category:	1
Watering Needs:	2
Sun Requirements:	4
Plant Zones:	3-10
Bloom Colors:	White, Purple
Bloom Time Range:	Spring, Fall
Average Time to Install:	9 hours
Approximate Bedding:	589sf
Mulch:	3.6 cuyds
Pine Straw:	14 bales
Rock:	7.3 tons at 3" thick
Other Cultivars Available to Sub:	Yes
Special Needs:	None

Till garden and amend soil with composted material such as mulched leaves or shredded pine.

Using the planting diagram, measure for plant placement and sit each plant in its proper place. Adjust placement based on the shape of the actual bed.

Dig each hole twice as wide as the root ball. Sprinkle in starter fertilizer to the bottom of the hole (follow directions on package for proper application). Set plant in hole. Push soil back around plant, tamping in tight with the handle end of the shovel to remove all air pockets. Tamp soil tight at top of root ball.

Repeat for each plant.

Water in all plants thoroughly.

Top beds with mulch, pine straw or other bedding materials to hold moisture and keep roots warm in winter and cool in summer.

Common Name	Kousa Dogwood
Scientific Name	Cornus Kousa
Status	Deciduous
Mature Size (H x W)	20x10
Pruning Category (1-5)	1
Watering Category (1-5)	2
Sun Category (1-5)	4
USDA Hardiness Zone:	3-8
Bloom Season	Spring

Common Name	Gold Mop Cypress
Scientific Name	Chamaecyparis
Status	Evergreen
Mature Size (H x W)	6x6
Pruning Category (1-5)	1
Watering Category (1-5)	1
Sun Category (1-5)	4
USDA Hardiness Zone:	6-9
Bloom Season	None

Common Name	Hinoki Cypress
Scientific Name	Chamaecyparis obtusa
Status	Evergreen
Mature Size (H x W)	5x4
Pruning Category (1-5)	1
Watering Category (1-5)	1
Sun Category (1-5)	4
USDA Hardiness Zone:	6-9
Bloom Season	None

Common Name	False Holly
Scientific Name	Osmanthus heterophyllus
Status	Evergreen
Mature Size (H x W)	3x3
Pruning Category (1-5)	2
Watering Category (1-5)	2
Sun Category (1-5)	3
USDA Hardiness Zone:	6-9
Bloom Season	Fall

Common Name	Crimson Fire Loropetalum
Scientific Name	Loropetalum chinense var. rubrum 'Crimson Fire'
Status	Evergreen
Mature Size (H x W)	4x4
Pruning Category (1-5)	2
Watering Category (1-5)	2
Sun Category (1-5)	3
USDA Hardiness Zone:	7-10
Bloom Season	Spring

Come Sit a Spell

Accent Gardens

Description

A simple little accent garden to welcome guests and provide color and scent sensations. Switch out the herbs each year for even more interest and variety. Use the blooms for dried arrangements or summer color indoors.

Ingredients

(1) Adagio Miscanthus Grass
(2) Guacamole Hosta
(2) Liriope
(1) Agapanthus
(1) Autumn Joy Sedum
(2) Colorblaze Coleus
(1) Mini Loropetalum

(1) Thyme
(1) Asiatic Lily
(3) Sage

1 - Adagio Grass
2 - Guacamole Hosta
3 - Variegated Liriope
4 - Agapanthus
5 - Colorblaze Coleus
6 - Jazz Hands Mini Loropetalum
7 - Thyme
8 - Asiatic Lily
9 - Sage
10 - Autumn Joy Sedum

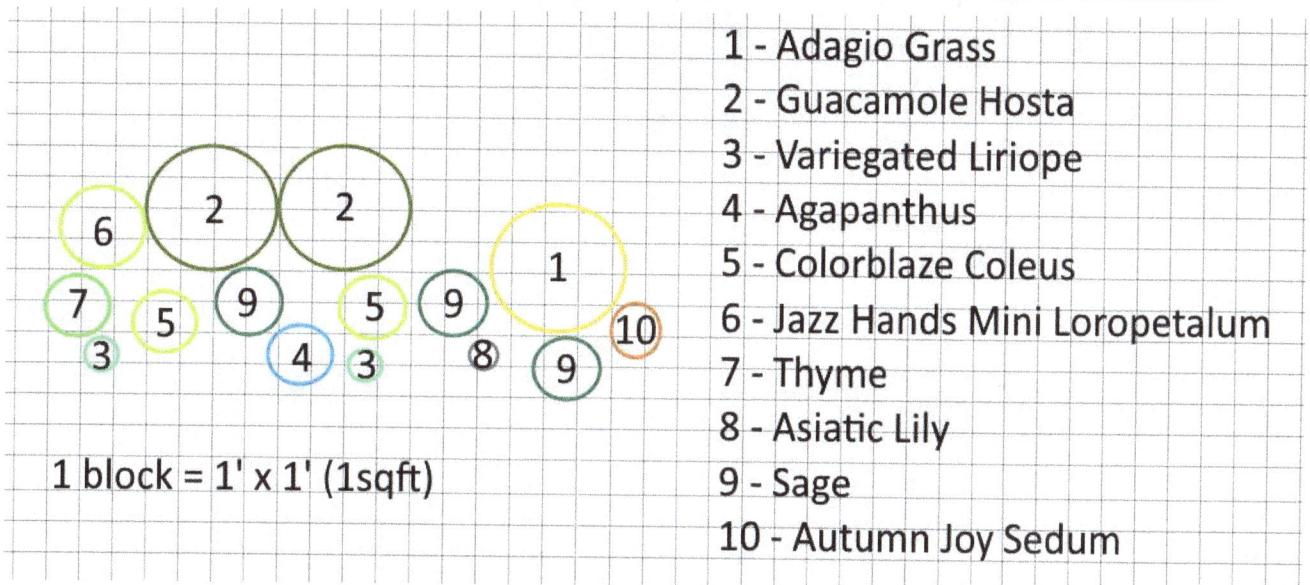

1 block = 1' x 1' (1sqft)

Assembly Instructions

Garden Size (Approximate):	19'L x 8'W
Pruning Category:	1
Watering Needs:	2
Sun Requirements:	4
Plant Zones:	3-11
Bloom Colors:	Purple, Blue, White, Pink
Bloom Time Range:	Spring-Fall
Average Time to Install:	8 hours
Approximate Bedding:	152sf
Mulch:	1 cuyds
Pine Straw:	4 bales
Rock:	1.9 tons at 3" thick
Other Cultivars Available to Sub:	Yes
Special Needs:	Sage doesn't tolerate heat well. Use as an annual in higher planting zones

Till garden and amend soil with composted material such as mulched leaves or shredded pine.

Using the planting diagram, measure for plant placement and sit each plant in its proper place. Adjust placement based on the shape of the actual bed.

Dig each hole twice as wide as the root ball. Sprinkle in starter fertilizer to the bottom of the hole (follow directions on package for proper application). Set plant in hole. Push soil back around plant, tamping in tight with the handle end of the shovel to remove all air pockets. Tamp soil tight at top of root ball.

Repeat for each plant.

Water in all plants thoroughly.

Top beds with mulch, pine straw or other bedding materials to hold moisture and keep roots warm in winter and cool in summer.

Common Name	Adagio Miscanthus Grass
Scientific Name	Miscanthus sinensis 'Adagio'
Status	Perennial
Mature Size (H x W)	5x5
Pruning Category (1-5)	1
Watering Category (1-5)	1
Sun Category (1-5)	4
USDA Hardiness Zone:	6-10
Bloom Season	Summer

Common Name	Liriope
Scientific Name	Liriope muscari
Status	Perennial
Mature Size (H x W)	2x2
Pruning Category (1-5)	1
Watering Category (1-5)	1
Sun Category (1-5)	4
USDA Hardiness Zone:	6-10
Bloom Season	Summer

Common Name	Mini Loropetalum
Scientific Name	Loropetalum chinense 'Beni-Hime'
Status	Evergreen
Mature Size (H x W)	3x3
Pruning Category (1-5)	2
Watering Category (1-5)	2
Sun Category (1-5)	3
USDA Hardiness Zone:	7-10
Bloom Season	Spring

Common Name	Guacamole Hosta
Scientific Name	Hosta 'Guacamole'
Status	Perennial
Mature Size (H x W)	4x4
Pruning Category (1-5)	1
Watering Category (1-5)	2
Sun Category (1-5)	2
USDA Hardiness Zone:	3-8
Bloom Season	Summer

Common Name	Colorblaze Coleus
Scientific Name	Solenostemon scutellarioides 'Color Blaze'
Status	Semi Tropical
Mature Size (H x W)	3x2
Pruning Category (1-5)	1
Watering Category (1-5)	2
Sun Category (1-5)	4
USDA Hardiness Zone:	10-11
Bloom Season	Summer

Common Name	Thyme
Scientific Name	Thymus vulgaris
Status	Perennial
Mature Size (H x W)	1x2
Pruning Category (1-5)	1
Watering Category (1-5)	2
Sun Category (1-5)	4
USDA Hardiness Zone:	5-10
Bloom Season	Summer

Common Name	Asiatic Lily
Scientific Name	Lilium auratum
Status	Perennial
Mature Size (H x W)	2x1
Pruning Category (1-5)	1
Watering Category (1-5)	3
Sun Category (1-5)	3
USDA Hardiness Zone:	4-9
Bloom Season	Spring

Common Name	Agapanthus
Scientific Name	Agapanthus africanus
Status	Perennial
Mature Size (H x W)	2.5x2.5
Pruning Category (1-5)	1
Watering Category (1-5)	2
Sun Category (1-5)	2
USDA Hardiness Zone:	8-11
Bloom Season	Spring

Common Name	Sage
Scientific Name	Salvia officinalis
Status	Perennial
Mature Size (H x W)	3x3
Pruning Category (1-5)	1
Watering Category (1-5)	2
Sun Category (1-5)	4
USDA Hardiness Zone:	5-8
Bloom Season	Fall

Common Name	Autumn Joy Sedum
Scientific Name	Hylotelephium telephium 'Autumn Joy'
Status	Perennial
Mature Size (H x W)	2x2
Pruning Category (1-5)	1
Watering Category (1-5)	1
Sun Category (1-5)	5
USDA Hardiness Zone:	3-8
Bloom Season	Fall

Shady Corners, Not Shady Neighbors

Description

You can't do anything about shady neighbors, but the corners around your home will be fresh and clean with this shade garden. Morning sun is ok but avoid the afternoon heat. In summer, use the blooms for arrangements or just stroll and enjoy the scent of the season.

Ingredients

(1) Dwarf Alberta Spruce   (1) GG Gerbing Azalea
(2) Big Leaf Hosta   (68) 4" Vinca
(1) Bloodgood Japanese Maple
(3) Hydrangea Arborescens
(1) Nikko Blue Hydrangea

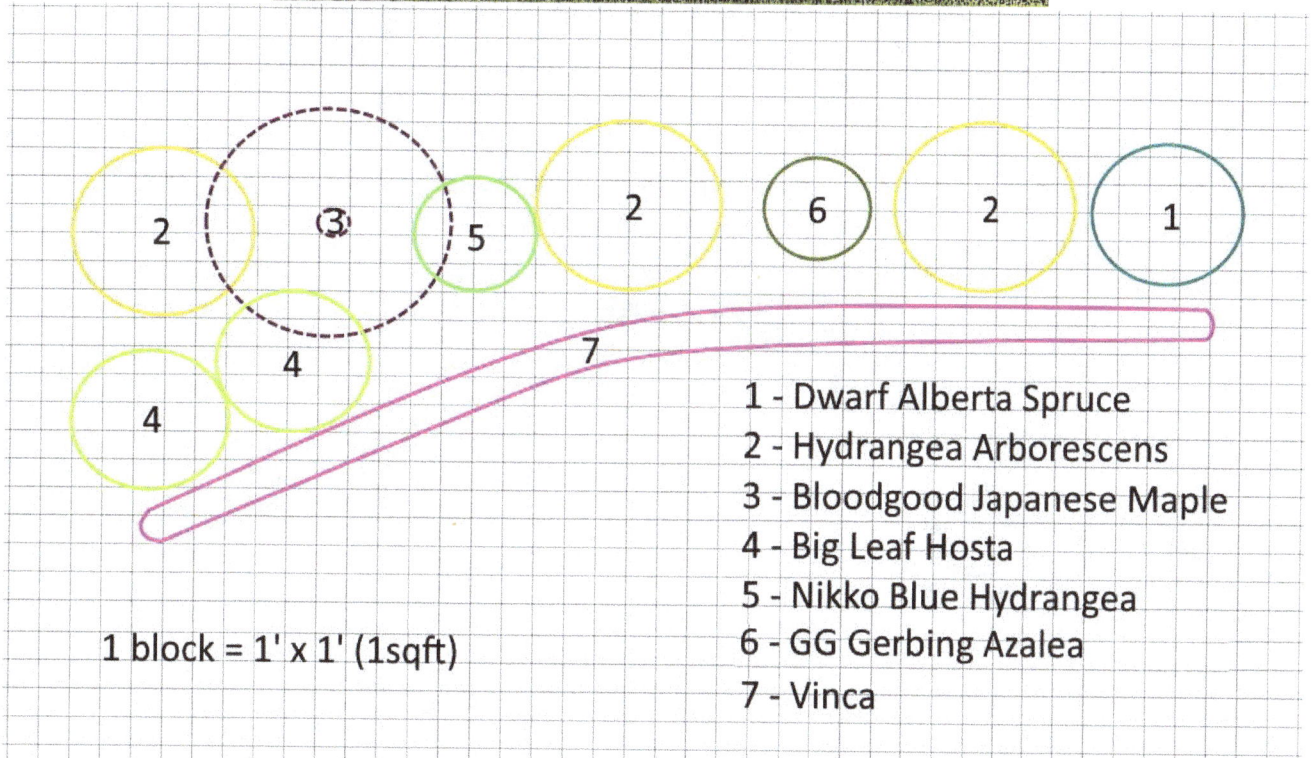

1 block = 1' x 1' (1sqft)

1 - Dwarf Alberta Spruce
2 - Hydrangea Arborescens
3 - Bloodgood Japanese Maple
4 - Big Leaf Hosta
5 - Nikko Blue Hydrangea
6 - GG Gerbing Azalea
7 - Vinca

Shady Corners, Not Shady Neighbors

Accent Gardens

Garden Size (Approximate):	38'L x 16'W
Pruning Category:	1
Watering Needs:	2
Sun Requirements:	3
Plant Zones:	3-9
Bloom Colors:	White, Blue, Pink
Bloom Time Range:	Spring-Summer
Average Time to Install:	9 hours
Approximate Bedding:	608sf
Mulch:	4 cuyds
Pine Straw:	15 bales
Rock:	17.6 tons at 3" thick
Other Cultivars Available to Sub:	Yes
Special Needs:	Mulch Dwarf Alberta Spruce heavily in summer in warmer areas to protect roots. Vinca is an annual, but readily reseeds itself.

Till garden and amend soil with composted material such as mulched leaves or shredded pine.

Using the planting diagram, measure for plant placement and sit each plant in its proper place. Adjust placement based on the shape of the actual bed.

Dig each hole twice as wide as the root ball. Sprinkle in starter fertilizer to the bottom of the hole (follow directions on package for proper application). Set plant in hole. Push soil back around plant, tamping in tight with the handle end of the shovel to remove all air pockets. Tamp soil tight at top of root ball.

Repeat for each plant.

Space annuals evenly by measuring with your hand or the handle of a tool.

Water in all plants thoroughly.

Top beds with mulch, pine straw or other bedding materials to hold moisture and keep roots warm in winter and cool in summer.

Common Name	Dwarf Alberta Spruce
Scientific Name	Picea glauca
Status	Evergreen
Mature Size (H x W)	5x4
Pruning Category (1-5)	1
Watering Category (1-5)	2
Sun Category (1-5)	3
USDA Hardiness Zone:	3-8
Bloom Season	None

Common Name	Hydrangea Arborescens
Scientific Name	Hydrangea Arborescens
Status	Deciduous
Mature Size (H x W)	6x6
Pruning Category (1-5)	1
Watering Category (1-5)	3
Sun Category (1-5)	3
USDA Hardiness Zone:	4-9
Bloom Season	Summer

Common Name	Bloodgood Japanese Maple
Scientific Name	Acer palmatum 'Bloodgood'
Status	Deciduous
Mature Size (H x W)	15x10
Pruning Category (1-5)	1
Watering Category (1-5)	2
Sun Category (1-5)	4
USDA Hardiness Zone:	5-8
Bloom Season	None

Common Name	G.G. Gerbing Azalea
Scientific Name	Rhododendron indicum 'GG Gerbing'
Status	Evergreen
Mature Size (H x W)	3x3
Pruning Category (1-5)	2
Watering Category (1-5)	3
Sun Category (1-5)	3
USDA Hardiness Zone:	7-9
Bloom Season	Spring

Common Name	Big Leaf Hosta
Scientific Name	Hosta
Status	Perennial
Mature Size (H x W)	4x4
Pruning Category (1-5)	1
Watering Category (1-5)	2
Sun Category (1-5)	2
USDA Hardiness Zone:	3-8
Bloom Season	Summer

Common Name	Nikko Blue Hydrangea
Scientific Name	Hydrangea macrophylla 'Nikko Blue'
Status	Deciduous
Mature Size (H x W)	3x3
Pruning Category (1-5)	1
Watering Category (1-5)	3
Sun Category (1-5)	2
USDA Hardiness Zone:	4-9
Bloom Season	Summer

Common Name	Vinca
Scientific Name	Catharanthus roseus
Status	Annual
Mature Size (H x W)	1.5x1.5
Pruning Category (1-5)	1
Watering Category (1-5)	1
Sun Category (1-5)	5
USDA Hardiness Zone:	4-8
Bloom Season	Summer

Cheeky Garden

Description

A blazing pink dogwood starts spring off just right in this beautiful small garden. The shade from the dogwood protects the plants below for a stunning visual show all through summer and fall. Evergreens in back hold the garden in place over winter until spring bursts with color once again.

Ingredients

(1) Pink Dogwood   (6) Autumn Fern

(3) Guacamole Hosta   (3) Distylium 'Vintage Jade'

(3) Dwarf Plum Yew   (3) Patriot Hosta

1 - Pink Dogwood
2 - Guacamole Hosta
3 - Dwarf Plum Yew
4 - Autumn Fern
5 - Distylium 'Vintage Jade'
6 - Patriot Hosta

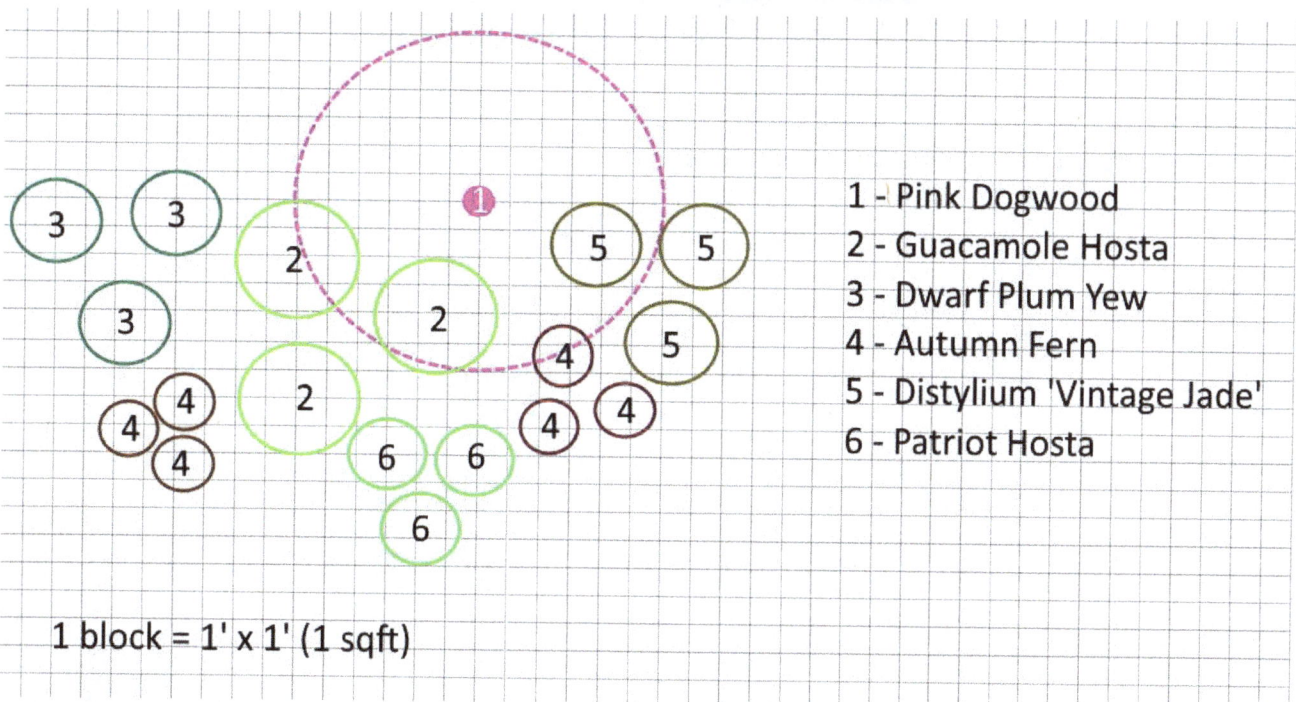

1 block = 1' x 1' (1 sqft)

Assembly Instructions

Garden Size (Approximate):	25'L x 19'W
Pruning Category:	1
Watering Needs:	2
Sun Requirements:	2
Plant Zones:	3-9
Bloom Colors:	Pink, Purple, White
Bloom Time Range:	Spring-Summer
Average Time to Install:	11 hours
Approximate Bedding:	475sf
Mulch:	3 cuyds
Pine Straw:	11 bales
Rock:	6 tons at 3" thick
Other Cultivars Available to Sub:	Yes
Special Needs:	Cut back failing foliage of ferns in early winter and mulch heavily for winter.

Till garden and amend soil with composted material such as mulched leaves or shredded pine.

Using the planting diagram, measure for plant placement and sit each plant in its proper place. Adjust placement based on the shape of the actual bed.

Dig each hole twice as wide as the root ball. Sprinkle in starter fertilizer to the bottom of the hole (follow directions on package for proper application). Set plant in hole. Push soil back around plant, tamping in tight with the handle end of the shovel to remove all air pockets. Tamp soil tight at top of root ball.

Repeat for each plant.

Water in all plants thoroughly.

Top beds with mulch, pine straw or other bedding materials to hold moisture and keep roots warm in winter and cool in summer.

Common Name	Pink Dogwood
Scientific Name	Cornus florida 'Rubra'
Status	Deciduous
Mature Size (H x W)	20x15
Pruning Category (1-5)	1
Watering Category (1-5)	2
Sun Category (1-5)	3
USDA Hardiness Zone:	3-8
Bloom Season	Spring

Common Name	Guacamole Hosta
Scientific Name	Hosta 'Guacamole'
Status	Perennial
Mature Size (H x W)	4x4
Pruning Category (1-5)	1
Watering Category (1-5)	2
Sun Category (1-5)	2
USDA Hardiness Zone:	3-8
Bloom Season	Summer

Common Name	Dwarf Plum Yew
Scientific Name	Cephalotaxus harringtonia 'Prostrata'
Status	Evergreen
Mature Size (H x W)	3x3
Pruning Category (1-5)	1
Watering Category (1-5)	2
Sun Category (1-5)	3
USDA Hardiness Zone:	4-8
Bloom Season	None

Common Name	Autumn Fern
Scientific Name	Dryopteris erythrosora
Status	Perennial
Mature Size (H x W)	2x2
Pruning Category (1-5)	1
Watering Category (1-5)	3
Sun Category (1-5)	2
USDA Hardiness Zone:	4-8
Bloom Season	None

Common Name	Vintage Jade Distylium
Scientific Name	Distylium 'Vintage Jade'
Status	Evergreen
Mature Size (H x W)	3x2.5
Pruning Category (1-5)	2
Watering Category (1-5)	2
Sun Category (1-5)	2
USDA Hardiness Zone:	7-9
Bloom Season	Spring

Common Name	Patriot Hosta
Scientific Name	Hosta 'Patriot'
Status	Perennial
Mature Size (H x W)	3x3
Pruning Category (1-5)	1
Watering Category (1-5)	2
Sun Category (1-5)	2
USDA Hardiness Zone:	3-8
Bloom Season	Summer

Flirty Fences

Description

The jasmine alone is enough to bring all the hummingbirds buzzing around. The daisies and gardenia will fill the entire yard with incredible summer scents. Plant close to a patio or other outdoor entertaining area for years of blooms and bird watching.

Ingredients

(5) Star Jasmine (on trellis)
(3) August Beauty Gardenia
(2) Caryopteris
(1) Fernleaf Yarrow
(3) Shasta Daisy
(20) Fire Witch Dianthus

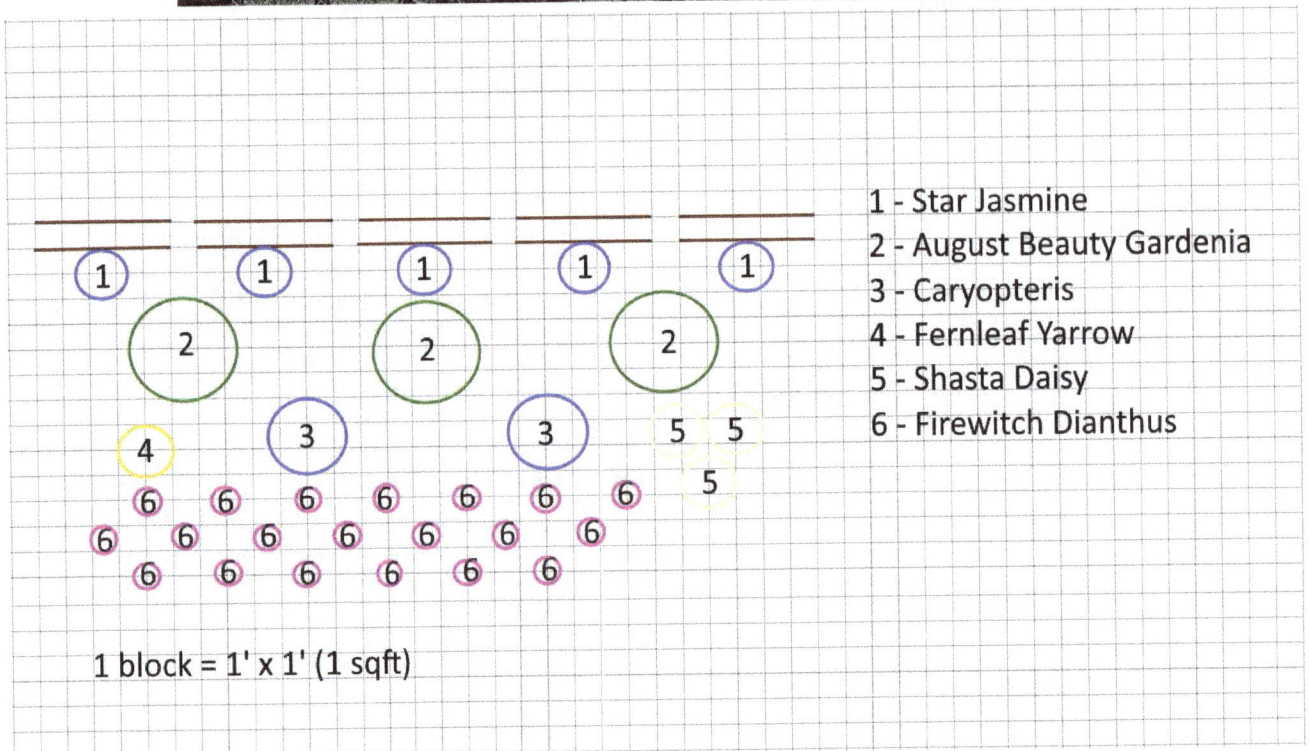

1 - Star Jasmine
2 - August Beauty Gardenia
3 - Caryopteris
4 - Fernleaf Yarrow
5 - Shasta Daisy
6 - Firewitch Dianthus

1 block = 1' x 1' (1 sqft)

Assembly Instructions

Garden Size (Approximate):	27'L x 14' W
Pruning Category:	1
Watering Needs:	2
Sun Requirements:	4
Plant Zones:	3-11
Bloom Colors:	White, Blue, Yellow, Purple
Bloom Time Range:	Spring-Fall
Average Time to Install:	12 hours
Approximate Bedding:	378sf
Mulch:	2.5 cuyds
Pine Straw:	9 bales
Rock:	4.75 tons at 3" thick
Other Cultivars Available to Sub:	Yes
Special Needs:	No

Till garden and amend soil with composted material such as mulched leaves or shredded pine.

Using the planting diagram, measure for plant placement and sit each plant in its proper place. Adjust placement based on the shape of the actual bed.

Dig each hole twice as wide as the root ball. Sprinkle in starter fertilizer to the bottom of the hole (follow directions on package for proper application). Set plant in hole. Push soil back around plant, tamping in tight with the handle end of the shovel to remove all air pockets. Tamp soil tight at top of root ball.

Repeat for each plant.

Water in all plants thoroughly.

Top beds with mulch, pine straw or other bedding materials to hold moisture and keep roots warm in winter and cool in summer.

Flirty Fences

Common Name	Star Jasmine
Scientific Name	Trachelospermum jasminoides
Status	Perennial
Mature Size (H x W)	vine
Pruning Category (1-5)	3
Watering Category (1-5)	2
Sun Category (1-5)	5
USDA Hardiness Zone:	7-10
Bloom Season	Summer

Common Name	Caryopteris
Scientific Name	Caryopteris
Status	Perennial
Mature Size (H x W)	3x3
Pruning Category (1-5)	1
Watering Category (1-5)	2
Sun Category (1-5)	4
USDA Hardiness Zone:	5-9
Bloom Season	Summer

Common Name	Shasta Daisy
Scientific Name	Leucanthemum x superbum
Status	Perennial
Mature Size (H x W)	2.5x2.5
Pruning Category (1-5)	1
Watering Category (1-5)	2
Sun Category (1-5)	4
USDA Hardiness Zone:	4-10
Bloom Season	Summer

Birds, Bees & Butterflies

Common Name	August Beauty Gardenia
Scientific Name	Gardenia jasminoides 'August Beauty'
Status	Evergreen
Mature Size (H x W)	5x5
Pruning Category (1-5)	2
Watering Category (1-5)	3
Sun Category (1-5)	4
USDA Hardiness Zone:	7-11
Bloom Season	Summer, Fall

Common Name	Fernleaf Yarrow
Scientific Name	Achillea filipendulina
Status	Perennial
Mature Size (H x W)	2x2
Pruning Category (1-5)	1
Watering Category (1-5)	1
Sun Category (1-5)	3
USDA Hardiness Zone:	3-7
Bloom Season	Spring

Common Name	Fire Witch Dianthus
Scientific Name	Dianthus gratianopolitanus 'Fire Witch'
Status	Perennial
Mature Size (H x W)	1.5x1.5
Pruning Category (1-5)	1
Watering Category (1-5)	2
Sun Category (1-5)	3
USDA Hardiness Zone:	3-9
Bloom Season	Summer

Bursting at the Seams

Birds, Bees & Butterflies

Description

These tight-knit companion plants will not disappoint throughout spring and summer. Zinnia are annuals in most areas, but let the heads go to seed and they will pop back up next year. At the end of the season, trim back dead foliage and mulch over winter to protect roots for a beautiful and sensual garden again next spring.

Ingredients

(1) Russian Sage
(3) Tri-Color Perennial Lantana
(3) Assorted Zinnia
(3) Autumn Joy Sedum
(6) Blackeyed Susan

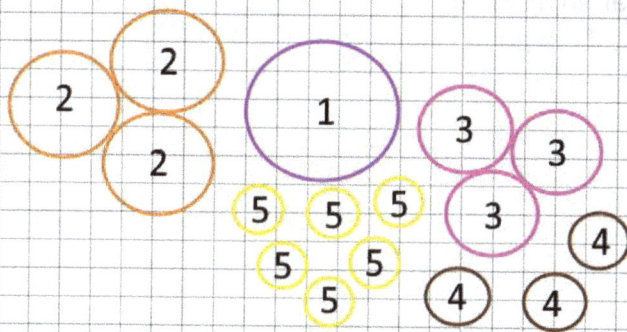

1 - Russian Sage
2 - Lantana (perennial tri color)
3 - Assorted Zinnia
4 - Autumn Joy Sedum
5 - Blackeyed Susan

1 block = 1' x 1' (1 sqft)

Assembly Instructions

Garden Size (Approximate):	21'L x 11'W
Pruning Category:	1
Watering Needs:	2
Sun Requirements:	5
Plant Zones:	3-11
Bloom Colors:	Blue, Yellow, Orange, Red, Pink
Bloom Time Range:	Summer-Fall
Average Time to Install:	8 hours
Approximate Bedding:	231sf
Mulch:	1.5 cuyds
Pine Straw:	6 bales
Rock:	3 tons at 3" thick
Other Cultivars Available to Sub:	Yes
Special Needs:	Zinnia are annuals in most areas. Allow heads to go to seed and they will return next year.

Till garden and amend soil with composted material such as mulched leaves or shredded pine.

Using the planting diagram, measure for plant placement and sit each plant in its proper place. Adjust placement based on the shape of the actual bed.

Dig each hole twice as wide as the root ball. Sprinkle in starter fertilizer to the bottom of the hole (follow directions on package for proper application). Set plant in hole. Push soil back around plant, tamping in tight with the handle end of the shovel to remove all air pockets. Tamp soil tight at top of root ball.

Repeat for each plant.

Water in all plants thoroughly.

Top beds with mulch, pine straw or other bedding materials to hold moisture and keep roots warm in winter and cool in summer.

Bursting at the Seams

Birds, Bees & Butterflies

Common Name	Russian Sage
Scientific Name	Perovskia atriplicifolia
Status	Perennial
Mature Size (H x W)	5x5
Pruning Category (1-5)	1
Watering Category (1-5)	2
Sun Category (1-5)	5
USDA Hardiness Zone:	5-10
Bloom Season	Fall

Common Name	Lantana
Scientific Name	Lantana
Status	Perennial
Mature Size (H x W)	3x5
Pruning Category (1-5)	1
Watering Category (1-5)	2
Sun Category (1-5)	5
USDA Hardiness Zone:	7-11
Bloom Season	Summer

Common Name	Zinnia
Scientific Name	Zinnia elegans
Status	Annual
Mature Size (H x W)	3x1
Pruning Category (1-5)	1
Watering Category (1-5)	2
Sun Category (1-5)	5
USDA Hardiness Zone:	4-11
Bloom Season	Summer

Common Name	Autumn Joy Sedum
Scientific Name	Hylotelephium telephium 'Autumn Joy'
Status	Perennial
Mature Size (H x W)	2x2
Pruning Category (1-5)	1
Watering Category (1-5)	1
Sun Category (1-5)	5
USDA Hardiness Zone:	3-8
Bloom Season	Fall

Common Name	Blackeyed Susan
Scientific Name	Rudbeckia hirta
Status	Perennial
Mature Size (H x W)	2x2
Pruning Category (1-5)	1
Watering Category (1-5)	2
Sun Category (1-5)	4
USDA Hardiness Zone:	3-9
Bloom Season	Summer

Description

These beauties will be rockin' in the sun all summer. Bees and butterflies won't be able to resist the plethora of blooms, the flavor of the flowers and the bouncy flowering stems. Trim back dead foliage after first frost and mulch over the bed to protect roots through the winter.

Ingredients

(3) Tall Garden Phlox
(1) Bee Balm
(3) Autumn Chiffon Encore Azalea
(1) Dwarf Butterfly Shrub
(3) Purple Cone Flower
(3) Whirling Butterflies
(9) Coreopsis

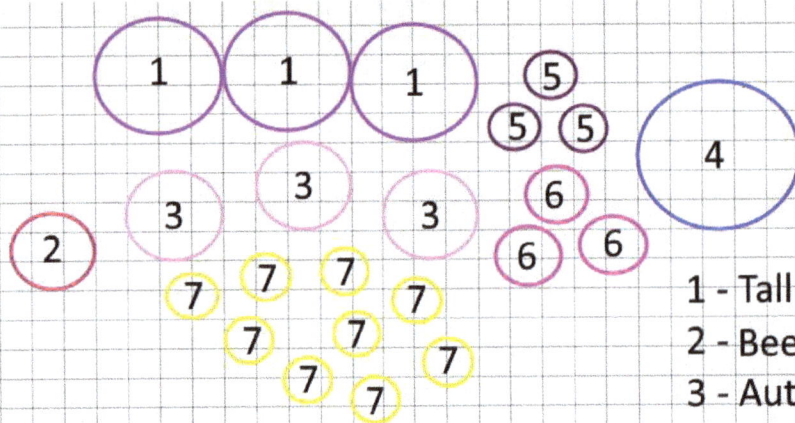

1 block = 1' x 1' (1 sqft)

1 - Tall Garden Phlox
2 - Bee Balm
3 - Autumn Chiffon Encore Azalea
4 - Dwarf Blue Butterfly Shrub
5 - Purple Cone Flower
6 - Whirling Butterflies
7 - Coreopsis

Sassy and Sunny

Birds, Bees & Butterflies

Assembly Instructions

Garden Size (Approximate):	25'L x 15'W
Pruning Category:	1
Watering Needs:	2
Sun Requirements:	4
Plant Zones:	3-11
Bloom Colors:	Pink, Blue, Purple, Yellow
Bloom Time Range:	Spring-Fall
Average Time to Install:	11 hours
Approximate Bedding:	375sf
Mulch:	2.3 cuyds
Pine Straw:	9 bales
Rock:	5 tons at 3" thick
Other Cultivars Available to Sub:	Yes
Special Needs:	No

Till garden and amend soil with composted material such as mulched leaves or shredded pine.

Using the planting diagram, measure for plant placement and sit each plant in its proper place. Adjust placement based on the shape of the actual bed.

Dig each hole twice as wide as the root ball. Sprinkle in starter fertilizer to the bottom of the hole (follow directions on package for proper application). Set plant in hole. Push soil back around plant, tamping in tight with the handle end of the shovel to remove all air pockets. Tamp soil tight at top of root ball.

Repeat for each plant.

Water in all plants thoroughly.

Top beds with mulch, pine straw or other bedding materials to hold moisture and keep roots warm in winter and cool in summer.

Sassy and Sunny

Common Name	Tall Garden Phlox
Scientific Name	Phlox paniculata
Status	Perennial
Mature Size (H x W)	3.5x2
Pruning Category (1-5)	1
Watering Category (1-5)	2
Sun Category (1-5)	3
USDA Hardiness Zone:	3-8
Bloom Season	Fall

Common Name	Autumn Chiffon Encore Azalea
Scientific Name	Rhododendron 'Robled' PP15862
Status	Evergreen
Mature Size (H x W)	3.5x3.5
Pruning Category (1-5)	2
Watering Category (1-5)	3
Sun Category (1-5)	4
USDA Hardiness Zone:	7-10
Bloom Season	Spring, Fall

Common Name	Purple Cone Flower
Scientific Name	Echinacea
Status	Perennial
Mature Size (H x W)	2x2
Pruning Category (1-5)	1
Watering Category (1-5)	2
Sun Category (1-5)	4
USDA Hardiness Zone:	3-9
Bloom Season	Summer

Birds, Bees & Butterflies

Common Name	Bee Balm
Scientific Name	Monarda
Status	Perennial
Mature Size (H x W)	3x3
Pruning Category (1-5)	1
Watering Category (1-5)	2
Sun Category (1-5)	4
USDA Hardiness Zone:	2-10
Bloom Season	Summer

Common Name	Dwarf Butterfly Shrub
Scientific Name	Buddleia
Status	Deciduous
Mature Size (H x W)	3x3
Pruning Category (1-5)	2
Watering Category (1-5)	2
Sun Category (1-5)	5
USDA Hardiness Zone:	5-11
Bloom Season	Summer

Common Name	Whirling Butterflies
Scientific Name	Gaura
Status	Perennial
Mature Size (H x W)	3x2
Pruning Category (1-5)	1
Watering Category (1-5)	1
Sun Category (1-5)	4
USDA Hardiness Zone:	5-9
Bloom Season	Summer

Common Name	Coreopsis
Scientific Name	Selleophutum Urb. Tuckermannia Nutt.
Status	Perennial
Mature Size (H x W)	2.5x1
Pruning Category (1-5)	1
Watering Category (1-5)	2
Sun Category (1-5)	4
USDA Hardiness Zone:	3-9
Bloom Season	Summer

Style for Miles

Description

The classic design and look of this garden bed will delight wildlife all season and is stunningly beautiful. The variety of blooms will make beautiful arrangements throughout the season. The bed is fully deciduous and perennial so cut back dead foliage at first front and mulch the bed well over winter. Trim roses in the late fall to resize for next spring.

Ingredients

(3) Limelight Hydrangea
(3) Knock Out Roses
(3) Endless Summer Hydrangea
(10) Stella d'Oro Daylily

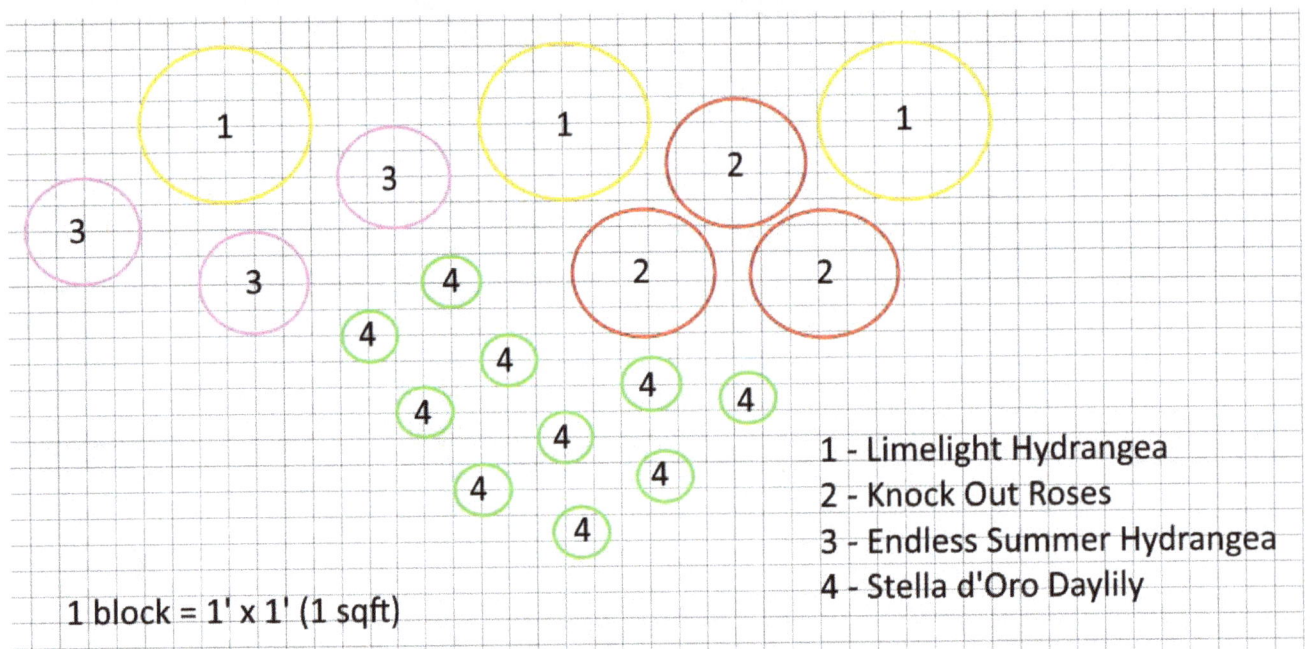

1 - Limelight Hydrangea
2 - Knock Out Roses
3 - Endless Summer Hydrangea
4 - Stella d'Oro Daylily

1 block = 1' x 1' (1 sqft)

Assembly Instructions

Garden Size (Approximate):	34'L x 20'W
Pruning Category:	1
Watering Needs:	3
Sun Requirements:	4
Plant Zones:	3-10
Bloom Colors:	White, Red, Purple, Yellow
Bloom Time Range:	Summer
Average Time to Install:	8 hours
Approximate Bedding:	680sf
Mulch:	4 cuyds
Pine Straw:	16 bales
Rock:	8.5 tons at 3" thick
Other Cultivars Available to Sub:	Yes
Special Needs:	Deadhead roses after blooming for more blooms. Prune back knock out roses to 18" at end of Fall

Till garden and amend soil with composted material such as mulched leaves or shredded pine.

Using the planting diagram, measure for plant placement and sit each plant in its proper place. Adjust placement based on the shape of the actual bed.

Dig each hole twice as wide as the root ball. Sprinkle in starter fertilizer to the bottom of the hole (follow directions on package for proper application). Set plant in hole. Push soil back around plant, tamping in tight with the handle end of the shovel to remove all air pockets. Tamp soil tight at top of root ball.

Repeat for each plant.

Water in all plants thoroughly.

Top beds with mulch, pine straw or other bedding materials to hold moisture and keep roots warm in winter and cool in summer.

Style for Miles

Birds, Bees & Butterflies

Common Name	Limelight Hydrangea
Scientific Name	Hydrangea paniculala 'Limelight'
Status	Deciduous
Mature Size (H x W)	6x6
Pruning Category (1-5)	1
Watering Category (1-5)	3
Sun Category (1-5)	4
USDA Hardiness Zone:	4-9
Bloom Season	Summer

Common Name	Knock Out Rose
Scientific Name	Rosa Radrazz
Status	Deciduous
Mature Size (H x W)	4x4
Pruning Category (1-5)	2
Watering Category (1-5)	2
Sun Category (1-5)	5
USDA Hardiness Zone:	5-10
Bloom Season	Summer

Common Name	Endless Summer Hydrangea
Scientific Name	Hydrangea macrophylla 'Bailmacfive' PPAF
Status	Deciduous
Mature Size (H x W)	3x3
Pruning Category (1-5)	1
Watering Category (1-5)	3
Sun Category (1-5)	3
USDA Hardiness Zone:	4-9
Bloom Season	Summer

Common Name	Stella d'Oro Daylily
Scientific Name	Hemerocallis 'Stella d'Oro'
Status	Perennial
Mature Size (H x W)	2x2
Pruning Category (1-5)	1
Watering Category (1-5)	2
Sun Category (1-5)	4
USDA Hardiness Zone:	3-9
Bloom Season	Summer

Serenity at Last

Birds, Bees & Butterflies

Description

Wildlife will flock to the colors and scents in this garden. Tuck this beauty away for a natural look with amazing color, texture and nasal sensation. The green in the Japanese Maple will brighten a slightly shade area as the agapanthus blooms add contrast and visual appeal.

Ingredients

(1) Dissectum Japanese Maple
(6) Caramel Heuchera
(3) George Tabor Azalea
(6) Agapanthus
(9) Chocolate Chip Ajuga

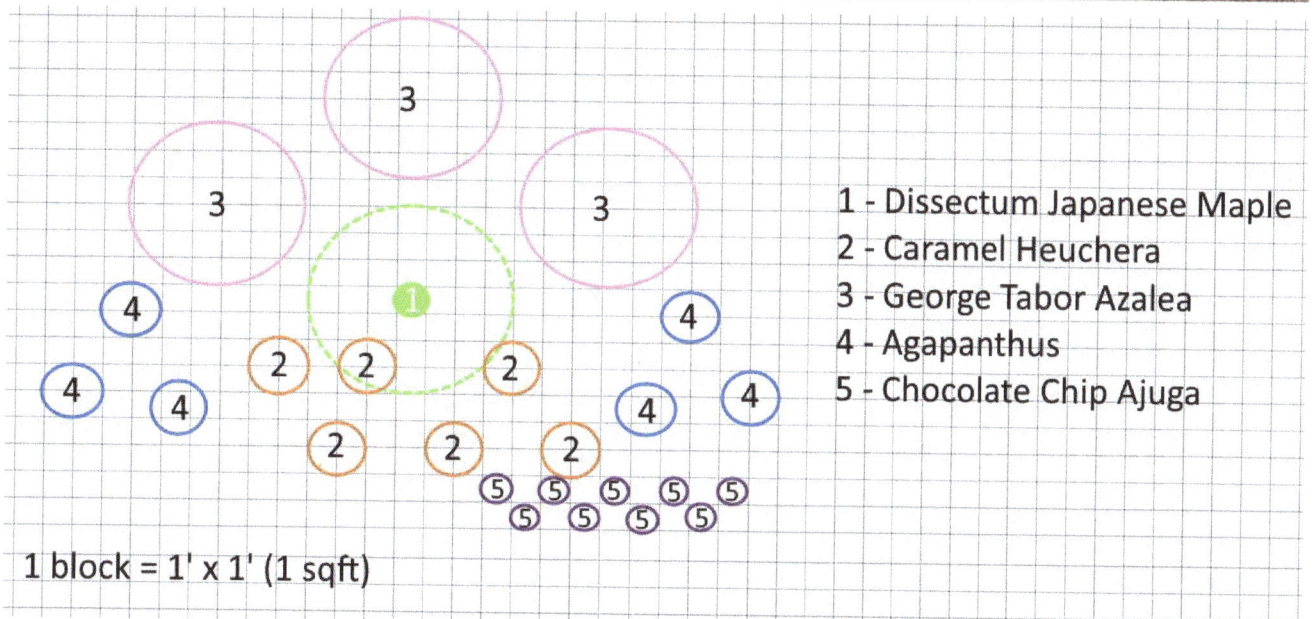

1 - Dissectum Japanese Maple
2 - Caramel Heuchera
3 - George Tabor Azalea
4 - Agapanthus
5 - Chocolate Chip Ajuga

1 block = 1' x 1' (1 sqft)

Assembly Instructions

Garden Size (Approximate):	25'L x 19'W
Pruning Category:	1
Watering Needs:	2
Sun Requirements:	3
Plant Zones:	4-11
Bloom Colors:	Orange, Pink, Blue
Bloom Time Range:	Spring-Summer
Average Time to Install:	12 hours
Approximate Bedding:	475sf
Mulch:	3 cuyds
Pine Straw:	11 bales
Rock:	6 tons at 3" thick
Other Cultivars Available to Sub:	Yes
Special Needs:	Regularly prune Japanese Maple to prevent any branches from touching the ground.

Till garden and amend soil with composted material such as mulched leaves or shredded pine.

Using the planting diagram, measure for plant placement and sit each plant in its proper place. Adjust placement based on the shape of the actual bed.

Dig each hole twice as wide as the root ball. Sprinkle in starter fertilizer to the bottom of the hole (follow directions on package for proper application). Set plant in hole. Push soil back around plant, tamping in tight with the handle end of the shovel to remove all air pockets. Tamp soil tight at top of root ball.

Repeat for each plant.

Water in all plants thoroughly.

Top beds with mulch, pine straw or other bedding materials to hold moisture and keep roots warm in winter and cool in summer.

Serenity at Last

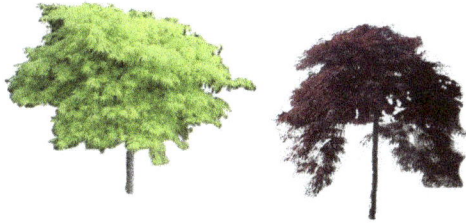

Birds, Bees & Butterflies

Common Name	Dissectum Japanese Maple
Scientific Name	Acer palmatum var dissectum
Status	Deciduous
Mature Size (H x W)	6x9
Pruning Category (1-5)	2
Watering Category (1-5)	2
Sun Category (1-5)	3
USDA Hardiness Zone:	5-8
Bloom Season	None

Common Name	Caramel Heuchera
Scientific Name	Heuchera 'Caramel'
Status	Perennial
Mature Size (H x W)	2x3
Pruning Category (1-5)	1
Watering Category (1-5)	2
Sun Category (1-5)	2
USDA Hardiness Zone:	4-9
Bloom Season	Summer

Common Name	George Tabor Azalea
Scientific Name	Rhododendron x 'George Tabor'
Status	Evergreen
Mature Size (H x W)	5x5
Pruning Category (1-5)	2
Watering Category (1-5)	3
Sun Category (1-5)	3
USDA Hardiness Zone:	7-9
Bloom Season	Spring

Common Name	Agapanthus
Scientific Name	Agapanthus africanus
Status	Perennial
Mature Size (H x W)	2.5x2.5
Pruning Category (1-5)	1
Watering Category (1-5)	2
Sun Category (1-5)	2
USDA Hardiness Zone:	8-11
Bloom Season	Spring

Common Name	Chocolate Chip Ajuga
Scientific Name	Ajuga reptans 'Chocolate Chip'
Status	Evergreen
Mature Size (H x W)	2x2
Pruning Category (1-5)	1
Watering Category (1-5)	3
Sun Category (1-5)	3
USDA Hardiness Zone:	4-9
Bloom Season	Spring

Description

A bright and cherry yellow garden with three season color. For a full sun area, this garden brings unmatched brilliance and vibrance. The first glimpse of spring will peek through when the forsythia shows off, sometimes even before the snow has melted in winter. Cut back dead foliage of the perennials in late fall and protect with a thick layer of mulch for winter.

Ingredients

(1) Witch Hazel
(1) Forsythia
(3) Sunshine Ligustrum
(3) Stella d'Oro Daylily
(5) Blackeyed Susan
(3) Calla Lily

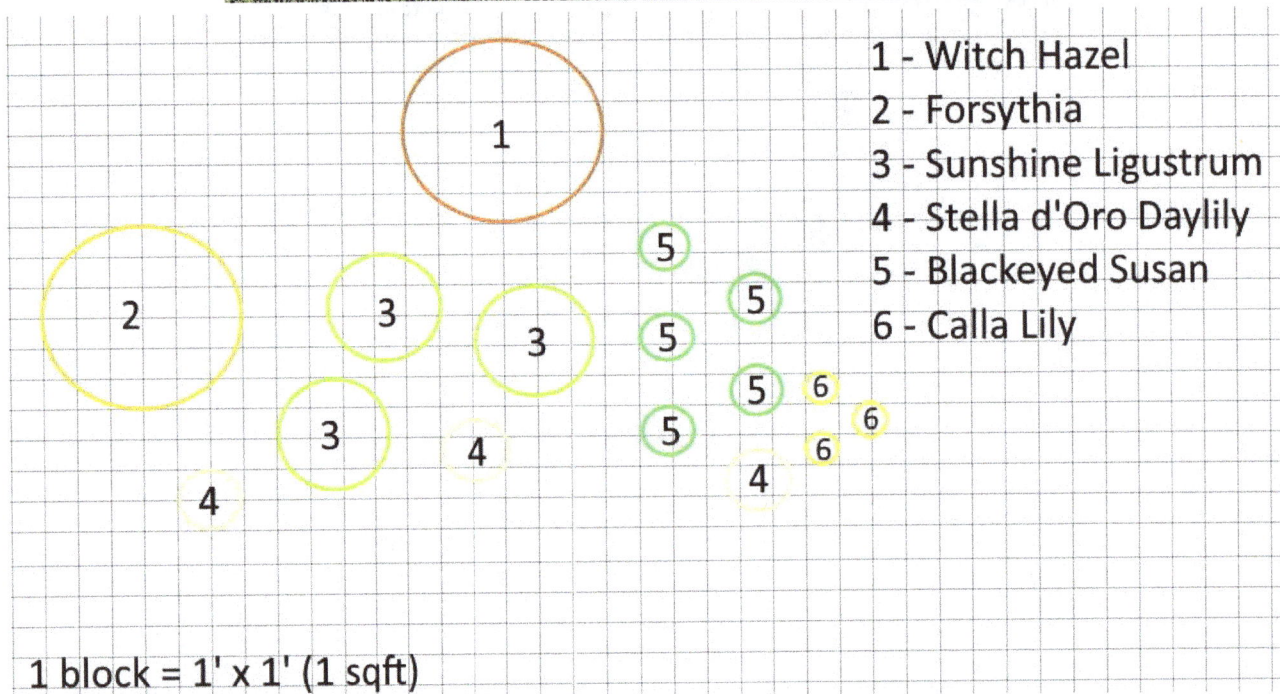

1 - Witch Hazel
2 - Forsythia
3 - Sunshine Ligustrum
4 - Stella d'Oro Daylily
5 - Blackeyed Susan
6 - Calla Lily

1 block = 1' x 1' (1 sqft)

Assembly Instructions

Garden Size (Approximate):	25'L x 16'W
Pruning Category:	2
Watering Needs:	2
Sun Requirements:	4
Plant Zones:	3-10
Bloom Colors:	Yellow
Bloom Time Range:	Spring-Fall
Average Time to Install:	8 hours
Approximate Bedding:	400sf
Mulch:	3 cuyds
Pine Straw:	10 bales
Rock:	5 tons at 3" thick
Other Cultivars Available to Sub:	Yes
Special Needs:	Mulch perennials heavily for winter.

Till garden and amend soil with composted material such as mulched leaves or shredded pine.

Using the planting diagram, measure for plant placement and sit each plant in its proper place. Adjust placement based on the shape of the actual bed.

Dig each hole twice as wide as the root ball. Sprinkle in starter fertilizer to the bottom of the hole (follow directions on package for proper application). Set plant in hole. Push soil back around plant, tamping in tight with the handle end of the shovel to remove all air pockets. Tamp soil tight at top of root ball.

Repeat for each plant.

Water in all plants thoroughly.

Top beds with mulch, pine straw or other bedding materials to hold moisture and keep roots warm in winter and cool in summer.

Common Name	Witch Hazel
Scientific Name	Hamamelis
Status	Deciduous
Mature Size (H x W)	6x6
Pruning Category (1-5)	1
Watering Category (1-5)	1
Sun Category (1-5)	3
USDA Hardiness Zone:	5-9
Bloom Season	Fall

Common Name	Forsythia
Scientific Name	Forsythia
Status	Deciduous
Mature Size (H x W)	8x8
Pruning Category (1-5)	2
Watering Category (1-5)	2
Sun Category (1-5)	4
USDA Hardiness Zone:	5-9
Bloom Season	Spring

Common Name	Sunshine Ligustrum
Scientific Name	Ligustrum sinense 'Sunshine'
Status	Evergreen
Mature Size (H x W)	4x4
Pruning Category (1-5)	4
Watering Category (1-5)	2
Sun Category (1-5)	5
USDA Hardiness Zone:	7-10
Bloom Season	None-Inconspicuous

Common Name	Stella d'Oro Daylily
Scientific Name	Hemerocallis 'Stella d'Oro'
Status	Perennial
Mature Size (H x W)	2x2
Pruning Category (1-5)	1
Watering Category (1-5)	2
Sun Category (1-5)	4
USDA Hardiness Zone:	3-9
Bloom Season	Summer

Common Name	Blackeyed Susan
Scientific Name	Rudbeckia hirta
Status	Perennial
Mature Size (H x W)	2x2
Pruning Category (1-5)	1
Watering Category (1-5)	2
Sun Category (1-5)	4
USDA Hardiness Zone:	3-9
Bloom Season	Summer

Common Name	Calla Lily
Scientific Name	Zantedeschia aethiopica
Status	Perennial
Mature Size (H x W)	1.5x1.5
Pruning Category (1-5)	1
Watering Category (1-5)	3
Sun Category (1-5)	4
USDA Hardiness Zone:	4-9
Bloom Season	Spring

Description

Even the man in the moon will be envious for this all white blooming garden. Bees and butterflies will flock to the bloom and the fabulous scents will provide plenty of pleasure all summer. Soft landscape lighting on this beauty at night will be a moon light delight for all who gaze upon it. Set up the garden where it can be seen from indoors for a magnificent focal point.

Ingredients

(1) Snowball Viburnum
(3) Radicans Gardenia
(3) August Beauty Gardenia
(3) Autumn Moonlight Encore Azalea
(3) Shasta Daisy

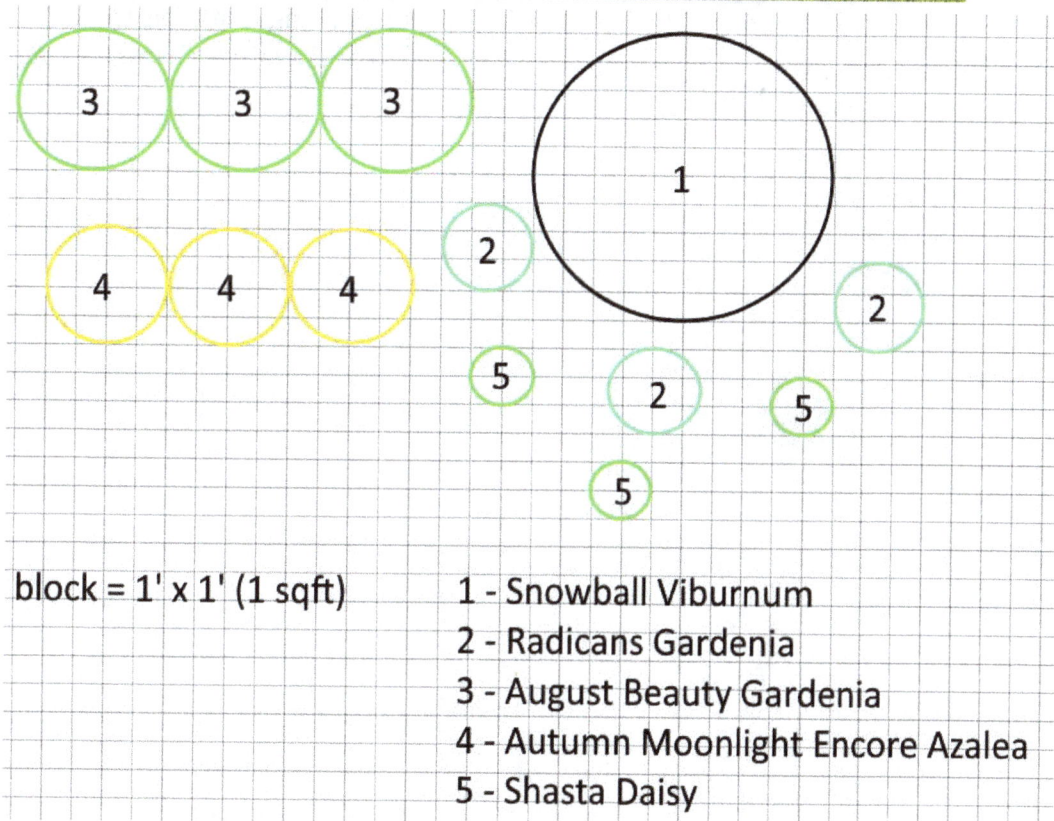

block = 1' x 1' (1 sqft)

1 - Snowball Viburnum
2 - Radicans Gardenia
3 - August Beauty Gardenia
4 - Autumn Moonlight Encore Azalea
5 - Shasta Daisy

Assembly Instructions

Garden Size (Approximate):	30'L x 17'W
Pruning Category:	2
Watering Needs:	3
Sun Requirements:	4
Plant Zones:	3-11
Bloom Colors:	White
Bloom Time Range:	Spring-Fall
Average Time to Install:	7 hours
Approximate Bedding:	510sf
Mulch:	3 cuyds
Pine Straw:	12 bales
Rock:	6.3 tons at 3" thick
Other Cultivars Available to Sub:	Yes
Special Needs:	

Till garden and amend soil with composted material such as mulched leaves or shredded pine.

Using the planting diagram, measure for plant placement and sit each plant in its proper place. Adjust placement based on the shape of the actual bed.

Dig each hole twice as wide as the root ball. Sprinkle in starter fertilizer to the bottom of the hole (follow directions on package for proper application). Set plant in hole. Push soil back around plant, tamping in tight with the handle end of the shovel to remove all air pockets. Tamp soil tight at top of root ball.

Repeat for each plant.

Water in all plants thoroughly.

Top beds with mulch, pine straw or other bedding materials to hold moisture and keep roots warm in winter and cool in summer.

Common Name	Snowball Viburnum
Scientific Name	Viburnum opulus 'Roseum'
Status	Deciduous
Mature Size (H x W)	10x10
Pruning Category (1-5)	1
Watering Category (1-5)	2
Sun Category (1-5)	3
USDA Hardiness Zone:	3-8
Bloom Season	Spring

Common Name	Radicans Gardenia
Scientific Name	Gardenia jasminoides 'Radicans Variegata'
Status	Evergreen
Mature Size (H x W)	3x3
Pruning Category (1-5)	2
Watering Category (1-5)	3
Sun Category (1-5)	4
USDA Hardiness Zone:	7-11
Bloom Season	Summer, Fall

Common Name	August Beauty Gardenia
Scientific Name	Gardenia jasminoides 'August Beauty'
Status	Evergreen
Mature Size (H x W)	5x5
Pruning Category (1-5)	2
Watering Category (1-5)	3
Sun Category (1-5)	4
USDA Hardiness Zone:	7-11
Bloom Season	Summer, Fall

Common Name	Autumn Moonlight Encore Azalea
Scientific Name	Rhododendron 'Mootum' PP18416
Status	Evergreen
Mature Size (H x W)	3x3
Pruning Category (1-5)	2
Watering Category (1-5)	3
Sun Category (1-5)	4
USDA Hardiness Zone:	7-10
Bloom Season	Spring, Fall

Common Name	Shasta Daisy
Scientific Name	Leucanthemum x superbum
Status	Perennial
Mature Size (H x W)	2.5x2.5
Pruning Category (1-5)	1
Watering Category (1-5)	2
Sun Category (1-5)	4
USDA Hardiness Zone:	4-10
Bloom Season	Summer

Description

It's bright! It's bold! It's brilliant! The color in this garden is the gift that just keeps on giving all summer with flowing crape myrtles, swaying canna lily and flirty day lilies out front. It's like a car load of sorority girls on summer break! Dwarf crape myrtles mean there's no pruning and the reblooming azaleas keep the color coming all summer.

Ingredients

(3) Dynamite Crape Myrtle
(3) Canna Lily
(6) Autumn Embers Encore Azalea
(3) Knock Out Roses
(2) Red Day Lily (reblooming)

1 - Dynamite Crape Myrtle
2 - Canna Lily
3 - Autumn Embers Encore Azalea
4 - Knock Out Roses
5 - Red Day Lily

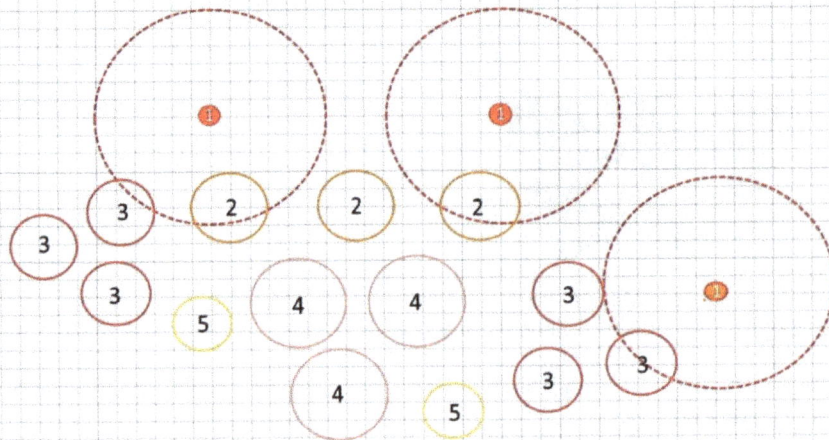

1 block = 1' x 1' (1 sqft)

Assembly Instructions

Garden Size (Approximate):	43'L x 24'W	
Pruning Category:	1	
Watering Needs:	3	
Sun Requirements:	4	
Plant Zones:	3-11	
Bloom Colors:	Red	
Bloom Time Range:	Spring-Fall	
Average Time to Install:	10 hours	
Approximate Bedding:	1032sf	
Mulch:	6 cuyds	
Pine Straw:	25 bales	
Rock:	13 tons	
Other Cultivars Available to Sub:	Yes	
Special Needs:	This cultivar of crape myrtle is considered dwarf. There is no need to cut back every year (also called "knuckling"). Cut back knock out roses to 18" tall at end of Fall.	

Till garden and amend soil with composted material such as mulched leaves or shredded pine.

Using the planting diagram, measure for plant placement and sit each plant in its proper place. Adjust placement based on the shape of the actual bed.

Dig each hole twice as wide as the root ball. Sprinkle in starter fertilizer to the bottom of the hole (follow directions on package for proper application). Set plant in hole. Push soil back around plant, tamping in tight with the handle end of the shovel to remove all air pockets. Tamp soil tight at top of root ball.

Repeat for each plant.

Water in all plants thoroughly.

Top beds with mulch, pine straw or other bedding materials to hold moisture and keep roots warm in winter and cool in summer.

Common Name	Dynamite Crape Myrtle
Scientific Name	Lagerstroemia indica 'Whit II' Dynamite
Status	Deciduous
Mature Size (H x W)	15x10
Pruning Category (1-5)	1
Watering Category (1-5)	2
Sun Category (1-5)	4
USDA Hardiness Zone:	6-11
Bloom Season	Summer

Common Name	Canna Lily
Scientific Name	Canna indica
Status	Perennial
Mature Size (H x W)	6x4
Pruning Category (1-5)	1
Watering Category (1-5)	3
Sun Category (1-5)	4
USDA Hardiness Zone:	4-9
Bloom Season	Summer

Common Name	Autumn Embers Encore Azalea
Scientific Name	Rhododendron 'Conleb'
Status	Evergreen
Mature Size (H x W)	4x4.5
Pruning Category (1-5)	2
Watering Category (1-5)	3
Sun Category (1-5)	4
USDA Hardiness Zone:	7-10
Bloom Season	Spring, Fall

Common Name	Knock Out Rose
Scientific Name	Rosa Radrazz
Status	Deciduous
Mature Size (H x W)	4x4
Pruning Category (1-5)	2
Watering Category (1-5)	2
Sun Category (1-5)	5
USDA Hardiness Zone:	5-10
Bloom Season	Summer

Common Name	Red Daylily
Scientific Name	Hemerocallis 'Red Hot Returns'
Status	Perennial
Mature Size (H x W)	2x2
Pruning Category (1-5)	1
Watering Category (1-5)	2
Sun Category (1-5)	4
USDA Hardiness Zone:	3-9
Bloom Season	Summer

Rhymes with Emu

Description

Subdued and serene, but full of color and texture. The veronica is sure to delight the bees and hummingbirds all season while the soft colors soothe the psyche. Mulch the entire bed heavily for the winter months.

Ingredients

(1) Dwarf Blue Butterfly Shrub
(2) Hyssop
(2) Dwarf Blue Spruce
(3) Veronica Spicata

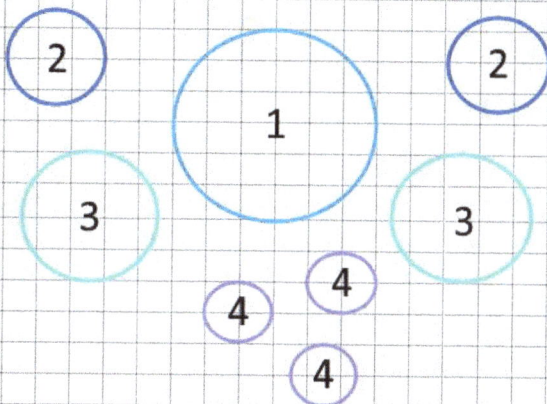

1 - Dwarf Blue Butterfly Shrub
2 - Hyssop
3 - Dwarf Blue Spruce
4 - Veronica Spicata

1 block = 1' x 1' (1 sqft)

Assembly Instructions

Garden Size (Approximate):	16'L x 13'W
Pruning Category:	1
Watering Needs:	2
Sun Requirements:	4
Plant Zones:	3-11
Bloom Colors:	Blue
Bloom Time Range:	Summer
Average Time to Install:	4 hours
Approximate Bedding:	208sf
Mulch:	1.5 cuyds
Pine Straw:	5 bales
Rock:	2.6 tons at 3" thick
Other Cultivars Available to Sub:	Yes
Special Needs:	Mulch dwarf blue spruce heavily in summer in warmer climates to protect it from heat.

Till garden and amend soil with composted material such as mulched leaves or shredded pine.

Using the planting diagram, measure for plant placement and sit each plant in its proper place. Adjust placement based on the shape of the actual bed.

Dig each hole twice as wide as the root ball. Sprinkle in starter fertilizer to the bottom of the hole (follow directions on package for proper application). Set plant in hole. Push soil back around plant, tamping in tight with the handle end of the shovel to remove all air pockets. Tamp soil tight at top of root ball.

Repeat for each plant.

Water in all plants thoroughly.

Top beds with mulch, pine straw or other bedding materials to hold moisture and keep roots warm in winter and cool in summer.

Common Name	Dwarf Butterfly Shrub
Scientific Name	Buddleia
Status	Deciduous
Mature Size (H x W)	3x3
Pruning Category (1-5)	2
Watering Category (1-5)	2
Sun Category (1-5)	5
USDA Hardiness Zone:	5-11
Bloom Season	Summer

Common Name	Hyssop
Scientific Name	Hyssopus officinalis
Status	Perennial
Mature Size (H x W)	2x2
Pruning Category (1-5)	1
Watering Category (1-5)	2
Sun Category (1-5)	4
USDA Hardiness Zone:	4-9
Bloom Season	Summer

Common Name	Dwarf Blue Spruce
Scientific Name	Picea pungens 'Globosa'
Status	Evergreen
Mature Size (H x W)	2x2
Pruning Category (1-5)	1
Watering Category (1-5)	2
Sun Category (1-5)	3
USDA Hardiness Zone:	3-8
Bloom Season	None

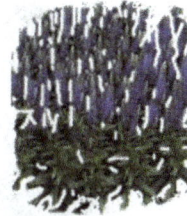

Common Name	Veronica Spicata
Scientific Name	Veronica spicata
Status	Perennial
Mature Size (H x W)	2.5x2.5
Pruning Category (1-5)	1
Watering Category (1-5)	2
Sun Category (1-5)	4
USDA Hardiness Zone:	4-8
Bloom Season	Summer

Description

Perfect and pretty in pink, this gentle garden is just too nice. Three season color softens any corner of the yard while still providing for all Mother Nature's creatures with fragrant and delicate blooms. Cut back declining perennial foliage as it wilts in late fall and mulch the roots for winter.

Ingredients

(1) Weeping Cherry Tree
(1) George Tabor Azalea
(3) Edward Goucher Abelia
(1) Autumn Joy Sedum
(1) Peach Drift Rose
(3) Harbor Dwarf Nandina

(3) Autumn Chiffon Encore Azalea
(2) Bee Balm

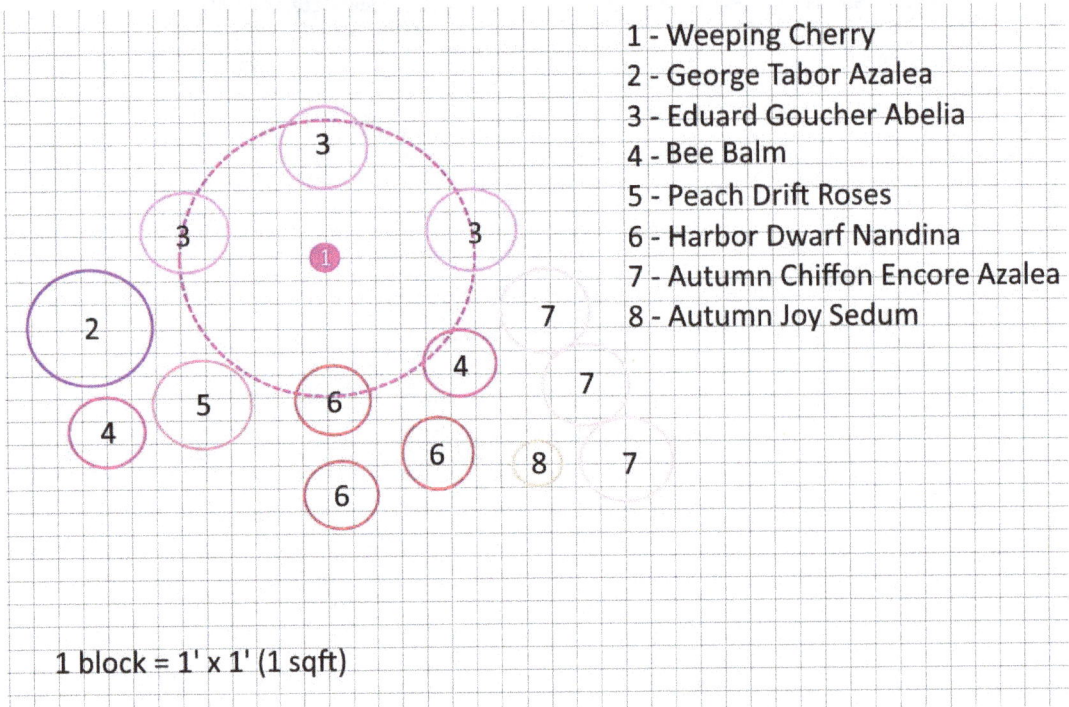

1 - Weeping Cherry
2 - George Tabor Azalea
3 - Eduard Goucher Abelia
4 - Bee Balm
5 - Peach Drift Roses
6 - Harbor Dwarf Nandina
7 - Autumn Chiffon Encore Azalea
8 - Autumn Joy Sedum

1 block = 1' x 1' (1 sqft)

Assembly Instructions

Garden Size (Approximate):	26'L x 19'W
Pruning Category:	2
Watering Needs:	2
Sun Requirements:	4
Plant Zones:	4-10
Bloom Colors:	Pink, Peach
Bloom Time Range:	Spring-Fall
Average Time to Install:	9 hours
Approximate Bedding:	494sf
Mulch:	3 cuyds
Pine Straw:	12 bales
Rock:	6 tons at 3" thick
Other Cultivars Available to Sub:	Yes
Special Needs:	Dead head roses throughout the season to get more blooms.

Till garden and amend soil with composted material such as mulched leaves or shredded pine.

Using the planting diagram, measure for plant placement and sit each plant in its proper place. Adjust placement based on the shape of the actual bed.

Dig each hole twice as wide as the root ball. Sprinkle in starter fertilizer to the bottom of the hole (follow directions on package for proper application). Set plant in hole. Push soil back around plant, tamping in tight with the handle end of the shovel to remove all air pockets. Tamp soil tight at top of root ball.

Repeat for each plant.

Water in all plants thoroughly.

Top beds with mulch, pine straw or other bedding materials to hold moisture and keep roots warm in winter and cool in summer.

Common Name	Weeping Cherry
Scientific Name	Prunus pendula
Status	Deciduous
Mature Size (H x W)	25x15
Pruning Category (1-5)	1
Watering Category (1-5)	2
Sun Category (1-5)	4
USDA Hardiness Zone:	4-8
Bloom Season	Spring

Common Name	George Tabor Azalea
Scientific Name	Rhododendron x 'George Tabor'
Status	Evergreen
Mature Size (H x W)	5x5
Pruning Category (1-5)	2
Watering Category (1-5)	3
Sun Category (1-5)	3
USDA Hardiness Zone:	7-9
Bloom Season	Spring

Common Name	Glossy Abelia
Scientific Name	Abelia x grandiflora
Status	Semi Deciduous
Mature Size (H x W)	3x3
Pruning Category (1-5)	1
Watering Category (1-5)	2
Sun Category (1-5)	4
USDA Hardiness Zone:	6-9
Bloom Season	Fall

Common Name	Bee Balm
Scientific Name	Monarda
Status	Perennial
Mature Size (H x W)	3x3
Pruning Category (1-5)	1
Watering Category (1-5)	2
Sun Category (1-5)	4
USDA Hardiness Zone:	2-10
Bloom Season	Summer

Common Name	Drift Rose
Scientific Name	Rosa 'Meijocos'
Status	Deciduous
Mature Size (H x W)	3x3
Pruning Category (1-5)	2
Watering Category (1-5)	2
Sun Category (1-5)	5
USDA Hardiness Zone:	5-10
Bloom Season	Summer

Common Name	Harbor Dwarf Nandina
Scientific Name	Nandina domestica 'Harbour Dwarf'
Status	Evergreen
Mature Size (H x W)	3x3
Pruning Category (1-5)	2
Watering Category (1-5)	2
Sun Category (1-5)	3
USDA Hardiness Zone:	5-10
Bloom Season	Summer

Common Name	Autumn Chiffon Encore Azalea
Scientific Name	Rhododendron 'Robled' PP15862
Status	Evergreen
Mature Size (H x W)	3.5x3.5
Pruning Category (1-5)	2
Watering Category (1-5)	3
Sun Category (1-5)	4
USDA Hardiness Zone:	7-10
Bloom Season	Spring, Fall

Common Name	Autumn Joy Sedum
Scientific Name	Hylotelephium telephium 'Autumn Joy'
Status	Perennial
Mature Size (H x W)	2x2
Pruning Category (1-5)	1
Watering Category (1-5)	1
Sun Category (1-5)	5
USDA Hardiness Zone:	3-8
Bloom Season	Fall

Magic Balls and Broomsticks

Description

No hocus pocus needed with this maintenance free garden. Add as a back drop to a colorful perennial garden or create a screen around pools, ponds or peering eyes of neighbors or passersby. The dark and light greens make a great addition for a fuss free side garden or a break at the top of a hill.

Ingredients

(5) Emerald Green Arborvitae
(5) Nana Globosa Dwarf Cryptomeria

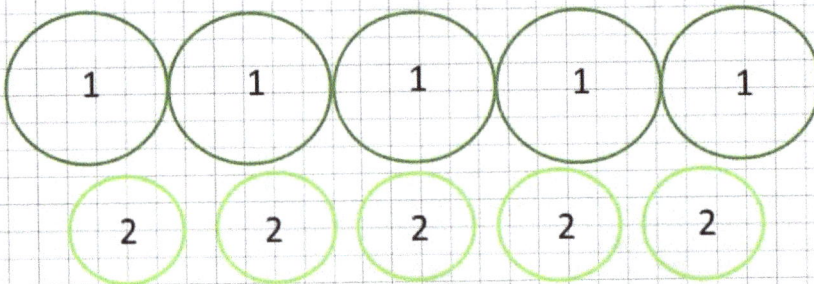

1 - Emerald Green Arborvitae
2 - Nana Globosa Dwarf Cryptomeria

1 block = 1' x 1' (1 sqft)

Assembly Instructions

Garden Size (Approximate):	28'L x 10'W
Pruning Category:	1
Watering Needs:	2
Sun Requirements:	4
Plant Zones:	4-9
Bloom Colors:	None
Bloom Time Range:	N/A
Average Time to Install:	8 hours
Approximate Bedding:	280sf
Mulch:	2 cuyds
Pine Straw:	7 bales
Rock:	3.5 tons at 3" thick
Other Cultivars Available to Sub:	Yes
Special Needs:	

Till garden and amend soil with composted material such as mulched leaves or shredded pine.

Using the planting diagram, measure for plant placement and sit each plant in its proper place. Adjust placement based on the shape of the actual bed.

Dig each hole twice as wide as the root ball. Sprinkle in starter fertilizer to the bottom of the hole (follow directions on package for proper application). Set plant in hole. Push soil back around plant, tamping in tight with the handle end of the shovel to remove all air pockets. Tamp soil tight at top of root ball.

Repeat for each plant.

Water in all plants thoroughly.

Top beds with mulch, pine straw or other bedding materials to hold moisture and keep roots warm in winter and cool in summer.

Common Name	Emerald Green Arborvitae
Scientific Name	Thuja occidentalis
Status	Evergreen
Mature Size (H x W)	15x5
Pruning Category (1-5)	1
Watering Category (1-5)	3
Sun Category (1-5)	4
USDA Hardiness Zone:	4-8
Bloom Season	None

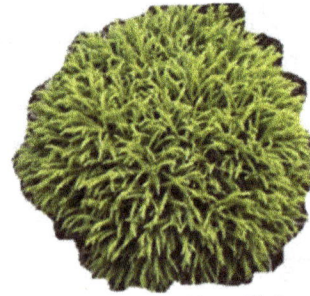

Common Name	Nana Globosa Dwarf Cryptomeria
Scientific Name	Cryptomeria japonica 'Globosa Nana'
Status	Evergreen
Mature Size (H x W)	4x4
Pruning Category (1-5)	1
Watering Category (1-5)	1
Sun Category (1-5)	3
USDA Hardiness Zone:	6-9
Bloom Season	None

Heavenly Hedge

Description

This straight-line design can serve for privacy, hedge, property lines or curve the shape to fill a need around the landscape. Plants grow to mature size shown and require very little pruning so maintenance is a snap. Evergreen means year-round color and interest.

Ingredients

(5) Gold Mop Cypress
(7) Purple Diamond Loropetalum
(5) Mardi Gras Abelia

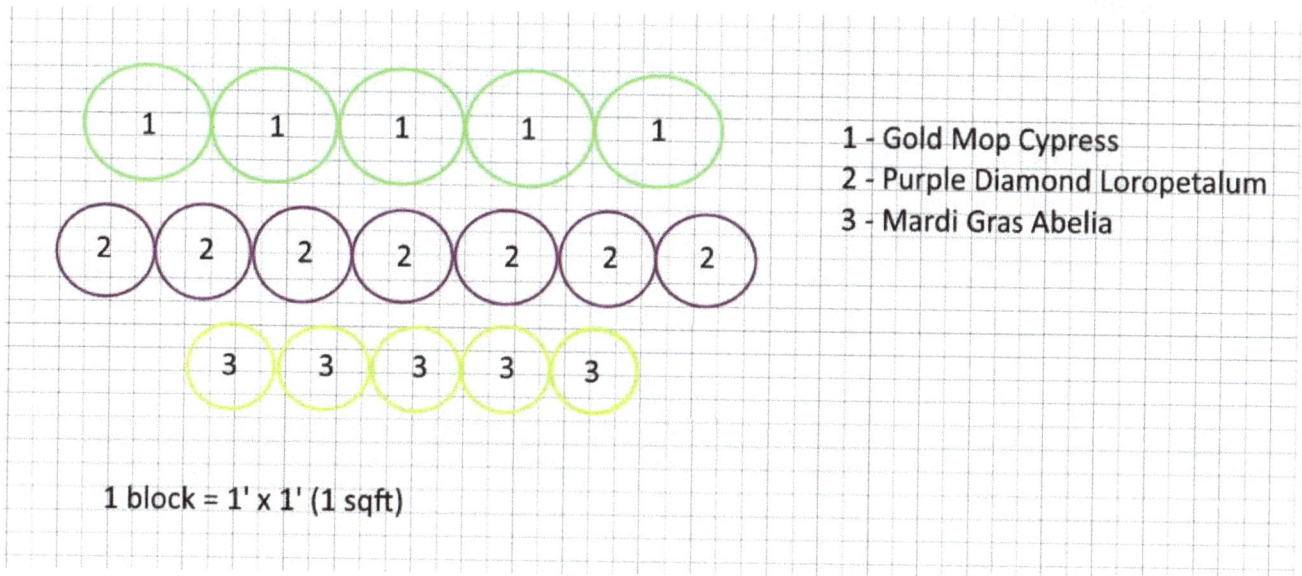

1 - Gold Mop Cypress
2 - Purple Diamond Loropetalum
3 - Mardi Gras Abelia

1 block = 1' x 1' (1 sqft)

Assembly Instructions

Garden Size (Approximate):	28'L x 15'W
Pruning Category:	1
Watering Needs:	2
Sun Requirements:	4
Plant Zones:	6-10
Bloom Colors:	Purple, Pink
Bloom Time Range:	Spring, Fall
Average Time to Install:	9 hours
Approximate Bedding:	420sf
Mulch:	2.5 cuyds
Pine Straw:	10 bales
Rock:	5.25 tons at 3" thick
Other Cultivars Available to Sub:	Yes
Special Needs:	

Till garden and amend soil with composted material such as mulched leaves or shredded pine.

Using the planting diagram, measure for plant placement and sit each plant in its proper place. Adjust placement based on the shape of the actual bed.

Dig each hole twice as wide as the root ball. Sprinkle in starter fertilizer to the bottom of the hole (follow directions on package for proper application). Set plant in hole. Push soil back around plant, tamping in tight with the handle end of the shovel to remove all air pockets. Tamp soil tight at top of root ball.

Repeat for each plant.

Water in all plants thoroughly.

Top beds with mulch, pine straw or other bedding materials to hold moisture and keep roots warm in winter and cool in summer.

Common Name	Gold Mop Cypress
Scientific Name	Chamaecyparis
Status	Evergreen
Mature Size (H x W)	6x6
Pruning Category (1-5)	1
Watering Category (1-5)	1
Sun Category (1-5)	4
USDA Hardiness Zone:	6-9
Bloom Season	None

Common Name	Purple Diamond Loropetalum
Scientific Name	Loropetalum chinense 'Shang-hi' PP18331
Status	Evergreen
Mature Size (H x W)	5x5
Pruning Category (1-5)	2
Watering Category (1-5)	2
Sun Category (1-5)	3
USDA Hardiness Zone:	7-10
Bloom Season	Spring

Common Name	Mardi Gras Abelia
Scientific Name	Abelia x grandiflora 'Mardi Gras'
Status	Semi Deciduous
Mature Size (H x W)	3x3
Pruning Category (1-5)	1
Watering Category (1-5)	2
Sun Category (1-5)	4
USDA Hardiness Zone:	6-9
Bloom Season	Fall

Buffed, Puffed and Fluffed

Description

A timeless color combination of white, red and lime green, this garden is bedazzled with style and texture. The fluffiness in back and front with the hard lines of the roses creates contrast which can be enlarged by repeating the pattern with more plants. Create a beautiful property line, cover up a troubled area or impress the company with a welcoming side garden near a parking area.

Ingredients

(3) Limelight Hydrangea
(3) Knock Out Roses
(21) Acorus Grass

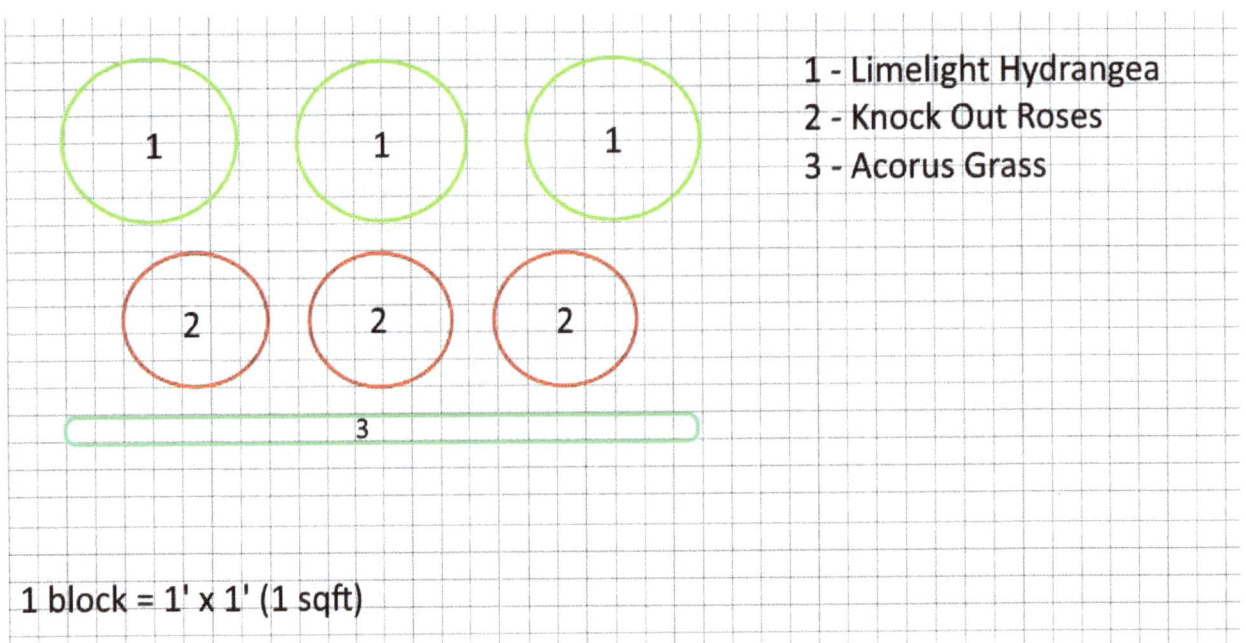

1 - Limelight Hydrangea
2 - Knock Out Roses
3 - Acorus Grass

1 block = 1' x 1' (1 sqft)

Buffed, Puffed and Fluffed

Assembly Instructions

Garden Size (Approximate):	22'L x 14' W
Pruning Category:	1
Watering Needs:	2
Sun Requirements:	4
Plant Zones:	4-10
Bloom Colors:	White, Red
Bloom Time Range:	Summer
Average Time to Install:	5 hours
Approximate Bedding:	308sf
Mulch:	2 cuyds
Pine Straw:	7 bales
Rock:	3.8 tons at 3" thick
Other Cultivars Available to Sub:	Yes
Special Needs:	Prune back knock out roses to 18" at end of Fall

Till garden and amend soil with composted material such as mulched leaves or shredded pine.

Using the planting diagram, measure for plant placement and sit each plant in its proper place. Adjust placement based on the shape of the actual bed.

Dig each hole twice as wide as the root ball. Sprinkle in starter fertilizer to the bottom of the hole (follow directions on package for proper application). Set plant in hole. Push soil back around plant, tamping in tight with the handle end of the shovel to remove all air pockets. Tamp soil tight at top of root ball.

Repeat for each plant.

Water in all plants thoroughly.

Top beds with mulch, pine straw or other bedding materials to hold moisture and keep roots warm in winter and cool in summer.

Common Name	Limelight Hydrangea
Scientific Name	Hydrangea paniculala 'Limelight'
Status	Deciduous
Mature Size (H x W)	6x6
Pruning Category (1-5)	1
Watering Category (1-5)	3
Sun Category (1-5)	4
USDA Hardiness Zone:	4-9
Bloom Season	Summer

Common Name	Knock Out Rose
Scientific Name	Rosa Radrazz
Status	Deciduous
Mature Size (H x W)	4x4
Pruning Category (1-5)	2
Watering Category (1-5)	2
Sun Category (1-5)	5
USDA Hardiness Zone:	5-10
Bloom Season	Summer

Common Name	Acorus Grass
Scientific Name	Acorus gramineus
Status	Perennial
Mature Size (H x W)	1X1
Pruning Category (1-5)	1
Watering Category (1-5)	1
Sun Category (1-5)	2
USDA Hardiness Zone:	6-9
Bloom Season	None

Beauty Queen

Description

The belle of the ball is the cluster of red Knock Out Roses. Their long season of brilliant red blooms is contrasted with the quaint stature of the Inkberry Holly. This holly is small, but it packs a mighty punch of dense color and consistent growth. Repeat the design to create a larger garden.

Ingredients

(3) Knock Out Roses (Red)
(7) Nordic Inkberry Holly

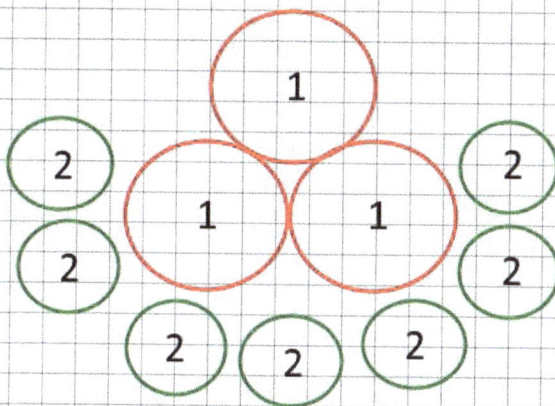

1 - Knock Out Roses
2 - Nordic Inkberry Holly

1 block = 1' x 1' (1 sqft)

Assembly Instructions

Garden Size (Approximate):	17L x 13W
Pruning Category:	3
Watering Needs:	2
Sun Requirements:	5
Plant Zones:	5-10
Bloom Colors:	Red
Bloom Time Range:	Summer
Average Time to Install:	5 hours
Approximate Bedding:	221sf
Mulch:	1.5 cuyds
Pine Straw:	5 bales
Rock:	2.75 tons at 3" thick
Other Cultivars Available to Sub:	Yes
Special Needs:	Prune back roses to 18" at end of Fall

Till garden and amend soil with composted material such as mulched leaves or shredded pine.

Using the planting diagram, measure for plant placement and sit each plant in its proper place. Adjust placement based on the shape of the actual bed.

Dig each hole twice as wide as the root ball. Sprinkle in starter fertilizer to the bottom of the hole (follow directions on package for proper application). Set plant in hole. Push soil back around plant, tamping in tight with the handle end of the shovel to remove all air pockets. Tamp soil tight at top of root ball.

Repeat for each plant.

Water in all plants thoroughly.

Top beds with mulch, pine straw or other bedding materials to hold moisture and keep roots warm in winter and cool in summer.

Common Name	Knock Out Rose
Scientific Name	Rosa Radrazz
Status	Deciduous
Mature Size (H x W)	4x4
Pruning Category (1-5)	2
Watering Category (1-5)	2
Sun Category (1-5)	5
USDA Hardiness Zone:	5-10
Bloom Season	Summer

Common Name	Nordic Inkberry Holly
Scientific Name	Ilex glabra
Status	Evergreen
Mature Size (H x W)	3x3
Pruning Category (1-5)	4
Watering Category (1-5)	2
Sun Category (1-5)	4
USDA Hardiness Zone:	5-8
Bloom Season	None-Inconspicuous

Prom Date

Description

Welcome spring with this lovely and innocent pink and white garden. The magnolia will be the envy of the neighborhood in early Spring with its delicate pink blooms. Keep the party going with white Knock Out Roses all summer bloomers, and twice a year blooms from reblooming Encore Azaleas.

Ingredients

(1) Saucer Magnolia
(2) Knock Out Roses (White)
(6) Autumn Carnation Encore Azalea
(3) Autumn Moonlight Encore Azalea

1 - Saucer Magnolia
2 - White Knock Out Roses
3 - Autumn Carnation Encore Azalea
4 - Autumn Moonlight Encore Azalea

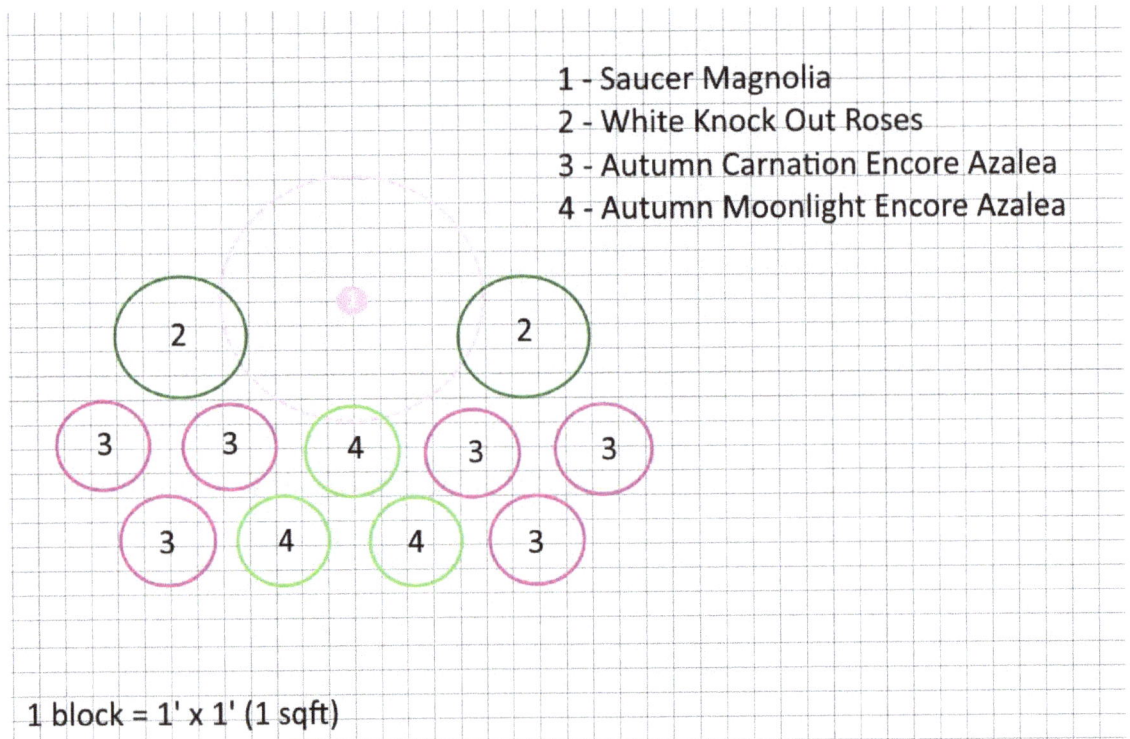

1 block = 1' x 1' (1 sqft)

Assembly Instructions

Garden Size (Approximate):	23'L x 17'W
Pruning Category:	2
Watering Needs:	3
Sun Requirements:	4
Plant Zones:	5-10
Bloom Colors:	Pink, White
Bloom Time Range:	Spring-Fall
Average Time to Install:	7 hours
Approximate Bedding:	391sf
Mulch:	2.5 cuyds
Pine Straw:	10 bales
Rock:	4.9 tons at 3" thick
Other Cultivars Available to Sub:	Yes
Special Needs:	Prune back knock out roses to 18" at end of Fall

Till garden and amend soil with composted material such as mulched leaves or shredded pine.

Using the planting diagram, measure for plant placement and sit each plant in its proper place. Adjust placement based on the shape of the actual bed.

Dig each hole twice as wide as the root ball. Sprinkle in starter fertilizer to the bottom of the hole (follow directions on package for proper application). Set plant in hole. Push soil back around plant, tamping in tight with the handle end of the shovel to remove all air pockets. Tamp soil tight at top of root ball.

Repeat for each plant.

Water in all plants thoroughly.

Top beds with mulch, pine straw or other bedding materials to hold moisture and keep roots warm in winter and cool in summer.

Common Name	Saucer Magnolia
Scientific Name	Magnolia x soulangeana
Status	Deciduous
Mature Size (H x W)	15x10
Pruning Category (1-5)	1
Watering Category (1-5)	2
Sun Category (1-5)	4
USDA Hardiness Zone:	7-9
Bloom Season	Spring

Common Name	Knock Out Rose
Scientific Name	Rosa Radrazz
Status	Deciduous
Mature Size (H x W)	4x4
Pruning Category (1-5)	2
Watering Category (1-5)	2
Sun Category (1-5)	5
USDA Hardiness Zone:	5-10
Bloom Season	Summer

Common Name	Autumn Carnation Encore Azalea
Scientific Name	Rhododendron 'Roblec' PP15339
Status	Evergreen
Mature Size (H x W)	4x4.5
Pruning Category (1-5)	2
Watering Category (1-5)	3
Sun Category (1-5)	4
USDA Hardiness Zone:	7-10
Bloom Season	Spring, Fall

Common Name	Autumn Moonlight Encore Azalea
Scientific Name	Rhododendron 'Mootum' PP18416
Status	Evergreen
Mature Size (H x W)	3x3
Pruning Category (1-5)	2
Watering Category (1-5)	3
Sun Category (1-5)	4
USDA Hardiness Zone:	7-10
Bloom Season	Spring, Fall

Spring Fling

Description

Be the best dressed house on the block with color, height, texture, blooms and interest. That's right, the neighbors will be green with envy, but not as green as this year-round garden landscape. Keep perennials and viburnum heavily mulched in winter for protection and in summer to keep roots cool and comfortable.

Ingredients

(3) Hardy Daisy Gardenia

(3) Blue Point Juniper

(3) Crimson Fire Loropetalum

(7) Radicans Gardenia

(3) Knock Out Roses (Red)

(3) Gold Mop Cypress

(5) Stella d'Oro Daylily

(1) Snowball Viburnum

(1) Limelight Hydrangea

(5) Autumn Embers Encore Azalea

(1) Hicks Yew

(5) Carissa Holly

(3) Shasta Daisy

(5) Carissa Holly

(3) Shasta Daisy

(5) Lamb's Ear

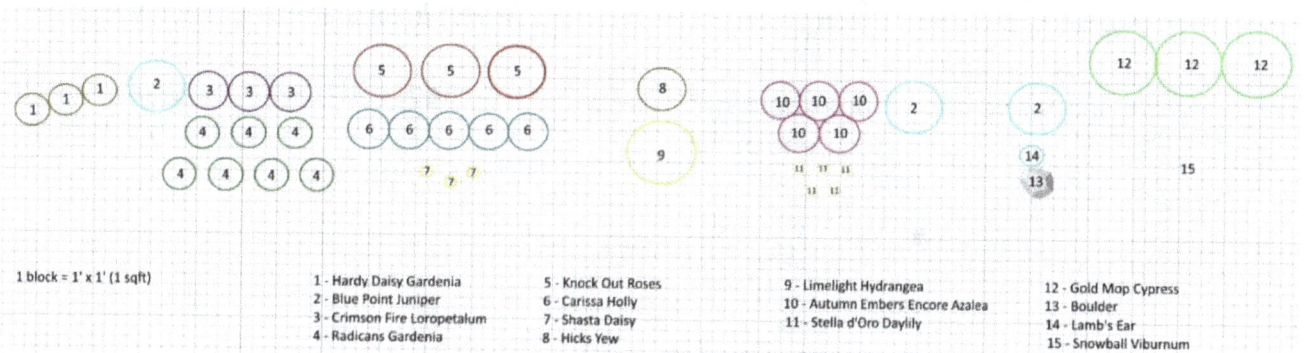

1 block = 1' x 1' (1 sqft)

1 - Hardy Daisy Gardenia
2 - Blue Point Juniper
3 - Crimson Fire Loropetalum
4 - Radicans Gardenia

5 - Knock Out Roses
6 - Carissa Holly
7 - Shasta Daisy
8 - Hicks Yew

9 - Limelight Hydrangea
10 - Autumn Embers Encore Azalea
11 - Stella d'Oro Daylily

12 - Gold Mop Cypress
13 - Boulder
14 - Lamb's Ear
15 - Snowball Viburnum

Assembly Instructions

Garden Size (Approximate):	123'L x 15'W
Pruning Category:	1
Watering Needs:	2
Sun Requirements:	4
Plant Zones:	3-11
Bloom Colors:	White, Purple, Red, Yellow, Blue
Bloom Time Range:	Spring-Fall
Average Time to Install:	30 hours
Approximate Bedding:	1,845sf
Mulch:	12 cuyds
Pine Straw:	44 bales
Rock:	23 tons at 3" thick
Other Cultivars Available to Sub:	Yes
Special Needs:	Prune knock out roses to 18" at end of Fall

Till garden and amend soil with composted material such as mulched leaves or shredded pine.

Using the planting diagram, set boulders by digging into the soil several inches to create a foundation slightly below the grade of the garden. Set the boulder on to the foundation then spread the removed soil around the boulders to bring the soil height back up to grade level.

Measure for plant placement and sit each plant in its proper place. Adjust placement based on the shape of the actual bed.

Dig each hole twice as wide as the root ball. Sprinkle in starter fertilizer to the bottom of the hole (follow directions on package for proper application). Set plant in hole. Push soil back around plant, tamping in tight with the handle end of the shovel to remove all air pockets. Tamp soil tight at top of root ball.

Repeat for each plant.

Water in all plants thoroughly.

Top beds with mulch, pine straw or other bedding materials to hold moisture and keep roots warm in winter and cool in summer.

Common Name	Hardy Daisy Gardenia
Scientific Name	Gardenia jasminoides 'Kleim's Hardy'
Status	Evergreen
Mature Size (H x W)	4x4
Pruning Category (1-5)	2
Watering Category (1-5)	3
Sun Category (1-5)	4
USDA Hardiness Zone:	7-11
Bloom Season	Summer, Fall

Common Name	Blue Point Juniper
Scientific Name	Juniperus chinensis 'Blue Point'
Status	Evergreen
Mature Size (H x W)	15x8
Pruning Category (1-5)	1
Watering Category (1-5)	1
Sun Category (1-5)	4
USDA Hardiness Zone:	6-9
Bloom Season	None

Common Name	Crimson Fire Loropetalum
Scientific Name	Loropetalum chinense var. rubrum 'Crimson Fire'
Status	Evergreen
Mature Size (H x W)	4x4
Pruning Category (1-5)	2
Watering Category (1-5)	2
Sun Category (1-5)	3
USDA Hardiness Zone:	7-10
Bloom Season	Spring

Common Name	Radicans Gardenia
Scientific Name	Gardenia jasminoides 'Radicans Variegata'
Status	Evergreen
Mature Size (H x W)	3x3
Pruning Category (1-5)	2
Watering Category (1-5)	3
Sun Category (1-5)	4
USDA Hardiness Zone:	7-11
Bloom Season	Summer, Fall

Common Name	Knock Out Rose
Scientific Name	Rosa Radrazz
Status	Deciduous
Mature Size (H x W)	4x4
Pruning Category (1-5)	2
Watering Category (1-5)	2
Sun Category (1-5)	5
USDA Hardiness Zone:	5-10
Bloom Season	Summer

Common Name	Carissa Holly
Scientific Name	Ilex cornuta 'Carissa'
Status	Evergreen
Mature Size (H x W)	4x4
Pruning Category (1-5)	4
Watering Category (1-5)	2
Sun Category (1-5)	4
USDA Hardiness Zone:	7-9
Bloom Season	None-Inconspicuous

Common Name	Shasta Daisy
Scientific Name	Leucanthemum x superbum
Status	Perennial
Mature Size (H x W)	2.5x2.5
Pruning Category (1-5)	1
Watering Category (1-5)	2
Sun Category (1-5)	4
USDA Hardiness Zone:	4-10
Bloom Season	Summer

Common Name	Hicks Yew
Scientific Name	Taxus x media
Status	Evergreen
Mature Size (H x W)	6x4
Pruning Category (1-5)	1
Watering Category (1-5)	2
Sun Category (1-5)	3
USDA Hardiness Zone:	4-8
Bloom Season	None

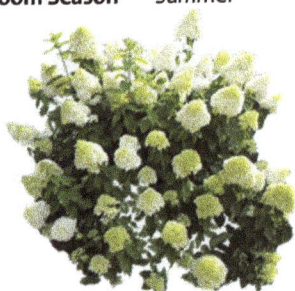

Common Name	Limelight Hydrangea
Scientific Name	Hydrangea paniculala 'Limelight'
Status	Deciduous
Mature Size (H x W)	6x6
Pruning Category (1-5)	1
Watering Category (1-5)	3
Sun Category (1-5)	4
USDA Hardiness Zone:	4-9
Bloom Season	Summer

Common Name	Autumn Embers Encore Azalea
Scientific Name	Rhododendron 'Conleb'
Status	Evergreen
Mature Size (H x W)	4x4.5
Pruning Category (1-5)	2
Watering Category (1-5)	3
Sun Category (1-5)	4
USDA Hardiness Zone:	7-10
Bloom Season	Spring, Fall

Common Name	Stella d'Oro Daylily
Scientific Name	Hemerocallis 'Stella d'Oro'
Status	Perennial
Mature Size (H x W)	2x2
Pruning Category (1-5)	1
Watering Category (1-5)	2
Sun Category (1-5)	4
USDA Hardiness Zone:	3-9
Bloom Season	Summer

Common Name	Gold Mop Cypress
Scientific Name	Chamaecyparis
Status	Evergreen
Mature Size (H x W)	6x6
Pruning Category (1-5)	1
Watering Category (1-5)	1
Sun Category (1-5)	4
USDA Hardiness Zone:	6-9
Bloom Season	None

Common Name	Lamb's Ear
Scientific Name	Stachys byzantina
Status	Perennial
Mature Size (H x W)	2x2
Pruning Category (1-5)	1
Watering Category (1-5)	2
Sun Category (1-5)	3
USDA Hardiness Zone:	4-8
Bloom Season	Summer

Common Name	Snowball Viburnum
Scientific Name	Viburnum opulus 'Roseum'
Status	Deciduous
Mature Size (H x W)	10x10
Pruning Category (1-5)	1
Watering Category (1-5)	2
Sun Category (1-5)	3
USDA Hardiness Zone:	3-8
Bloom Season	Spring

Nook, Nook - Who's There?

Description

Small spaces always seem to be the hardest to design. This petite garden has a lot of "wow" when seen from the street. The colors, textures and heights give plenty of interest. The appearance is neat and clean and has a variety of evergreen, perennial and deciduous plants so the front isn't bare in the winter. The curved turf-line frames it all in for a finished look.

Ingredients

(6) Variegated Liriope
(1) Dwarf Blue Spruce
(1) Sasanqua Camellia
(3) Tiarella Foam Flower
(2) Nikko Blue Hydrangea
(1) Limelight Hydrangea

(4) Carissa Holly
(1) White Dogwood
(4) Autumn Fern
(1) Hosta

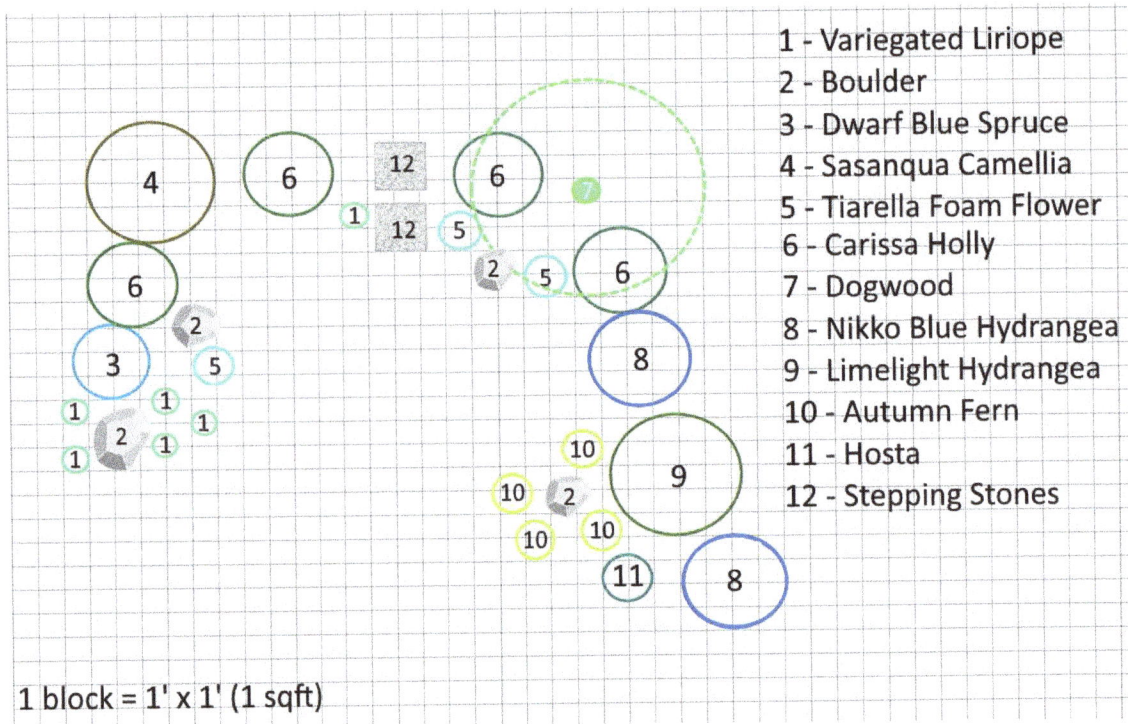

1 - Variegated Liriope
2 - Boulder
3 - Dwarf Blue Spruce
4 - Sasanqua Camellia
5 - Tiarella Foam Flower
6 - Carissa Holly
7 - Dogwood
8 - Nikko Blue Hydrangea
9 - Limelight Hydrangea
10 - Autumn Fern
11 - Hosta
12 - Stepping Stones

1 block = 1' x 1' (1 sqft)

Assembly Instructions

Garden Size (Approximate):	28'L x 23'W
Pruning Category:	1
Watering Needs:	2
Sun Requirements:	3
Plant Zones:	3-10
Bloom Colors:	Red, White, Blue
Bloom Time Range:	Spring-Fall
Average Time to Install:	12 hours
Approximate Bedding:	644sf
Mulch:	4 cuyds
Pine Straw:	15 bales
Rock:	8 tons at 3" thick
Other Cultivars Available to Sub:	Yes
Special Needs:	Mulch dwarf blue spruce heavily in summer in warmer climates to protect it from heat.

Till garden and amend soil with composted material such as mulched leaves or shredded pine.

Using the planting diagram, set boulders by digging into the soil several inches to create a foundation slightly below the grade of the garden. Set the boulder on to the foundation then spread the removed soil around the boulders to bring the soil height back up to grade level. Repeat for stepping stones.

Measure for plant placement and sit each plant in its proper place. Adjust placement based on the shape of the actual bed.

Dig each hole twice as wide as the root ball. Sprinkle in starter fertilizer to the bottom of the hole (follow directions on package for proper application). Set plant in hole. Push soil back around plant, tamping in tight with the handle end of the shovel to remove all air pockets. Tamp soil tight at top of root ball.

Repeat for each plant.

Water in all plants thoroughly.

Top beds with mulch, pine straw or other bedding materials to hold moisture and keep roots warm in winter and cool in summer.

Common Name	Liriope
Scientific Name	Liriope muscari
Status	Perennial
Mature Size (H x W)	2x2
Pruning Category (1-5)	1
Watering Category (1-5)	1
Sun Category (1-5)	4
USDA Hardiness Zone:	6-10
Bloom Season	Summer

Common Name	Dwarf Blue Spruce
Scientific Name	Picea pungens 'Globosa'
Status	Evergreen
Mature Size (H x W)	2x2
Pruning Category (1-5)	1
Watering Category (1-5)	2
Sun Category (1-5)	3
USDA Hardiness Zone:	3-8
Bloom Season	None

Common Name	Sasanqua Camellia
Scientific Name	Camellia sasanqua
Status	Evergreen
Mature Size (H x W)	12x6
Pruning Category (1-5)	1
Watering Category (1-5)	2
Sun Category (1-5)	3
USDA Hardiness Zone:	7-10
Bloom Season	Spring

Common Name	Tiarella Foam Flower
Scientific Name	Tiarella
Status	Perennial
Mature Size (H x W)	2x2
Pruning Category (1-5)	1
Watering Category (1-5)	3
Sun Category (1-5)	3
USDA Hardiness Zone:	4-9
Bloom Season	Summer

Common Name	Carissa Holly
Scientific Name	Ilex cornuta 'Carissa'
Status	Evergreen
Mature Size (H x W)	4x4
Pruning Category (1-5)	4
Watering Category (1-5)	2
Sun Category (1-5)	4
USDA Hardiness Zone:	7-9
Bloom Season	None-Inconspicuous

Common Name	White Dogwood
Scientific Name	Cornus florida
Status	Deciduous
Mature Size (H x W)	20x15
Pruning Category (1-5)	1
Watering Category (1-5)	2
Sun Category (1-5)	2
USDA Hardiness Zone:	3-8
Bloom Season	Spring

Common Name	Nikko Blue Hydrangea
Scientific Name	Hydrangea macrophylla 'Nikko Blue'
Status	Deciduous
Mature Size (H x W)	3x3
Pruning Category (1-5)	1
Watering Category (1-5)	3
Sun Category (1-5)	2
USDA Hardiness Zone:	4-9
Bloom Season	Summer

Common Name	Limelight Hydrangea
Scientific Name	Hydrangea paniculala 'Limelight'
Status	Deciduous
Mature Size (H x W)	6x6
Pruning Category (1-5)	1
Watering Category (1-5)	3
Sun Category (1-5)	4
USDA Hardiness Zone:	4-9
Bloom Season	Summer

Common Name	Autumn Fern
Scientific Name	Dryopteris erythrosora
Status	Perennial
Mature Size (H x W)	2x2
Pruning Category (1-5)	1
Watering Category (1-5)	3
Sun Category (1-5)	2
USDA Hardiness Zone:	4-8
Bloom Season	None

Common Name	Big Leaf Hosta
Scientific Name	Hosta
Status	Perennial
Mature Size (H x W)	4x4
Pruning Category (1-5)	1
Watering Category (1-5)	2
Sun Category (1-5)	2
USDA Hardiness Zone:	3-8
Bloom Season	Summer

Eye Candy

Curb Appeal

Description

It's a simple design, but visually, it draws your eye to what's important, which is the front door. Repeat the pattern on the opposite side to really draw the eye towards the door. Guests will delight in the cleanness and simplicity of the lines and the variation in colors adds year-round interest.

Ingredients

(2) Satsuki Azalea   (5) Wintergreen Boxwood
(1) Pieris Japonica   (1) Mini Loropetalum
(3) Nordic Inkberry Holly (1) Sasanqua Camellia
(3) Blue Spruce Sedum
(1) Emerald Green Arborvitae

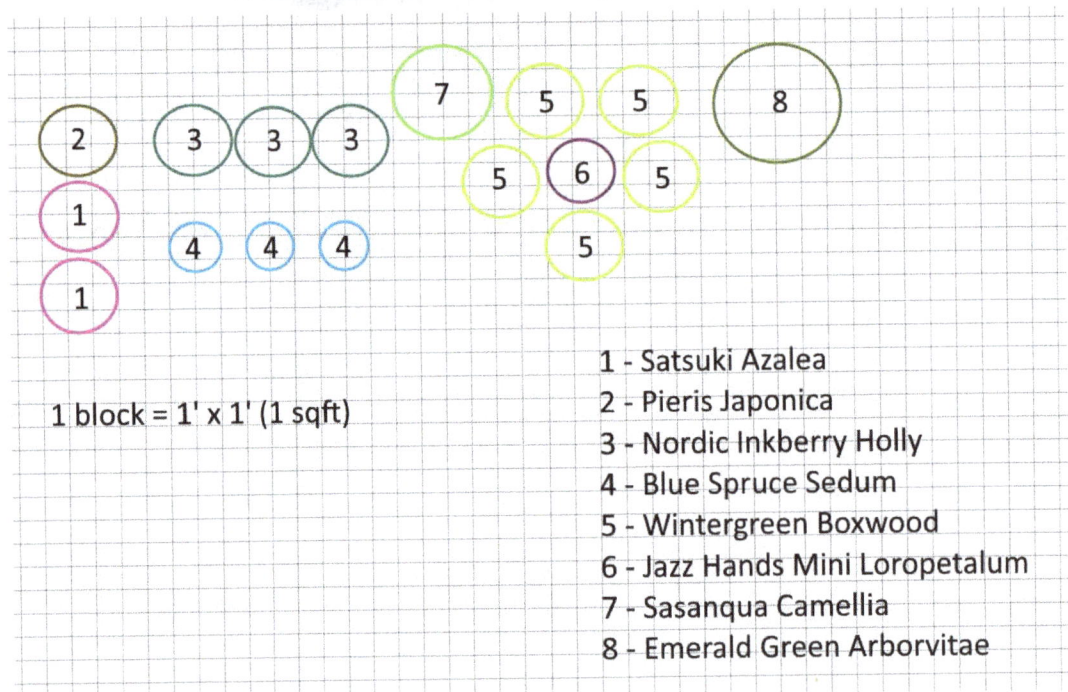

1 block = 1' x 1' (1 sqft)

1 - Satsuki Azalea
2 - Pieris Japonica
3 - Nordic Inkberry Holly
4 - Blue Spruce Sedum
5 - Wintergreen Boxwood
6 - Jazz Hands Mini Loropetalum
7 - Sasanqua Camellia
8 - Emerald Green Arborvitae

Assembly Instructions

Garden Size (Approximate):	32'L x 12'W
Pruning Category:	3
Watering Needs:	3
Sun Requirements:	4
Plant Zones:	3-10
Bloom Colors:	Pink, Purple, Red
Bloom Time Range:	Fall-Spring
Average Time to Install:	10 hours
Approximate Bedding:	384sf
Mulch:	2.5 cuyds
Pine Straw:	9 bales
Rock:	4.8 tons
Other Cultivars Available to Sub:	Yes
Special Needs:	

Till garden and amend soil with composted material such as mulched leaves or shredded pine.

Using the planting diagram, measure for plant placement and sit each plant in its proper place. Adjust placement based on the shape of the actual bed.

Dig each hole twice as wide as the root ball. Sprinkle in starter fertilizer to the bottom of the hole (follow directions on package for proper application). Set plant in hole. Push soil back around plant, tamping in tight with the handle end of the shovel to remove all air pockets. Tamp soil tight at top of root ball.

Repeat for each plant.

Water in all plants thoroughly.

Top beds with mulch, pine straw or other bedding materials to hold moisture and keep roots warm in winter and cool in summer.

Common Name	Satsuki Azalea
Scientific Name	Rhododendron indicum 'Satsuki azalea'
Status	Evergreen
Mature Size (H x W)	3x3
Pruning Category (1-5)	2
Watering Category (1-5)	3
Sun Category (1-5)	3
USDA Hardiness Zone:	7-9
Bloom Season	Spring

Common Name	Pieris
Scientific Name	Pieris japonica
Status	Evergreen
Mature Size (H x W)	3x3
Pruning Category (1-5)	2
Watering Category (1-5)	2
Sun Category (1-5)	2
USDA Hardiness Zone:	5-9
Bloom Season	Winter

Common Name	Nordic Inkberry Holly
Scientific Name	Ilex glabra
Status	Evergreen
Mature Size (H x W)	3x3
Pruning Category (1-5)	4
Watering Category (1-5)	2
Sun Category (1-5)	4
USDA Hardiness Zone:	5-8
Bloom Season	None-Inconspicuous

Common Name	Blue Spruce Sedum
Scientific Name	Petrosedum rupestre 'Blue Spruce'
Status	Perennial
Mature Size (H x W)	1x3
Pruning Category (1-5)	1
Watering Category (1-5)	1
Sun Category (1-5)	5
USDA Hardiness Zone:	3-9
Bloom Season	Fall

Common Name	Wintergreen Boxwood
Scientific Name	Buxus microphylla 'Wintergreen'
Status	Evergreen
Mature Size (H x W)	3x4
Pruning Category (1-5)	4
Watering Category (1-5)	3
Sun Category (1-5)	4
USDA Hardiness Zone:	4-9
Bloom Season	None

Common Name	Mini Loropetalum
Scientific Name	Loropetalum chinense 'Beni-Hime'
Status	Evergreen
Mature Size (H x W)	3x3
Pruning Category (1-5)	2
Watering Category (1-5)	2
Sun Category (1-5)	3
USDA Hardiness Zone:	7-10
Bloom Season	Spring

Common Name	Sasanqua Camellia
Scientific Name	Camellia sasanqua
Status	Evergreen
Mature Size (H x W)	12x6
Pruning Category (1-5)	1
Watering Category (1-5)	2
Sun Category (1-5)	3
USDA Hardiness Zone:	7-10
Bloom Season	Spring

Common Name	Emerald Green Arborvitae
Scientific Name	Thuja occidentalis
Status	Evergreen
Mature Size (H x W)	15x5
Pruning Category (1-5)	1
Watering Category (1-5)	3
Sun Category (1-5)	4
USDA Hardiness Zone:	4-8
Bloom Season	None

Description

Foundation gardens don't have to stay at the foundation of the house. Take over troubled areas by extending the front beds. Reduce the size of water-gobbling turf areas and add color and interest and lower maintenance time. Seasonal blooming adds more than height and texture to this small but powerful landscape bed.

Ingredients

(1) Tonto Crape Myrtle
(1) Yule Tide Camellia
(3) False Holly
(3) Radicans Gardenia
(1) Clethra Alnifolia
(1) Twist and Shout Hydrangea

(3) Tea Olive
(3) Dwarf Plum Yew

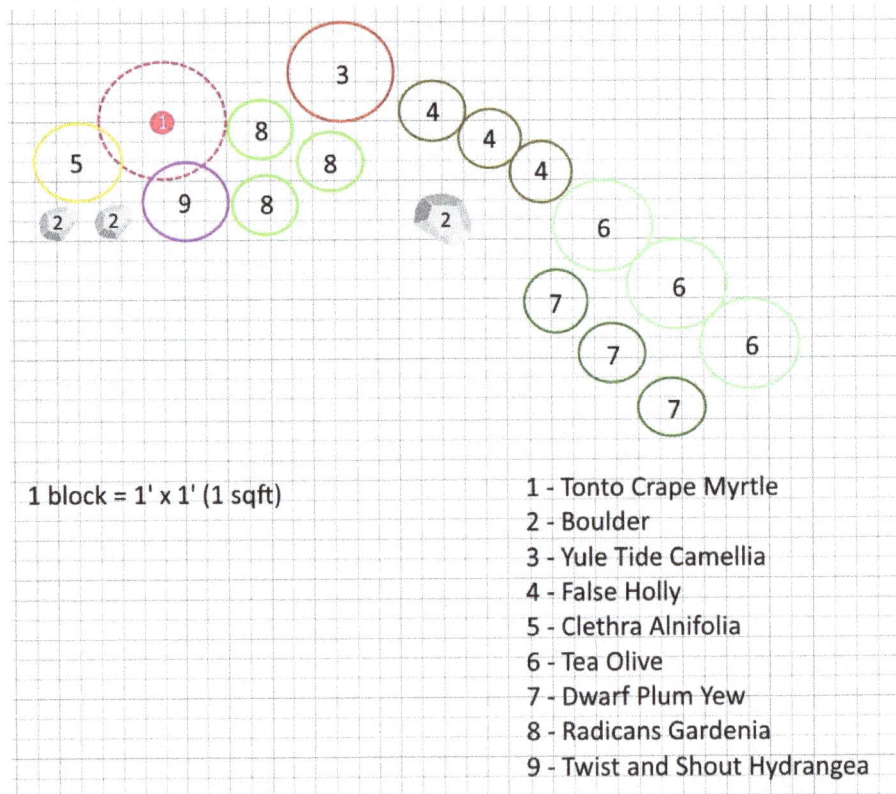

1 block = 1' x 1' (1 sqft)

1 - Tonto Crape Myrtle
2 - Boulder
3 - Yule Tide Camellia
4 - False Holly
5 - Clethra Alnifolia
6 - Tea Olive
7 - Dwarf Plum Yew
8 - Radicans Gardenia
9 - Twist and Shout Hydrangea

Assembly Instructions

Garden Size (Approximate):	36'L x 21'W
Pruning Category:	1
Watering Needs:	2
Sun Requirements:	3
Plant Zones:	3-11
Bloom Colors:	Pink, Red, White, Purple
Bloom Time Range:	Spring-Fall
Average Time to Install:	10 hours
Approximate Bedding:	756sf
Mulch:	4cuyds
Pine Straw:	18 bales
Rock:	9.5 tons at 3" thick
Other Cultivars Available to Sub:	Yes
Special Needs:	This cultivar of crape myrtle is considered dwarf. There is no need to cut back every year (also called "knuckling"). Clethra can tolerate salt spray in coastal areas.

Till garden and amend soil with composted material such as mulched leaves or shredded pine.

Using the planting diagram, set boulders by digging into the soil several inches to create a foundation slightly below the grade of the garden. Set the boulder on to the foundation then spread the removed soil around the boulders to bring the soil height back up to grade level.

Measure for plant placement and sit each plant in its proper place. Adjust placement based on the shape of the actual bed.

Dig each hole twice as wide as the root ball. Sprinkle in starter fertilizer to the bottom of the hole (follow directions on package for proper application). Set plant in hole. Push soil back around plant, tamping in tight with the handle end of the shovel to remove all air pockets. Tamp soil tight at top of root ball.

Repeat for each plant.

Water in all plants thoroughly.

Top beds with mulch, pine straw or other bedding materials to hold moisture and keep roots warm in winter and cool in summer.

Encore Performance

Curb Appeal

Common Name	Tonto Crape Myrtle
Scientific Name	Lagerstroemia indica x fauriei 'Tonto'
Status	Deciduous
Mature Size (H x W)	15x10
Pruning Category (1-5)	1
Watering Category (1-5)	2
Sun Category (1-5)	4
USDA Hardiness Zone:	6-11
Bloom Season	Summer

Common Name	Sasanqua Camellia
Scientific Name	Camellia sasanqua
Status	Evergreen
Mature Size (H x W)	12x6
Pruning Category (1-5)	1
Watering Category (1-5)	2
Sun Category (1-5)	3
USDA Hardiness Zone:	7-10
Bloom Season	Spring

Common Name	False Holly
Scientific Name	Osmanthus heterophyllus
Status	Evergreen
Mature Size (H x W)	3x3
Pruning Category (1-5)	2
Watering Category (1-5)	2
Sun Category (1-5)	3
USDA Hardiness Zone:	6-9
Bloom Season	Fall

Common Name	Clethra Alnifolia
Scientific Name	Clethra Alnifolia
Status	Deciduous
Mature Size (H x W)	5x4
Pruning Category (1-5)	1
Watering Category (1-5)	3
Sun Category (1-5)	2
USDA Hardiness Zone:	3-9
Bloom Season	Summer

Common Name	Tea Olive
Scientific Name	Osmanthus fragrans
Status	Evergreen
Mature Size (H x W)	6x6
Pruning Category (1-5)	3
Watering Category (1-5)	2
Sun Category (1-5)	3
USDA Hardiness Zone:	8-10
Bloom Season	Spring

Common Name	Dwarf Plum Yew
Scientific Name	Cephalotaxus harringtonia 'Prostrata'
Status	Evergreen
Mature Size (H x W)	3x3
Pruning Category (1-5)	1
Watering Category (1-5)	2
Sun Category (1-5)	3
USDA Hardiness Zone:	4-8
Bloom Season	None

Common Name	Radicans Gardenia
Scientific Name	Gardenia jasminoides 'Radicans Variegata'
Status	Evergreen
Mature Size (H x W)	3x3
Pruning Category (1-5)	2
Watering Category (1-5)	3
Sun Category (1-5)	4
USDA Hardiness Zone:	7-11
Bloom Season	Summer, Fall

Common Name	Twist and Shout Hydrangea
Scientific Name	Hydrangea macrophylla 'PIIHM-I'
Status	Deciduous
Mature Size (H x W)	4x4
Pruning Category (1-5)	1
Watering Category (1-5)	3
Sun Category (1-5)	3
USDA Hardiness Zone:	4-9
Bloom Season	Summer

Description

Neat and clean is key with this small garden design. Low shrubs let in light at the front of the house and the color and texture welcomes guests with a tidy "Hello"! Spring blooms add more color and the varying evergreens keep interest in the colder months.

Ingredients

(1) Mary Nell Holly
(3) Sunshine Ligustrum
(3) Otto Luyken Laurel
(7) Asiatic Lily

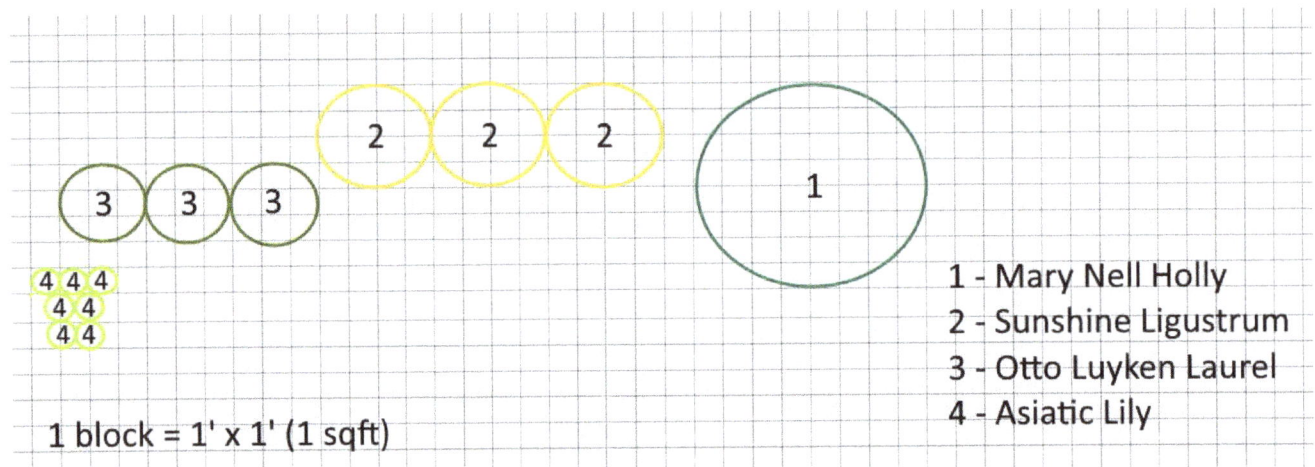

1 - Mary Nell Holly
2 - Sunshine Ligustrum
3 - Otto Luyken Laurel
4 - Asiatic Lily

1 block = 1' x 1' (1 sqft)

Business in the Front, Party in the Back

Assembly Instructions

Garden Size (Approximate):	31'L x 10'W
Pruning Category:	3
Watering Needs:	2
Sun Requirements:	3
Plant Zones:	4-10
Bloom Colors:	White
Bloom Time Range:	Spring
Average Time to Install:	7 hours
Approximate Bedding:	310sf
Mulch:	2 cuyds
Pine Straw:	7 bales
Rock:	3.9 tons at 3" thick
Other Cultivars Available to Sub:	Yes
Special Needs:	

Till garden and amend soil with composted material such as mulched leaves or shredded pine.

Using the planting diagram, measure for plant placement and sit each plant in its proper place. Adjust placement based on the shape of the actual bed.

Dig each hole twice as wide as the root ball. Sprinkle in starter fertilizer to the bottom of the hole (follow directions on package for proper application). Set plant in hole. Push soil back around plant, tamping in tight with the handle end of the shovel to remove all air pockets. Tamp soil tight at top of root ball.

Repeat for each plant.

Water in all plants thoroughly.

Top beds with mulch, pine straw or other bedding materials to hold moisture and keep roots warm in winter and cool in summer.

Common Name	Mary Nell Holly
Scientific Name	Ilex x 'Mary Nell'
Status	Evergreen
Mature Size (H x W)	15x8
Pruning Category (1-5)	5
Watering Category (1-5)	2
Sun Category (1-5)	4
USDA Hardiness Zone:	7-9
Bloom Season	None-Inconspicuous

Common Name	Sunshine Ligustrum
Scientific Name	Ligustrum sinense 'Sunshine'
Status	Evergreen
Mature Size (H x W)	4x4
Pruning Category (1-5)	4
Watering Category (1-5)	2
Sun Category (1-5)	5
USDA Hardiness Zone:	7-10
Bloom Season	None-Inconspicuous

Common Name	Otto Luyken Laurel
Scientific Name	Prunus laurocerasus
Status	Evergreen
Mature Size (H x W)	3.5x3.5
Pruning Category (1-5)	3
Watering Category (1-5)	2
Sun Category (1-5)	3
USDA Hardiness Zone:	6-8
Bloom Season	Spring

Common Name	Asiatic Lily
Scientific Name	Lilium auratum
Status	Perennial
Mature Size (H x W)	2x1
Pruning Category (1-5)	1
Watering Category (1-5)	3
Sun Category (1-5)	3
USDA Hardiness Zone:	4-9
Bloom Season	Spring

Rock and Roll

Design Elements

Description

Create a mountain retreat and hang out all year around the fire. Leave open spaces between boulders to add Adirondack chairs for comfort and use the boulder seating for over flow for guests or kids making smores. Add solar lighting behind the boulders for additional ambiance. Stack firewood behind the tall set to keep the area neat and clean.

Ingredients

(10) tons boulders   (3) Miscanthus Grass
(2) Cryptomeria   (1) Blue Point Juniper
(1) Emerald Green Arborvitae
(1) ton slate chips (base)
(1) Deodar Cedar
(2) Purple Diamond Loropetalum

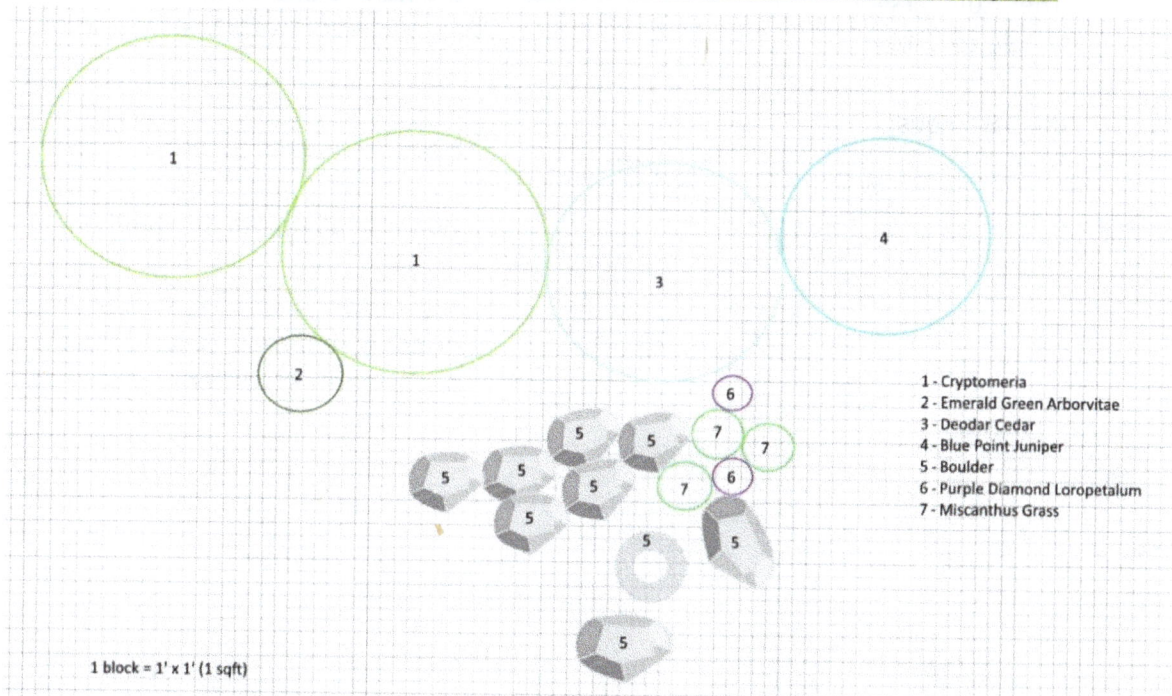

1 - Cryptomeria
2 - Emerald Green Arborvitae
3 - Deodar Cedar
4 - Blue Point Juniper
5 - Boulder
6 - Purple Diamond Loropetalum
7 - Miscanthus Grass

1 block = 1' x 1' (1 sqft)

Assembly Instructions

Garden Size (Approximate):	73'L x 53'W
Pruning Category:	1
Watering Needs:	2
Sun Requirements:	4
Plant Zones:	4-10
Bloom Colors:	Purple
Bloom Time Range:	Summer
Average Time to Install:	24 hours
Approximate Bedding:	3,869sf
Mulch:	21 cuyds
Pine Straw:	69 bales
Rock:	1 ton slate chips; 4.5 tons rock outer area at 3" thick
Other Cultivars Available to Sub:	Yes
Special Needs:	

Till garden and amend soil with composted material such as mulched leaves or shredded pine.

Using the planting diagram, set boulders by digging into the soil several inches to create a foundation slightly below the grade of the garden. Set the boulder on to the foundation then spread the removed soil around the boulders to bring the soil height back up to grade level.

After placing boulders for the fire pit, dig out a deeper interior to the "pit" to keep the fire further down inside the fire ring.

Measure for plant placement and sit each plant in its proper place. Adjust placement based on the shape of the actual bed.

Dig each hole twice as wide as the root ball. Sprinkle in starter fertilizer to the bottom of the hole (follow directions on package for proper application). Set plant in hole. Push soil back around plant, tamping in tight with the handle end of the shovel to remove all air pockets. Tamp soil tight at top of root ball.

Repeat for each plant.

Water in all plants thoroughly.

Top beds with mulch, pine straw or other bedding materials to hold moisture and keep roots warm in winter and cool in summer.

Common Name	Cryptomeria
Scientific Name	Cryptomeria japonica
Status	Evergreen
Mature Size (H x W)	50x30
Pruning Category (1-5)	1
Watering Category (1-5)	1
Sun Category (1-5)	4
USDA Hardiness Zone:	6-9
Bloom Season	None

Common Name	Emerald Green Arborvitae
Scientific Name	Thuja occidentalis
Status	Evergreen
Mature Size (H x W)	15x5
Pruning Category (1-5)	1
Watering Category (1-5)	3
Sun Category (1-5)	4
USDA Hardiness Zone:	4-8
Bloom Season	None

Common Name	Deodar Cedar
Scientific Name	Cedrus deodara
Status	Evergreen
Mature Size (H x W)	50x30
Pruning Category (1-5)	1
Watering Category (1-5)	2
Sun Category (1-5)	3
USDA Hardiness Zone:	6-7
Bloom Season	None

Common Name	Blue Point Juniper
Scientific Name	Juniperus chinensis 'Blue Point'
Status	Evergreen
Mature Size (H x W)	15x8
Pruning Category (1-5)	1
Watering Category (1-5)	1
Sun Category (1-5)	4
USDA Hardiness Zone:	6-9
Bloom Season	None

Common Name	Purple Diamond Loropetalum
Scientific Name	Loropetalum chinense 'Shang-hi' PP18331
Status	Evergreen
Mature Size (H x W)	5x5
Pruning Category (1-5)	2
Watering Category (1-5)	2
Sun Category (1-5)	3
USDA Hardiness Zone:	7-10
Bloom Season	Spring

Common Name	Adagio Miscanthus Grass
Scientific Name	Miscanthus sinensis 'Adagio'
Status	Perennial
Mature Size (H x W)	5x5
Pruning Category (1-5)	1
Watering Category (1-5)	1
Sun Category (1-5)	4
USDA Hardiness Zone:	6-10
Bloom Season	Summer

Comfy Cozy

Description

Read a book. Chat with a friend. Greet a neighbor.
This little nook garden is cozy and comfortable.
Low maintenance grasses and iris' make it a snap
to maintain. Repeat the pattern in a couple of
locations to tie the landscape together.
Substitute daylily or a different iris to add a new
flair to the color palette.

Ingredients

(3) Adagio Grass
(3) Blue Flag Iris
(1) Medium Garden Boulder

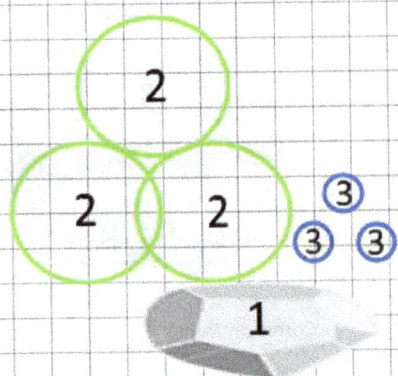

1 - Boulder
2 - Adagio Grass
3 - Blue Flag Iris

1 block = 1' x 1' (1 sqft)

Assembly Instructions

Garden Size (Approximate):	10'L x 11'W
Pruning Category:	1
Watering Needs:	2
Sun Requirements:	3
Plant Zones:	3-10
Bloom Colors:	Blue, White
Bloom Time Range:	Spring-Summer
Average Time to Install:	4 hours
Approximate Bedding:	110sf
Mulch:	0.50 cuyds
Pine Straw:	2 bales
Rock:	1.4 tons at 3" thick
Other Cultivars Available to Sub:	Yes
Special Needs:	

Till garden and amend soil with composted material such as mulched leaves or shredded pine.

Using the planting diagram, set boulders by digging into the soil several inches to create a foundation slightly below the grade of the garden. Set the boulder on to the foundation then spread the removed soil around the boulders to bring the soil height back up to grade level.

Measure for plant placement and sit each plant in its proper place. Adjust placement based on the shape of the actual bed.

Dig each hole twice as wide as the root ball. Sprinkle in starter fertilizer to the bottom of the hole (follow directions on package for proper application). Set plant in hole. Push soil back around plant, tamping in tight with the handle end of the shovel to remove all air pockets. Tamp soil tight at top of root ball.

Repeat for each plant.

Water in all plants thoroughly.

Top beds with mulch, pine straw or other bedding materials to hold moisture and keep roots warm in winter and cool in summer.

Common Name	Adagio Miscanthus Grass
Scientific Name	Miscanthus sinensis 'Adagio'
Status	Perennial
Mature Size (H x W)	5x5
Pruning Category (1-5)	1
Watering Category (1-5)	1
Sun Category (1-5)	4
USDA Hardiness Zone:	6-10
Bloom Season	Summer

Common Name	Blue Flag Iris
Scientific Name	Iris versicolor
Status	Perennial
Mature Size (H x W)	2x2
Pruning Category (1-5)	1
Watering Category (1-5)	4
Sun Category (1-5)	2
USDA Hardiness Zone:	3-8
Bloom Season	Spring

Description

Get creative with ways to make a garden your own. Guests will delight at the door to a secret garden, a hidden treasure, a pass through for neighbors, or nowhere at all! No walls needed. Just two posts and a door that can work or not. The visual interest is amazing and no fence is required.

Ingredients

(2) Gold Cone Juniper
(6) Glossy Abelia
(2) 6" x 6" x 8' Pressure Treated Posts
(2) Bags Quick Setting Concrete
(1) Door
(1) Set Door Hardware (or gate hardware)

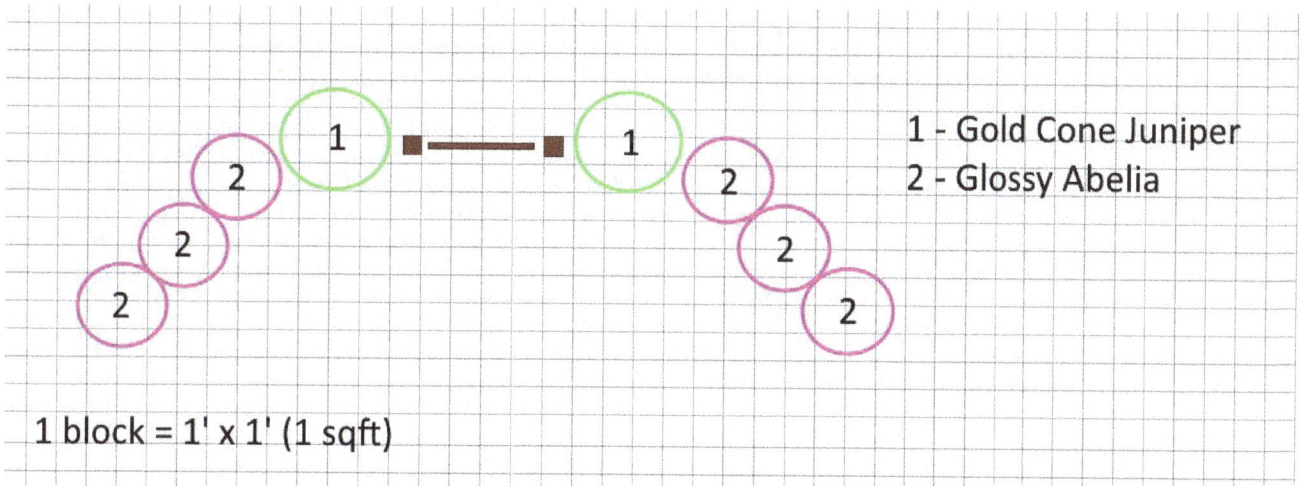

1 - Gold Cone Juniper
2 - Glossy Abelia

1 block = 1' x 1' (1 sqft)

Assembly Instructions

Garden Size (Approximate):	28'L x 10'W
Pruning Category:	1
Watering Needs:	1
Sun Requirements:	4
Plant Zones:	6-9
Bloom Colors:	Pink
Bloom Time Range:	Fall
Average Time to Install:	12 hours
Approximate Bedding:	280sf
Mulch:	2 cuyds
Pine Straw:	7 bales
Rock:	3.5 tons at 3" thick
Other Cultivars Available to Sub:	Yes
Special Needs:	

Till garden and amend soil with composted material such as mulched leaves or shredded pine.

Using the planting diagram, dig out holes for posts at least 12" deep. Based on the size of your door, leave enough post above ground match the height of the door. Set posts in hole and add one bag of quick dry cement to each hole and add appropriate amount of water. You'll need to secure the posts in an upright position until the concrete dries and the posts are steady.

After concrete is set, hang door with hardware and add a latch to create a working door.

Measure for plant placement and sit each plant in its proper place. Adjust placement based on the shape of the actual bed.

Dig each hole twice as wide as the root ball. Sprinkle in starter fertilizer to the bottom of the hole (follow directions on package for proper application). Set plant in hole. Push soil back around plant, tamping in tight with the handle end of the shovel to remove all air pockets. Tamp soil tight at top of root ball.

Repeat for each plant.

Water in all plants thoroughly.

Top beds with mulch, pine straw or other bedding materials to hold moisture and keep roots warm in winter and cool in summer.

Common Name	Gold Cone Juniper
Scientific Name	Juniperus communis 'Gold Cone'
Status	Evergreen
Mature Size (H x W)	15x8
Pruning Category (1-5)	1
Watering Category (1-5)	1
Sun Category (1-5)	4
USDA Hardiness Zone:	6-9
Bloom Season	None

Common Name	Glossy Abelia
Scientific Name	Abelia x grandiflora
Status	Semi Deciduous
Mature Size (H x W)	3x3
Pruning Category (1-5)	1
Watering Category (1-5)	2
Sun Category (1-5)	4
USDA Hardiness Zone:	6-9
Bloom Season	Fall

Common Scents

Description

Create your very own bird watching sanctuary. Attract them with the blooms and house them in their very own stylish condos. Choose bird houses with different heights and colors for the best effect. The posts here match to keep the focus on the garden and design elements. Paint the posts black and they will blend into the plantings.

Ingredients

(4) Tea Olive (Osmanthus)
(1) Dwarf Butterfly Shrub
(1 qt) Paint for Posts
(7) Bird Houses
(3) Peach Drift Roses
(2) Stella d'oro Daylily
(14) "L" Brackets with Screws
(1) Tube Waterproof Adhesive
(6) 6" x 6" x 8' Pressure Treated Posts
(6) bags Quick Setting Concrete

(1) Red Daylily
(1) Forsythia
(3) Bee Balm
(3) Blackeyed Susan

1 - Tea Olive
2 - Blue Butterfly Shrub
3 - Forsythia
4 - Bee Balm
5 - Blackeyed Susan
6 - Peach Drift Roses
7 - Stella d'Oro Daylily
8 - Red Daylily
9 - Bird House

1 block = 1' x 1' (1 sqft)

Assembly Instructions

Garden Size (Approximate):	19'L x 14'W
Pruning Category:	2
Watering Needs:	2
Sun Requirements:	4
Plant Zones:	2-11
Bloom Colors:	White, Blue, Pink, Yellow, Peach, Red
Bloom Time Range:	Spring-Summer
Average Time to Install:	40 hours
Approximate Bedding:	266sf
Mulch:	1.5 cuyds
Pine Straw:	6 bales
Rock:	3.3 tons at 3" thick
Other Cultivars Available to Sub:	Yes
Special Needs:	
	Dead head roses throughout the season to get more blooms.

Till garden and amend soil with composted material such as mulched leaves or shredded pine.

Measure and cut posts to desired lengths. Paint posts and set aside to dry. Dig holes to keep post at least 12" below grade. Set posts with fast setting concrete and allow them to dry.

Set bird houses on top of posts and add a bead of water-proof adhesive between the top of the post and the bottom of the birdhouse. Use the "L" brackets to secure each house to its post (one bracket on each side of the post).

Measure for plant placement and sit each plant in its proper place. Adjust placement based on the shape of the actual bed.

Dig each hole twice as wide as the root ball. Sprinkle in starter fertilizer to the bottom of the hole (follow directions on package for proper application). Set plant in hole. Push soil back around plant, tamping in tight with the handle end of the shovel to remove all air pockets. Tamp soil tight at top of root ball.

Repeat for each plant.

Water in all plants thoroughly.

Top beds with mulch, pine straw or other bedding materials to hold moisture and keep roots warm in winter and cool in summer.

Common Name	Tea Olive
Scientific Name	Osmanthus fragrans
Status	Evergreen
Mature Size (H x W)	6x6
Pruning Category (1-5)	3
Watering Category (1-5)	2
Sun Category (1-5)	3
USDA Hardiness Zone:	8-10
Bloom Season	Spring

Common Name	Dwarf Butterfly Shrub
Scientific Name	Buddleia
Status	Deciduous
Mature Size (H x W)	3x3
Pruning Category (1-5)	2
Watering Category (1-5)	2
Sun Category (1-5)	5
USDA Hardiness Zone:	5-11
Bloom Season	Summer

Common Name	Forsythia
Scientific Name	Forsythia
Status	Deciduous
Mature Size (H x W)	8x8
Pruning Category (1-5)	2
Watering Category (1-5)	2
Sun Category (1-5)	4
USDA Hardiness Zone:	5-9
Bloom Season	Spring

Common Name	Bee Balm
Scientific Name	Monarda
Status	Perennial
Mature Size (H x W)	3x3
Pruning Category (1-5)	1
Watering Category (1-5)	2
Sun Category (1-5)	4
USDA Hardiness Zone:	2-10
Bloom Season	Summer

Common Name	Blackeyed Susan
Scientific Name	Rudbeckia hirta
Status	Perennial
Mature Size (H x W)	2x2
Pruning Category (1-5)	1
Watering Category (1-5)	2
Sun Category (1-5)	4
USDA Hardiness Zone:	3-9
Bloom Season	Summer

Common Name	Drift Rose
Scientific Name	Rosa 'Meijocos'
Status	Deciduous
Mature Size (H x W)	3x3
Pruning Category (1-5)	2
Watering Category (1-5)	2
Sun Category (1-5)	5
USDA Hardiness Zone:	5-10
Bloom Season	Summer

Common Name	Stella d'Oro Daylily
Scientific Name	Hemerocallis 'Stella d'Oro'
Status	Perennial
Mature Size (H x W)	2x2
Pruning Category (1-5)	1
Watering Category (1-5)	2
Sun Category (1-5)	4
USDA Hardiness Zone:	3-9
Bloom Season	Summer

Common Name	Red Daylily
Scientific Name	Hemerocallis 'Red Hot Returns'
Status	Perennial
Mature Size (H x W)	2x2
Pruning Category (1-5)	1
Watering Category (1-5)	2
Sun Category (1-5)	4
USDA Hardiness Zone:	3-9
Bloom Season	Summer

Pot Garden

Design Elements

Description

Pot? Potted? What's the difference, really? Set up this amazing garden on a patio, in a bed or on a balcony. It's compact, versatile and you can change interest by changing out pots or rearranging from time to time. Grow herbs, flowers or trailing vines. Switch out plants every season or plant it and forget it.

Ingredients

(14) Varying Color/and Size Pots
Potting Soil (Volume based on pots)
Pine Cones, Mulch or Other Organic Fill

(1) Dill	(1) Basil
(1) Liatris	(1) Hyssop
(1) Borage	(1) Yellow Flag Iris
(3) Cilantro	(1) Rosemary
(6) Pansy	(1) Oregano
(2) Hosta	(3) Chives
(3) Marigold	(1) Thyme

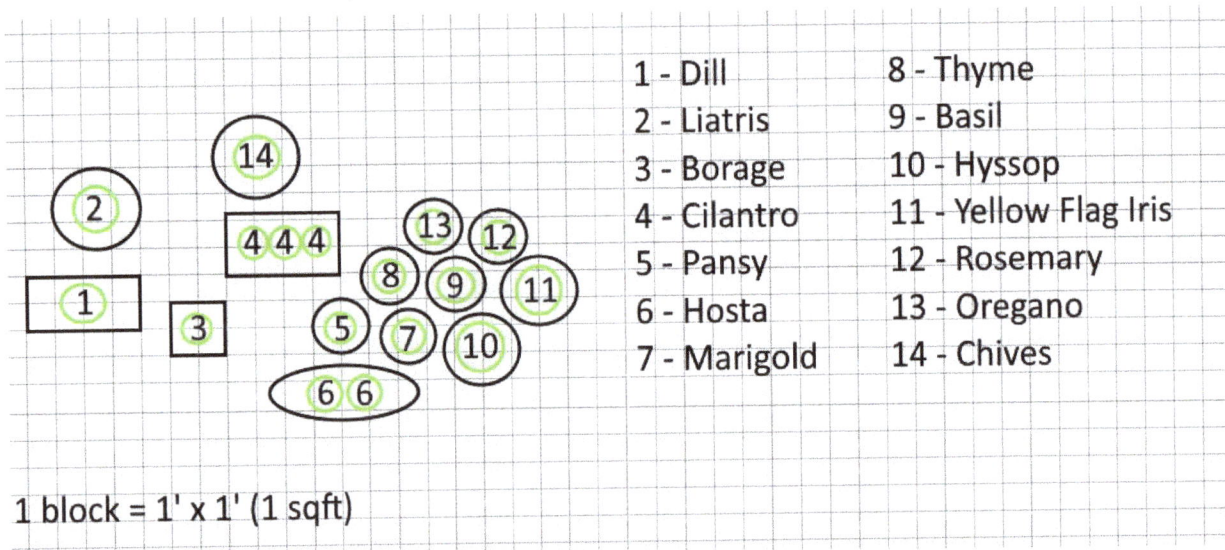

(4) Bags Gravel or Pebbles

1 - Dill	8 - Thyme
2 - Liatris	9 - Basil
3 - Borage	10 - Hyssop
4 - Cilantro	11 - Yellow Flag Iris
5 - Pansy	12 - Rosemary
6 - Hosta	13 - Oregano
7 - Marigold	14 - Chives

1 block = 1' x 1' (1 sqft)

130

Pot Garden

Assembly Instructions

Garden Size (Approximate):	20'L x 11'W
Pruning Category:	1
Watering Needs:	3
Sun Requirements:	3
Plant Zones:	2-11
Bloom Colors:	White, Pink, Purple, Blue, Yellow
Bloom Time Range:	Spring-Summer, Winter
Average Time to Install:	18 hours
Approximate Bedding:	220sf
Mulch:	(3) 3 cuft bags
Pine Straw:	NA
Rock:	(10) 5lb bags
Other Cultivars Available to Sub:	Yes
Special Needs:	

Set pots out based on planting design.

Fill bottom 2" of pot with pebbles (or gravel or other rock) for drainage.

Fill ½ the pot with organic materials such as leaf debris, shredded bark, pine cones, etc. Fill remaining ½ of pot with potting soil.

Place plants inside pots and tamp lightly to secure roots.

Water in all plants thoroughly.

Add mulch, mini pine bark nuggets, rock or other bedding material to top of pots to keep soil moist.

Protect pots from freezing in winter. Many ceramic pots will crack during winter months.

Common Name	Dill
Scientific Name	Anethum graveolens
Status	Perennial
Mature Size (H x W)	3x2
Pruning Category (1-5)	1
Watering Category (1-5)	1
Sun Category (1-5)	4
USDA Hardiness Zone:	3-11
Bloom Season	Summer

Common Name	Liatris
Scientific Name	Liatris spicata
Status	Perennial
Mature Size (H x W)	3x2
Pruning Category (1-5)	1
Watering Category (1-5)	2
Sun Category (1-5)	4
USDA Hardiness Zone:	5-9
Bloom Season	Summer

Common Name	Borage
Scientific Name	Borago officinalis
Status	Annual
Mature Size (H x W)	2x2
Pruning Category (1-5)	1
Watering Category (1-5)	2
Sun Category (1-5)	4
USDA Hardiness Zone:	NA
Bloom Season	Summer

Common Name	Cilantro
Scientific Name	Coriandum sativum
Status	Perennial
Mature Size (H x W)	3x3
Pruning Category (1-5)	1
Watering Category (1-5)	2
Sun Category (1-5)	4
USDA Hardiness Zone:	3-11
Bloom Season	Summer

Common Name	Pansy
Scientific Name	Viola tricolor var hortensis
Status	Annual
Mature Size (H x W)	2x1
Pruning Category (1-5)	1
Watering Category (1-5)	2
Sun Category (1-5)	3
USDA Hardiness Zone:	NA
Bloom Season	Winter

Common Name	Patriot Hosta
Scientific Name	Hosta 'Patriot'
Status	Perennial
Mature Size (H x W)	3x3
Pruning Category (1-5)	1
Watering Category (1-5)	2
Sun Category (1-5)	2
USDA Hardiness Zone:	3-8
Bloom Season	Summer

Common Name	Marigold
Scientific Name	Tagetes
Status	Perennial
Mature Size (H x W)	2x2
Pruning Category (1-5)	1
Watering Category (1-5)	2
Sun Category (1-5)	4
USDA Hardiness Zone:	2-11
Bloom Season	Summer

Common Name	Thyme
Scientific Name	Thymus vulgaris
Status	Perennial
Mature Size (H x W)	1x2
Pruning Category (1-5)	1
Watering Category (1-5)	2
Sun Category (1-5)	4
USDA Hardiness Zone:	5-10
Bloom Season	Summer

Common Name	Basil
Scientific Name	Ocimum basilicum
Status	Perennial
Mature Size (H x W)	2x1
Pruning Category (1-5)	1
Watering Category (1-5)	2
Sun Category (1-5)	4
USDA Hardiness Zone:	2-11
Bloom Season	Summer

Common Name	Hyssop
Scientific Name	Hyssopus officinalis
Status	Perennial
Mature Size (H x W)	2x2
Pruning Category (1-5)	1
Watering Category (1-5)	2
Sun Category (1-5)	4
USDA Hardiness Zone:	4-9
Bloom Season	Summer

Common Name	Yellow Flag Iris
Scientific Name	Iris pseudacorus
Status	Perennial
Mature Size (H x W)	2x2
Pruning Category (1-5)	1
Watering Category (1-5)	4
Sun Category (1-5)	2
USDA Hardiness Zone:	3-8
Bloom Season	Spring

Common Name	Rosemary
Scientific Name	Rosmarinus officinalis
Status	Perennial
Mature Size (H x W)	3x4
Pruning Category (1-5)	1
Watering Category (1-5)	2
Sun Category (1-5)	4
USDA Hardiness Zone:	5-10
Bloom Season	Summer

Common Name	Oregano
Scientific Name	Origanum vulgare
Status	Perennial
Mature Size (H x W)	3x2
Pruning Category (1-5)	1
Watering Category (1-5)	2
Sun Category (1-5)	4
USDA Hardiness Zone:	5-10
Bloom Season	Summer

Common Name	Chives
Scientific Name	Allium schoenoprasum
Status	Perennial
Mature Size (H x W)	2x2
Pruning Category (1-5)	1
Watering Category (1-5)	2
Sun Category (1-5)	4
USDA Hardiness Zone:	3-9
Bloom Season	Summer

Zen Vogue

Description

Everyone needs some stress relief. Create a quiet area to soothe and nurture. Simple plants and no maintenance make this a truly restful area. Add a hammock or chair for some afternoon relaxation.

Ingredients

(1) Fatsia
(1) Mini Loropetalum
(1) Statuary
(1) Dissectum Japanese Maple
(1) Nordic Inkberry Holly
(9) Polished Stones (Varying Sizes)

(1) Gumpo Azalea
(1) Vase

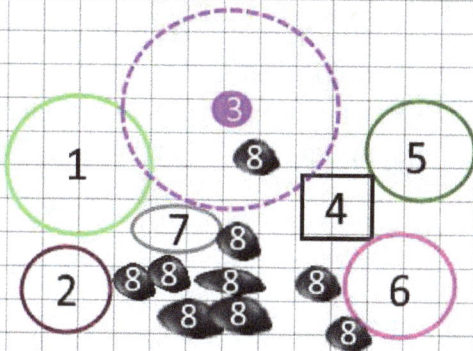

1 - Fatsia
2 - Mini Loropetalum
3 - Dissectum Japanese Maple
4 - Statuary
5 - Nordic Inkberry Holly
6 - Gumpo Azalea
7 - Vase
8 - Polished Stones

1 block = 1' x 1' (1 sqft)

Zen Vogue

Assembly Instructions

Garden Size (Approximate):	13'L x 11'W
Pruning Category:	1
Watering Needs:	1
Sun Requirements:	2
Plant Zones:	5-11
Bloom Colors:	Purple, Pink
Bloom Time Range:	Spring-Summer
Average Time to Install:	6 hours
Approximate Bedding:	143sf
Mulch:	1 cuyds
Pine Straw:	3 bales
Rock:	1 ton at 3" thick
Other Cultivars Available to Sub:	Yes
Special Needs:	
	No

Till garden and amend soil with composted material such as mulched leaves or shredded pine.

Using the planting diagram, set stones and statuary by digging into the soil several inches to create a foundation slightly below the grade of the garden. Set the items on to the foundation then spread the removed soil around to bring the soil height back up to grade level.

Measure for plant placement and sit each plant in its proper place. Adjust placement based on the shape of the actual bed.

Dig each hole twice as wide as the root ball. Sprinkle in starter fertilizer to the bottom of the hole (follow directions on package for proper application). Set plant in hole. Push soil back around plant, tamping in tight with the handle end of the shovel to remove all air pockets. Tamp soil tight at top of root ball.

Repeat for each plant.

Water in all plants thoroughly.

Top beds with mulch, pine straw or other bedding materials to hold moisture and keep roots warm in winter and cool in summer.

Common Name	Fatsia
Scientific Name	Fatsia japonica
Status	Evergreen
Mature Size (H x W)	5x5
Pruning Category (1-5)	1
Watering Category (1-5)	3
Sun Category (1-5)	3
USDA Hardiness Zone:	7-11
Bloom Season	Fall

Common Name	Mini Loropetalum
Scientific Name	Loropetalum chinense 'Beni-Hime'
Status	Evergreen
Mature Size (H x W)	3x3
Pruning Category (1-5)	2
Watering Category (1-5)	2
Sun Category (1-5)	3
USDA Hardiness Zone:	7-10
Bloom Season	Spring

Common Name	Dissectum Japanese Maple
Scientific Name	Acer palmatum var dissectum
Status	Deciduous
Mature Size (H x W)	6x9
Pruning Category (1-5)	2
Watering Category (1-5)	2
Sun Category (1-5)	3
USDA Hardiness Zone:	5-8
Bloom Season	None

Common Name	Nordic Inkberry Holly
Scientific Name	Ilex glabra
Status	Evergreen
Mature Size (H x W)	3x3
Pruning Category (1-5)	4
Watering Category (1-5)	2
Sun Category (1-5)	4
USDA Hardiness Zone:	5-8
Bloom Season	None-Inconspicuous

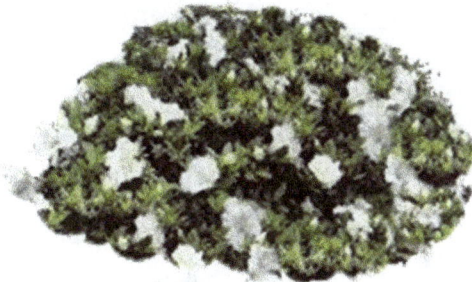

Common Name	Gumpo Azalea
Scientific Name	Rhododendron 'Gumpo'
Status	Evergreen
Mature Size (H x W)	3x3
Pruning Category (1-5)	2
Watering Category (1-5)	3
Sun Category (1-5)	3
USDA Hardiness Zone:	7-9
Bloom Season	Spring

Afternoon Tea

Description

Boulder steps accent this hill top get away. Add a bistro table to enjoy breakfast. No hill? No problem. Recreate the look on a flat surface with garden boulders instead of steps. Simple, shady plantings welcome you in and invite you to return when your visit is finished.

Ingredients

(4) tons step boulders
(1) Dwarf Mugo Pine
(3) Japanese Painted Fern
(1) Miscanthus Grass
(1) Bearded Iris

(3) Hosta
(1) Fatsia
(1) Foxtail Fern
(3) Autumn Fern

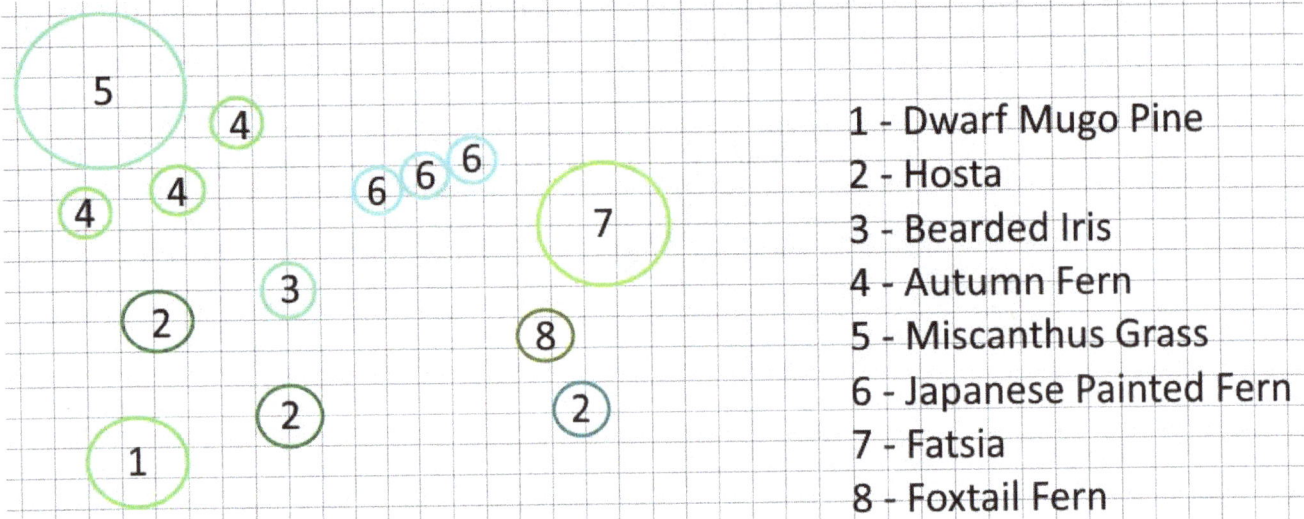

1 - Dwarf Mugo Pine
2 - Hosta
3 - Bearded Iris
4 - Autumn Fern
5 - Miscanthus Grass
6 - Japanese Painted Fern
7 - Fatsia
8 - Foxtail Fern

1 block = 1' x 1' (1 sqft)

Assembly Instructions

Garden Size (Approximate):	20'L x 16'W
Pruning Category:	1
Watering Needs:	3
Sun Requirements:	3
Plant Zones:	3-11
Bloom Colors:	Blue, Purple, White
Bloom Time Range:	Spring-Fall
Average Time to Install:	14 hours
Approximate Bedding:	320sf
Mulch:	2 cuyds
Pine Straw:	7 bales
Rock:	4 tons at 3" thick
Other Cultivars Available to Sub:	Yes
Special Needs:	

Till garden and amend soil with composted material such as mulched leaves or shredded pine.

Using the planting diagram, set step boulders by digging into the soil several inches to create a flat area to set the stones. Be sure stones are secure (don't wobble). Soil can be packed back under and around each step to secure it. Always start at the bottom of the hill and work your way to the top when setting stones. Set each subsequent stone slightly on top of the previous stone.

Measure for plant placement and sit each plant in its proper place. Adjust placement based on the shape of the actual bed.

Dig each hole twice as wide as the root ball. Sprinkle in starter fertilizer to the bottom of the hole (follow directions on package for proper application). Set plant in hole. Push soil back around plant, tamping in tight with the handle end of the shovel to remove all air pockets. Tamp soil tight at top of root ball.

Repeat for each plant.

Water in all plants thoroughly.

Top beds with mulch, pine straw or other bedding materials to hold moisture and keep roots warm in winter and cool in summer.

Common Name	Dwarf Mugo Pine
Scientific Name	Pinus mugo
Status	Evergreen
Mature Size (H x W)	4x3
Pruning Category (1-5)	1
Watering Category (1-5)	1
Sun Category (1-5)	3
USDA Hardiness Zone:	3-7
Bloom Season	None-Inconspicuous

Common Name	Big Leaf Hosta
Scientific Name	Hosta
Status	Perennial
Mature Size (H x W)	4x4
Pruning Category (1-5)	1
Watering Category (1-5)	2
Sun Category (1-5)	2
USDA Hardiness Zone:	3-8
Bloom Season	Summer

Common Name	Bearded Iris
Scientific Name	Iris germanica
Status	Perennial
Mature Size (H x W)	2x2
Pruning Category (1-5)	1
Watering Category (1-5)	4
Sun Category (1-5)	3
USDA Hardiness Zone:	3-8
Bloom Season	Spring

Common Name	Autumn Fern
Scientific Name	Dryopteris erythrosora
Status	Perennial
Mature Size (H x W)	2x2
Pruning Category (1-5)	1
Watering Category (1-5)	3
Sun Category (1-5)	2
USDA Hardiness Zone:	4-8
Bloom Season	None

Common Name	Adagio Miscanthus Grass
Scientific Name	Miscanthus sinensis 'Adagio'
Status	Perennial
Mature Size (H x W)	5x5
Pruning Category (1-5)	1
Watering Category (1-5)	1
Sun Category (1-5)	4
USDA Hardiness Zone:	6-10
Bloom Season	Summer

Common Name	Japanese Painted Fern
Scientific Name	Athyrium niponicum
Status	Perennial
Mature Size (H x W)	2x2
Pruning Category (1-5)	1
Watering Category (1-5)	3
Sun Category (1-5)	2
USDA Hardiness Zone:	4-8
Bloom Season	None

Common Name	Fatsia
Scientific Name	Fatsia japonica
Status	Evergreen
Mature Size (H x W)	5x5
Pruning Category (1-5)	1
Watering Category (1-5)	3
Sun Category (1-5)	3
USDA Hardiness Zone:	7-11
Bloom Season	Fall

Common Name	Foxtail Fern
Scientific Name	Asparagus aethiopicus
Status	Perennial
Mature Size (H x W)	2x2
Pruning Category (1-5)	1
Watering Category (1-5)	3
Sun Category (1-5)	2
USDA Hardiness Zone:	4-8
Bloom Season	None

Description

Retaining walls seem to be a necessity these days for most new houses. Hilly slopes and terraced gardens are no problem. Keep it simple, especially when it's difficult to climb a wall to prune or weed. Choose maintenance free bed covers like slate chips, egg rock or pea gravel. Drought tolerant plants cut down on extra watering in hot weather.

Ingredients

(9) Ice Plant
(10) Dianthus
(1) Agave
(3) Hens and Chicks
(1) Cordyline
(3) Dwarf Plum Yew

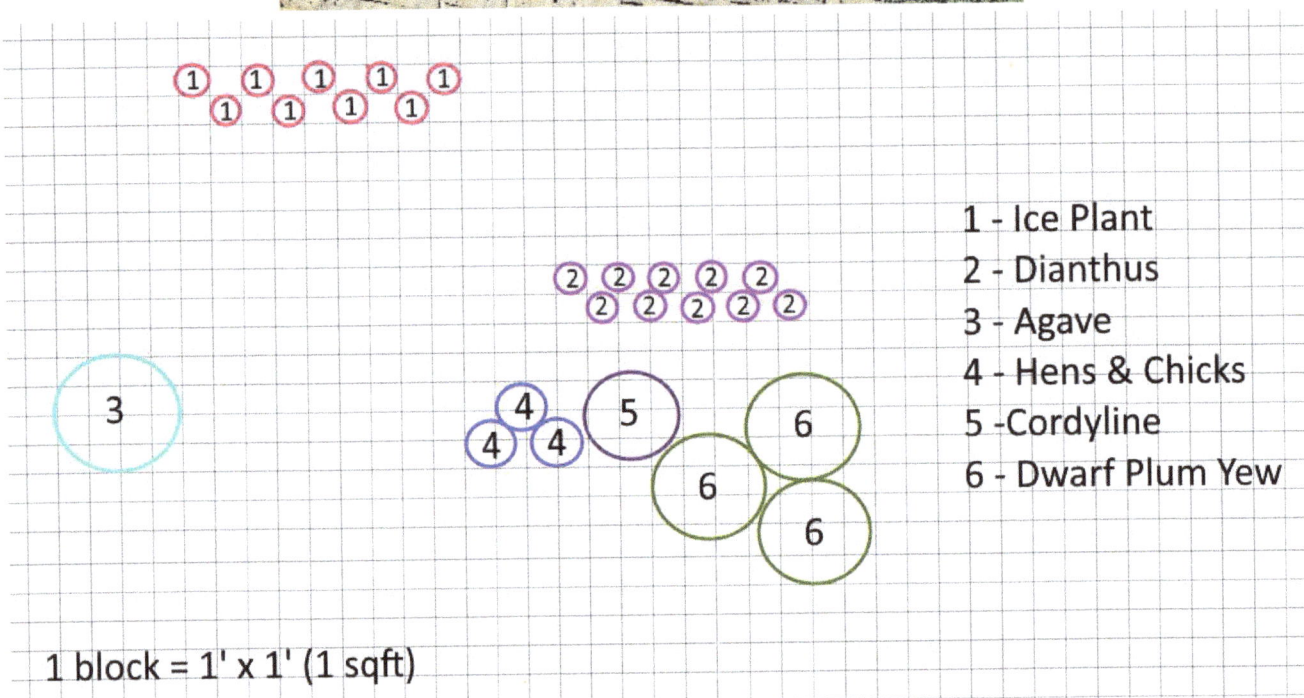

1 - Ice Plant
2 - Dianthus
3 - Agave
4 - Hens & Chicks
5 - Cordyline
6 - Dwarf Plum Yew

1 block = 1' x 1' (1 sqft)

Assembly Instructions

Garden Size (Approximate):	28'L x 22'W
Pruning Category:	1
Watering Needs:	1
Sun Requirements:	4
Plant Zones:	3-11
Bloom Colors:	Purple
Bloom Time Range:	Summer
Average Time to Install:	9 hours
Approximate Bedding:	616sf
Mulch:	4 cuyds
Pine Straw:	15 bales
Rock:	7.7 tons at 3" thick
Other Cultivars Available to Sub:	Yes
Special Needs:	Protect succulents from freezing temps (below 40 degrees F)

Till garden and amend soil with composted material such as mulched leaves or shredded pine.

Using the planting diagram, measure for plant placement and sit each plant in its proper place. Adjust placement based on the shape of the actual bed.

Dig each hole twice as wide as the root ball. Sprinkle in starter fertilizer to the bottom of the hole (follow directions on package for proper application). Set plant in hole. Push soil back around plant, tamping in tight with the handle end of the shovel to remove all air pockets. Tamp soil tight at top of root ball.

Repeat for each plant.

Water in all plants thoroughly.

Top beds with mulch, pine straw or other bedding materials to hold moisture and keep roots warm in winter and cool in summer.

Common Name	Ice Plant
Scientific Name	Aizoaceae
Status	Perennial
Mature Size (H x W)	1x1
Pruning Category (1-5)	1
Watering Category (1-5)	2
Sun Category (1-5)	3
USDA Hardiness Zone:	6-8
Bloom Season	Summer

Common Name	Fire Witch Dianthus
Scientific Name	Dianthus gratianopolitanus 'Fire Witch'
Status	Perennial
Mature Size (H x W)	1.5x1.5
Pruning Category (1-5)	1
Watering Category (1-5)	2
Sun Category (1-5)	3
USDA Hardiness Zone:	3-9
Bloom Season	Summer

Common Name	Agave
Scientific Name	Agave shawii x attenuata 'Blue Flame'
Status	Succulent
Mature Size (H x W)	5x5
Pruning Category (1-5)	1
Watering Category (1-5)	1
Sun Category (1-5)	5
USDA Hardiness Zone:	8-10
Bloom Season	None

Common Name	Hens and Chicks
Scientific Name	Sempervivum tectorum
Status	Succulent
Mature Size (H x W)	2x2
Pruning Category (1-5)	1
Watering Category (1-5)	1
Sun Category (1-5)	5
USDA Hardiness Zone:	3-8
Bloom Season	None

Common Name	Cordyline
Scientific Name	Cordyline fruticosa
Status	Tropical
Mature Size (H x W)	3x2
Pruning Category (1-5)	1
Watering Category (1-5)	1
Sun Category (1-5)	5
USDA Hardiness Zone:	10-11
Bloom Season	Summer

Common Name	Dwarf Plum Yew
Scientific Name	Cephalotaxus harringtonia 'Prostrata'
Status	Evergreen
Mature Size (H x W)	3x3
Pruning Category (1-5)	1
Watering Category (1-5)	2
Sun Category (1-5)	3
USDA Hardiness Zone:	4-8
Bloom Season	None

Rain, No Rain... Whatever

Description

Whatever the weather, this garden doesn't care. It's also virtually care-free. Low maintenance grasses and sedum keep it water free, maintenance free and problem free. Use rock as a bed cover for drainage and weed control. Install the garden with or without the dry creek bed to the right. The stacked stone wall is fieldstone, dry stacked to form a small wall, but doesn't actually "retain" anything.

Ingredients

(5) tons fieldstone boulders
(1) Garden Boulder
(2) tons 10" river rock
(3) Color Guard Yucca
(3) Miscanthus Grass
(1) Autumn Joy Sedum

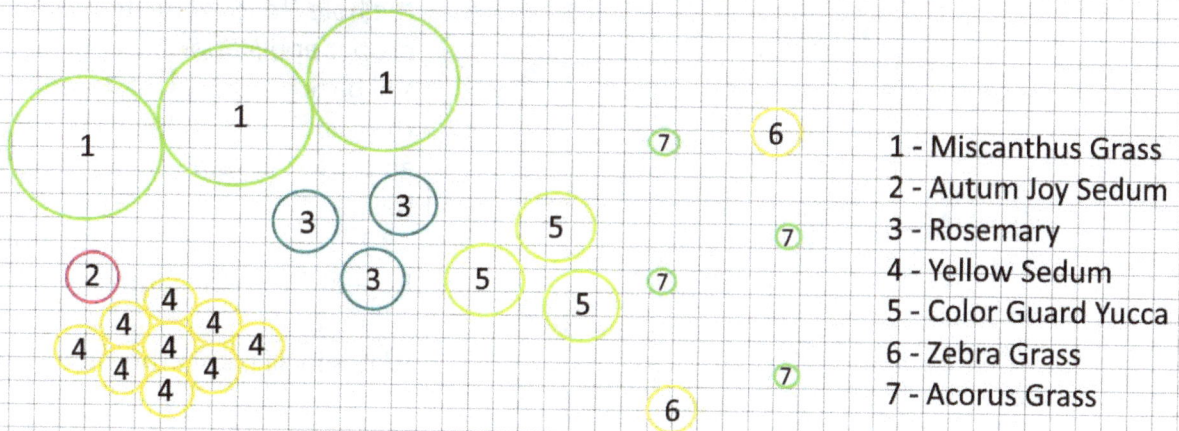

(3) Rosemary
(9) Yellow Sedum
(2) Zebra Grass
(4) Acorus Grass

1 - Miscanthus Grass
2 - Autum Joy Sedum
3 - Rosemary
4 - Yellow Sedum
5 - Color Guard Yucca
6 - Zebra Grass
7 - Acorus Grass

1 block = 1' x 1' (1 sqft)

Assembly Instructions

Garden Size (Approximate):	31'L x 18'W
Pruning Category:	1
Watering Needs:	1
Sun Requirements:	4
Plant Zones:	3-11
Bloom Colors:	White, Pink, Purple
Bloom Time Range:	Summer, Fall
Average Time to Install:	50 hours
Approximate Bedding:	558sf
Mulch:	3 cuyds
Pine Straw:	13 bales
Rock:	7 tons
Other Cultivars Available to Sub:	Yes
Special Needs:	

Till garden and amend soil with composted material such as mulched leaves or shredded pine.

To set a dry creek bed, dig out the area to form an indention in the soil to give the water a slope to run against. Starting at the outer edge, set the larger stones to resemble a border. Work your way toward the center, placing stones, flat side down, to form a dry creek bed.

Using the planting diagram, set boulders for wall by digging out a foundation for the lowest course of the wall. Set the boulder on to the foundation then spread the removed soil around the boulders to bring the soil height back up to grade level. Set the next course of stones slightly off-set on top of the first. Use the natural contours of the rock to dry stack and keep the stones from wobbling.

Measure for plant placement and sit each plant in its proper place. Adjust placement based on the shape of the actual bed.

Dig each hole twice as wide as the root ball. Sprinkle in starter fertilizer to the bottom of the hole (follow directions on package for proper application). Set plant in hole. Push soil back around plant, tamping in tight with the handle end of the shovel to remove all air pockets. Tamp soil tight at top of root ball.

Repeat for each plant.

Water in all plants thoroughly.

Top beds with mulch, pine straw or other bedding materials to hold moisture and keep roots warm in winter and cool in summer.

Common Name	Adagio Miscanthus Grass
Scientific Name	Miscanthus sinensis 'Adagio'
Status	Perennial
Mature Size (H x W)	5x5
Pruning Category (1-5)	1
Watering Category (1-5)	1
Sun Category (1-5)	4
USDA Hardiness Zone:	6-10
Bloom Season	Summer

Common Name	Autumn Joy Sedum
Scientific Name	Hylotelephium telephium 'Autumn Joy'
Status	Perennial
Mature Size (H x W)	2x2
Pruning Category (1-5)	1
Watering Category (1-5)	1
Sun Category (1-5)	5
USDA Hardiness Zone:	3-8
Bloom Season	Fall

Common Name	Rosemary
Scientific Name	Rosmarinus officinalis
Status	Perennial
Mature Size (H x W)	3x4
Pruning Category (1-5)	1
Watering Category (1-5)	2
Sun Category (1-5)	4
USDA Hardiness Zone:	5-10
Bloom Season	Summer

Common Name	Color Guard Yucca
Scientific Name	Yucca filamentosa 'Color Guard'
Status	Succulent
Mature Size (H x W)	2x2
Pruning Category (1-5)	1
Watering Category (1-5)	1
Sun Category (1-5)	5
USDA Hardiness Zone:	5-11
Bloom Season	Summer

Common Name	Zebra Grass
Scientific Name	Miscanthus sinensis 'Zebrinus'
Status	Perennial
Mature Size (H x W)	3x3
Pruning Category (1-5)	1
Watering Category (1-5)	1
Sun Category (1-5)	3
USDA Hardiness Zone:	5-9
Bloom Season	None

Common Name	Acorus Grass
Scientific Name	Acorus gramineus
Status	Perennial
Mature Size (H x W)	1x1
Pruning Category (1-5)	1
Watering Category (1-5)	1
Sun Category (1-5)	2
USDA Hardiness Zone:	6-9
Bloom Season	None

Description

Plant this maintenance free garden for a visually stunning open landscape. It is drought tolerant, heat tolerant and easy to look at as an accent garden, or repeat patterns to create a full backyard oasis. Maintenance free bedding is a bonus or add your favorite mulch or other stone for a unique drought-tolerant garden.

Ingredients

(4) tons field stone boulders   (1) Cane Yucca
(2) tons slate chips (bedding)   (6) Heliopsis
(3) Rosemary   (3) Yucca
(2) Miscanthus Grass
(1) Dwarf Butterfly Shrub

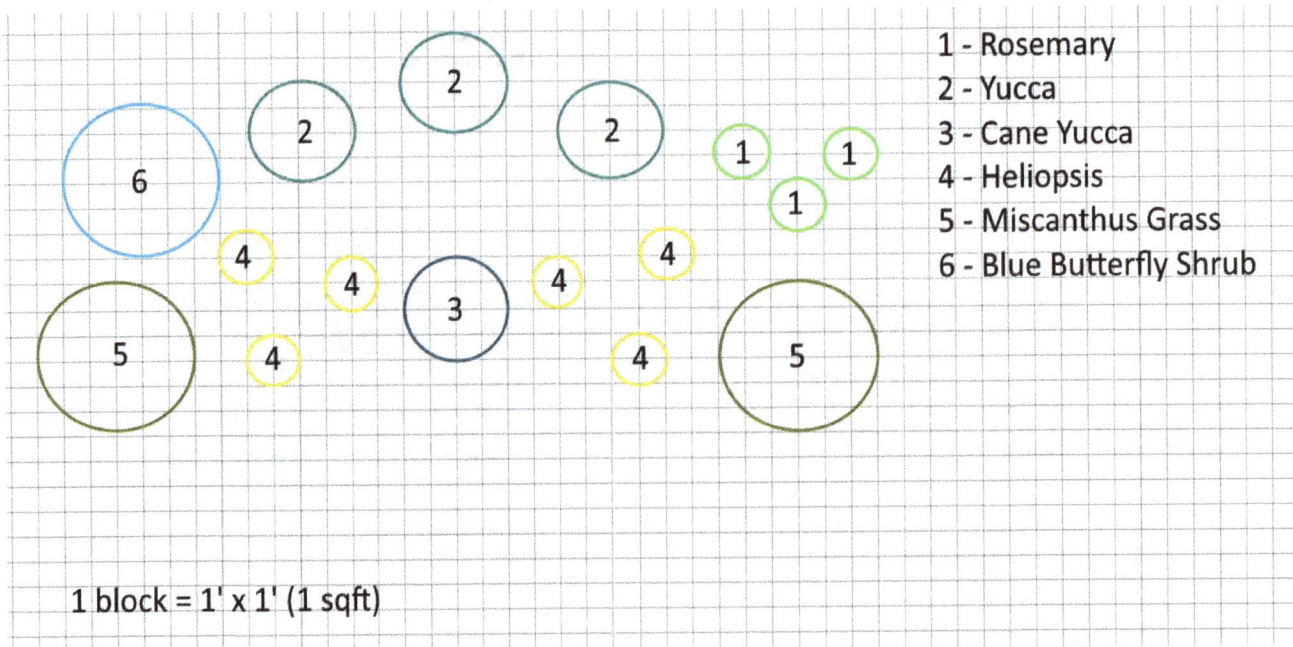

1 - Rosemary
2 - Yucca
3 - Cane Yucca
4 - Heliopsis
5 - Miscanthus Grass
6 - Blue Butterfly Shrub

1 block = 1' x 1' (1 sqft)

Assembly Instructions

Garden Size (Approximate):	31'L x 16'W
Pruning Category:	1
Watering Needs:	1
Sun Requirements:	4
Plant Zones:	3-11
Bloom Colors:	Purple, White, Yellow, Blue
Bloom Time Range:	Summer
Average Time to Install:	30 hours
Approximate Bedding:	496sf
Mulch:	3 cuyds
Pine Straw:	12 bales
Rock:	2 tons slate chips; 4 tons outer areas
Other Cultivars Available to Sub:	Yes
Special Needs:	

Till garden and amend soil with composted material such as mulched leaves or shredded pine.

Using the planting diagram, set boulders for wall by digging out a foundation for the lowest course of the wall. Set the boulder on to the foundation then spread the removed soil around the boulders to bring the soil height back up to grade level. Set the next course of stones slightly off-set on top of the first. Use the natural contours of the rock to dry stack and keep the stones from wobbling.

Measure for plant placement and sit each plant in its proper place. Adjust placement based on the shape of the actual bed.

Dig each hole twice as wide as the root ball. Sprinkle in starter fertilizer to the bottom of the hole (follow directions on package for proper application). Set plant in hole. Push soil back around plant, tamping in tight with the handle end of the shovel to remove all air pockets. Tamp soil tight at top of root ball.

Repeat for each plant.

Water in all plants thoroughly.

Top beds with mulch, pine straw or other bedding materials to hold moisture and keep roots warm in winter and cool in summer.

Common Name	Rosemary
Scientific Name	Rosmarinus officinalis
Status	Perennial
Mature Size (H x W)	3x4
Pruning Category (1-5)	1
Watering Category (1-5)	2
Sun Category (1-5)	4
USDA Hardiness Zone:	5-10
Bloom Season	Summer

Common Name	Yucca
Scientific Name	Yucca nana
Status	Succulent
Mature Size (H x W)	4x4
Pruning Category (1-5)	1
Watering Category (1-5)	1
Sun Category (1-5)	5
USDA Hardiness Zone:	5-11
Bloom Season	Summer

Common Name	Cane Yucca
Scientific Name	Yucca gigantea
Status	Succulent
Mature Size (H x W)	6x4
Pruning Category (1-5)	1
Watering Category (1-5)	1
Sun Category (1-5)	5
USDA Hardiness Zone:	5-11
Bloom Season	Summer

Common Name	Heliopsis
Scientific Name	Heliopsis helianthoides
Status	Perennial
Mature Size (H x W)	2x2
Pruning Category (1-5)	1
Watering Category (1-5)	2
Sun Category (1-5)	4
USDA Hardiness Zone:	3-9
Bloom Season	Summer

Common Name	Adagio Miscanthus Grass
Scientific Name	Miscanthus sinensis 'Adagio'
Status	Perennial
Mature Size (H x W)	5x5
Pruning Category (1-5)	1
Watering Category (1-5)	1
Sun Category (1-5)	4
USDA Hardiness Zone:	6-10
Bloom Season	Summer

Common Name	Dwarf Butterfly Shrub
Scientific Name	Buddleia
Status	Deciduous
Mature Size (H x W)	3x3
Pruning Category (1-5)	2
Watering Category (1-5)	2
Sun Category (1-5)	5
USDA Hardiness Zone:	5-11
Bloom Season	Summer

The Bee's Knees

Description

This garden isn't technically all edible. Forsythia adds a dash of color and attracts bees for pollination, which every garden needs. Marigolds deter pests and the petals are edible. Dry and save rosemary and basil for your chicken and stews in the winter. Switch out herbs seasonally for more variety.

Ingredients

(2) Forsythia   (1) Basil
(1) Rosemary   (1) Thyme
(1) Fothergilla   (3) Chives
(3) Marigold

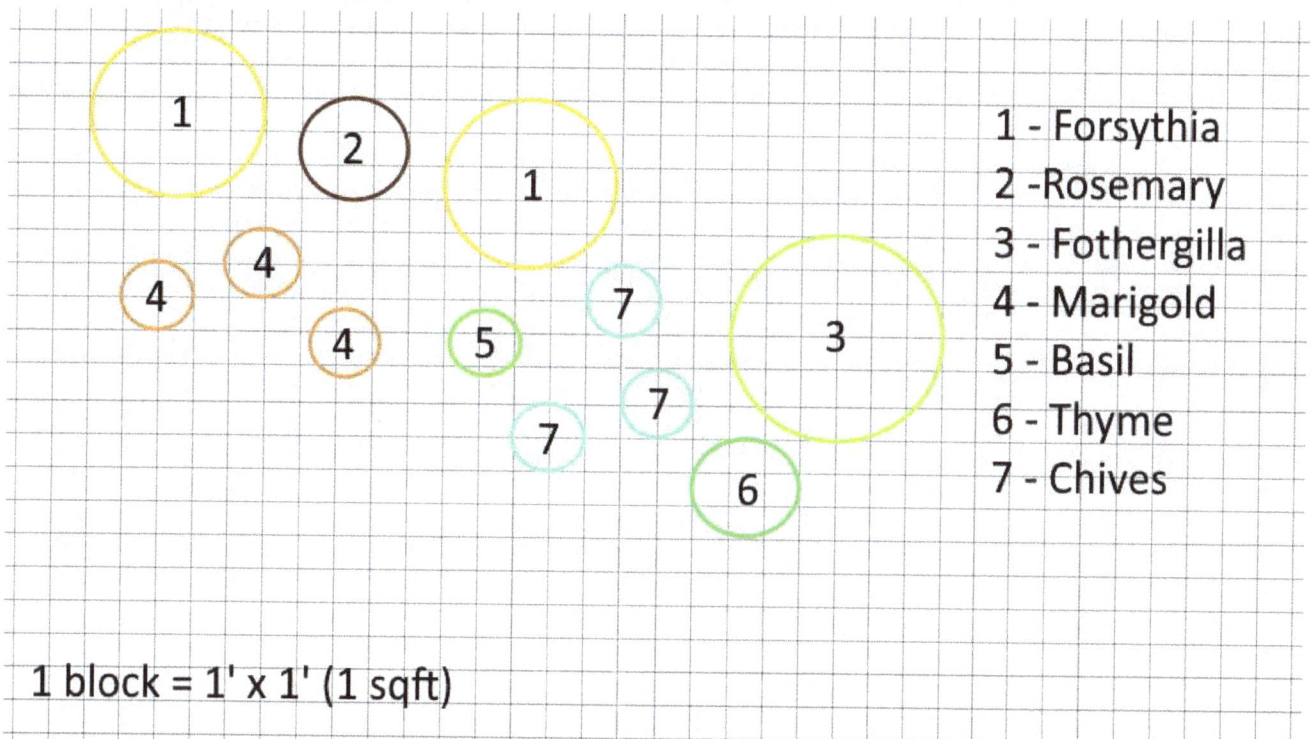

1 - Forsythia
2 - Rosemary
3 - Fothergilla
4 - Marigold
5 - Basil
6 - Thyme
7 - Chives

1 block = 1' x 1' (1 sqft)

Assembly Instructions

Garden Size (Approximate):	24'L x 15'W
Pruning Category:	1
Watering Needs:	2
Sun Requirements:	4
Plant Zones:	2-11
Bloom Colors:	Yellow, Purple, White, Blue
Bloom Time Range:	Spring-Summer
Average Time to Install:	5 hours
Approximate Bedding:	360sf
Mulch:	2 cuyds
Pine Straw:	9 bales
Rock:	4.5tons at 3" thick
Other Cultivars Available to Sub:	Yes
Special Needs:	

Till garden and amend soil with composted material such as mulched leaves or shredded pine.

Using the planting diagram, measure for plant placement and sit each plant in its proper place. Adjust placement based on the shape of the actual bed.

Dig each hole twice as wide as the root ball. Sprinkle in starter fertilizer to the bottom of the hole (follow directions on package for proper application). Set plant in hole. Push soil back around plant, tamping in tight with the handle end of the shovel to remove all air pockets. Tamp soil tight at top of root ball.

Repeat for each plant.

Water in all plants thoroughly.

Top beds with mulch, pine straw or other bedding materials to hold moisture and keep roots warm in winter and cool in summer.

Common Name	Forsythia
Scientific Name	Forsythia
Status	Deciduous
Mature Size (H x W)	8x8
Pruning Category (1-5)	2
Watering Category (1-5)	2
Sun Category (1-5)	4
USDA Hardiness Zone:	5-9
Bloom Season	Spring

Common Name	Rosemary
Scientific Name	Rosmarinus officinalis
Status	Perennial
Mature Size (H x W)	3x4
Pruning Category (1-5)	1
Watering Category (1-5)	2
Sun Category (1-5)	4
USDA Hardiness Zone:	5-10
Bloom Season	Summer

Common Name	Fothergilla
Scientific Name	Fothergilla gardenii
Status	Deciduous
Mature Size (H x W)	4x4
Pruning Category (1-5)	1
Watering Category (1-5)	2
Sun Category (1-5)	3
USDA Hardiness Zone:	4-9
Bloom Season	Spring

Common Name	Marigold
Scientific Name	Tagetes
Status	Perennial
Mature Size (H x W)	2x2
Pruning Category (1-5)	1
Watering Category (1-5)	2
Sun Category (1-5)	4
USDA Hardiness Zone:	2-11
Bloom Season	Summer

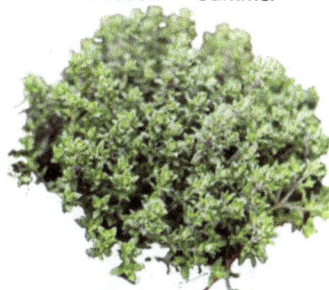

Common Name	Basil
Scientific Name	Ocimum basilicum
Status	Perennial
Mature Size (H x W)	2x1
Pruning Category (1-5)	1
Watering Category (1-5)	2
Sun Category (1-5)	4
USDA Hardiness Zone:	2-11
Bloom Season	Summer

Common Name	Thyme
Scientific Name	Thymus vulgaris
Status	Perennial
Mature Size (H x W)	1x2
Pruning Category (1-5)	1
Watering Category (1-5)	2
Sun Category (1-5)	4
USDA Hardiness Zone:	5-10
Bloom Season	Summer

Common Name	Chives
Scientific Name	Allium schoenoprasum
Status	Perennial
Mature Size (H x W)	2x2
Pruning Category (1-5)	1
Watering Category (1-5)	2
Sun Category (1-5)	4
USDA Hardiness Zone:	3-9
Bloom Season	Summer

Tootie Fruity – Hold the Fruit

Description

Although technically, the flower leads to the fruit, citrus isn't included in this bountiful garden. Always check which parts of which plants are edible and consider your own allergies before consuming something new.   This garden not only feeds the body, it feeds the soul with its beautiful blooms and pollinating flowers. Dry herbs for later use and freeze for freshness.

Ingredients

(3) Hyssop
(1) Witch Hazel
(2) Bee Balm
(5) Borage
(5) Nasturtium

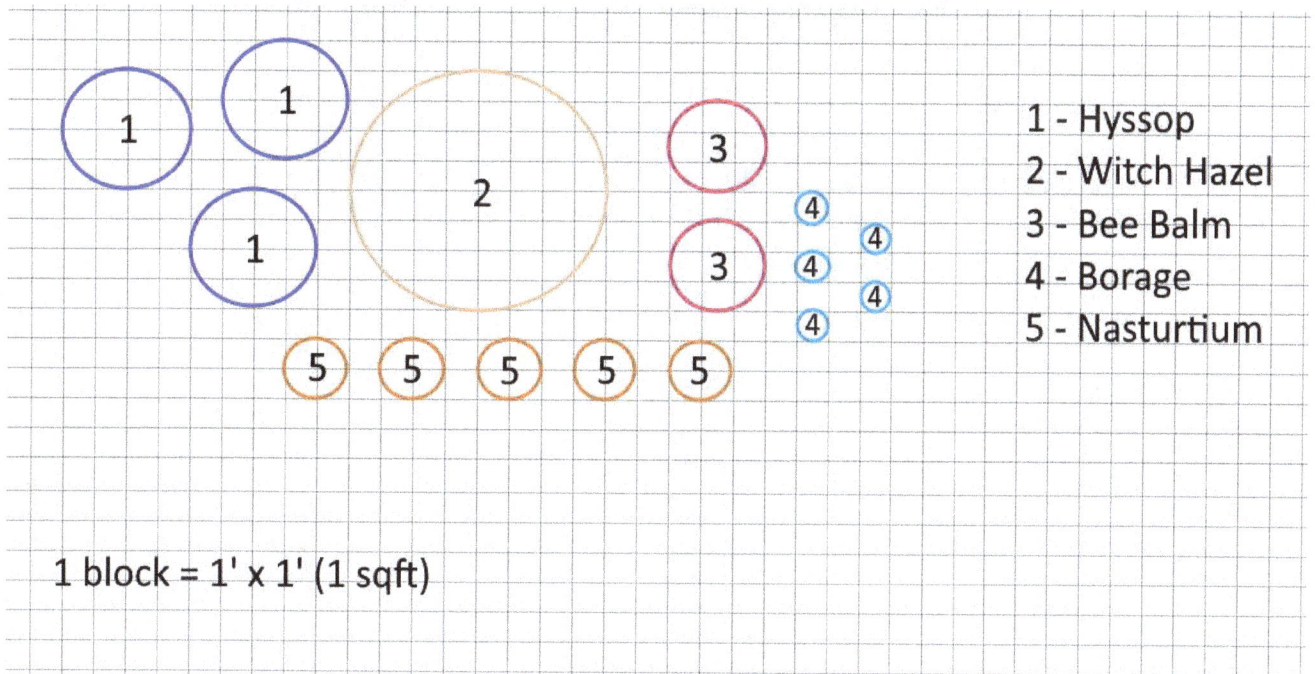

1 - Hyssop
2 - Witch Hazel
3 - Bee Balm
4 - Borage
5 - Nasturtium

1 block = 1' x 1' (1 sqft)

Tootie Fruity – Hold the Fruit

Edible Gardens

Assembly Instructions

Garden Size (Approximate):	26'L x 12'W
Pruning Category:	1
Watering Needs:	2
Sun Requirements:	4
Plant Zones:	2-10
Bloom Colors:	Blue, Yellow, Pink, Orange, Red
Bloom Time Range:	Summer-Fall
Average Time to Install:	8 hours
Approximate Bedding:	312sf
Mulch:	2 cuyds
Pine Straw:	8 bales
Rock:	4 tons at 3" thick
Other Cultivars Available to Sub:	Yes
Special Needs:	Nasturtium has a tendency to be aggressive.

Till garden and amend soil with composted material such as mulched leaves or shredded pine.

Using the planting diagram, measure for plant placement and sit each plant in its proper place. Adjust placement based on the shape of the actual bed.

Dig each hole twice as wide as the root ball. Sprinkle in starter fertilizer to the bottom of the hole (follow directions on package for proper application). Set plant in hole. Push soil back around plant, tamping in tight with the handle end of the shovel to remove all air pockets. Tamp soil tight at top of root ball.

Repeat for each plant.

Water in all plants thoroughly.

Top beds with mulch, pine straw or other bedding materials to hold moisture and keep roots warm in winter and cool in summer.

Common Name	Hyssop
Scientific Name	Hyssopus officinalis
Status	Perennial
Mature Size (H x W)	2x2
Pruning Category (1-5)	1
Watering Category (1-5)	2
Sun Category (1-5)	4
USDA Hardiness Zone:	4-9
Bloom Season	Summer

Common Name	Witch Hazel
Scientific Name	Hamamelis
Status	Deciduous
Mature Size (H x W)	6x6
Pruning Category (1-5)	1
Watering Category (1-5)	1
Sun Category (1-5)	3
USDA Hardiness Zone:	5-9
Bloom Season	Fall

Common Name	Bee Balm
Scientific Name	Monarda
Status	Perennial
Mature Size (H x W)	3x3
Pruning Category (1-5)	1
Watering Category (1-5)	2
Sun Category (1-5)	4
USDA Hardiness Zone:	2-10
Bloom Season	Summer

Common Name	Borage
Scientific Name	Borago officinalis
Status	Annual
Mature Size (H x W)	2x2
Pruning Category (1-5)	1
Watering Category (1-5)	2
Sun Category (1-5)	4
USDA Hardiness Zone:	NA
Bloom Season	Summer

Common Name	Nasturtium
Scientific Name	Tropaeolum
Status	Perennial
Mature Size (H x W)	2x5
Pruning Category (1-5)	1
Watering Category (1-5)	2
Sun Category (1-5)	4
USDA Hardiness Zone:	4-8
Bloom Season	Summer

Description

With the uprising of all sorts of cooking shows these days, it's no wonder we all don't have our nooks and crannies full of home-grown spices and herbs. This design establishes a basic herb garden. Substitute plants based on your own likes and needs. Keep space and height in mind as many veggies tend to get large over the season. Switch out varieties every few seasons to keep the soil balanced. Use organic insecticides like Neem Oil to protect your bounty from unwanted pests.

Ingredients

(1) Dill
(3) Chives
(3) Cilantro
(3) Oregano
(3) Basil

(3) Thyme
(3) Marigold
(3) Dandelion Weed
(3) Obedient Plant

1 - Dill
2 - Chives
3 - Cilantro
4 - Oregano
5 - Basil
6 - Thyme
7 - Marigold
8 - Dandelion
9 - Obedient Plant

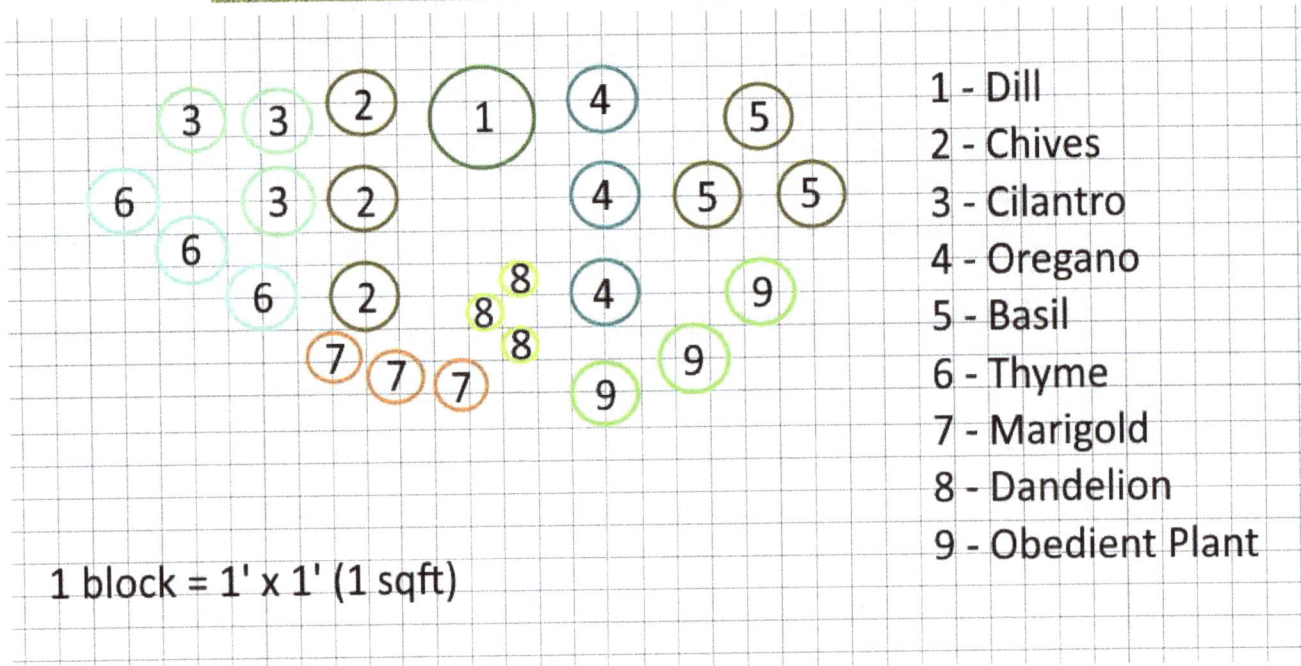

1 block = 1' x 1' (1 sqft)

Assembly Instructions

Garden Size (Approximate):	22'L x 11'W
Pruning Category:	1
Watering Needs:	2
Sun Requirements:	4
Plant Zones:	2-11
Bloom Colors:	White, Purple, Yellow, Orange
Bloom Time Range:	Summer-Fall
Average Time to Install:	13 hours
Approximate Bedding:	242sf
Mulch:	1.5 cuyds
Pine Straw:	6 bales
Rock:	3 tons at 3" thick
Other Cultivars Available to Sub:	Yes
Special Needs:	

Till garden and amend soil with composted material such as mulched leaves or shredded pine.

Using the planting diagram, measure for plant placement and sit each plant in its proper place. Adjust placement based on the shape of the actual bed.

Dig each hole twice as wide as the root ball. Sprinkle in starter fertilizer to the bottom of the hole (follow directions on package for proper application). Set plant in hole. Push soil back around plant, tamping in tight with the handle end of the shovel to remove all air pockets. Tamp soil tight at top of root ball.

Repeat for each plant.

Water in all plants thoroughly.

Top beds with mulch, pine straw or other bedding materials to hold moisture and keep roots warm in winter and cool in summer.

Common Name Dill
Scientific Name Anethum graveolens
Status Perennial
Mature Size (H x W) 3x2
Pruning Category (1-5) 1
Watering Category (1-5) 1
Sun Category (1-5) 4
USDA Hardiness Zone: 3-11
Bloom Season Summer

Common Name Chives
Scientific Name Allium schoenoprasum
Status Perennial
Mature Size (H x W) 2x2
Pruning Category (1-5) 1
Watering Category (1-5) 2
Sun Category (1-5) 4
USDA Hardiness Zone: 3-9
Bloom Season Summer

Common Name Cilantro
Scientific Name Coriandum sativum
Status Perennial
Mature Size (H x W) 3x3
Pruning Category (1-5) 1
Watering Category (1-5) 2
Sun Category (1-5) 4
USDA Hardiness Zone: 3-11
Bloom Season Summer

Common Name Oregano
Scientific Name Origanum vulgare
Status Perennial
Mature Size (H x W) 3x2
Pruning Category (1-5) 1
Watering Category (1-5) 2
Sun Category (1-5) 4
USDA Hardiness Zone: 5-10
Bloom Season Summer

Common Name Basil
Scientific Name Ocimum basilicum
Status Perennial
Mature Size (H x W) 2x1
Pruning Category (1-5) 1
Watering Category (1-5) 2
Sun Category (1-5) 4
USDA Hardiness Zone: 2-11
Bloom Season Summer

Common Name Thyme
Scientific Name Thymus vulgaris
Status Perennial
Mature Size (H x W) 1x2
Pruning Category (1-5) 1
Watering Category (1-5) 2
Sun Category (1-5) 4
USDA Hardiness Zone: 5-10
Bloom Season Summer

Common Name	Marigold
Scientific Name	Tagetes
Status	Perennial
Mature Size (H x W)	2x2
Pruning Category (1-5)	1
Watering Category (1-5)	2
Sun Category (1-5)	4
USDA Hardiness Zone:	2-11
Bloom Season	Summer

Common Name	Dandelion Weed
Scientific Name	Taraxacum
Status	Perennial
Mature Size (H x W)	1x1
Pruning Category (1-5)	3
Watering Category (1-5)	1
Sun Category (1-5)	5
USDA Hardiness Zone:	3-10
Bloom Season	Summer

Common Name	Obedient Plant
Scientific Name	Physostegia virginia
Status	Perennial
Mature Size (H x W)	2x1
Pruning Category (1-5)	1
Watering Category (1-5)	2
Sun Category (1-5)	4
USDA Hardiness Zone:	3-10
Bloom Season	Fall

Description

Fill your landscape with edible delights. Save money on herbs by drying and freezing for later use. Rosemary is not just a tasty herb, it also smells wonderful and makes a great addition to dried arrangements. Keep cilantro on hand for your favorite salsa recipe and to freshly garnish your plates. Dry and share herbs with friends or create an herb swapping co-op to keep a full selection of fresh herbs.

Ingredients

(3) Hyssop
(1) Thyme
(3) Cilantro
(3) Rosemary
(1) Oregano

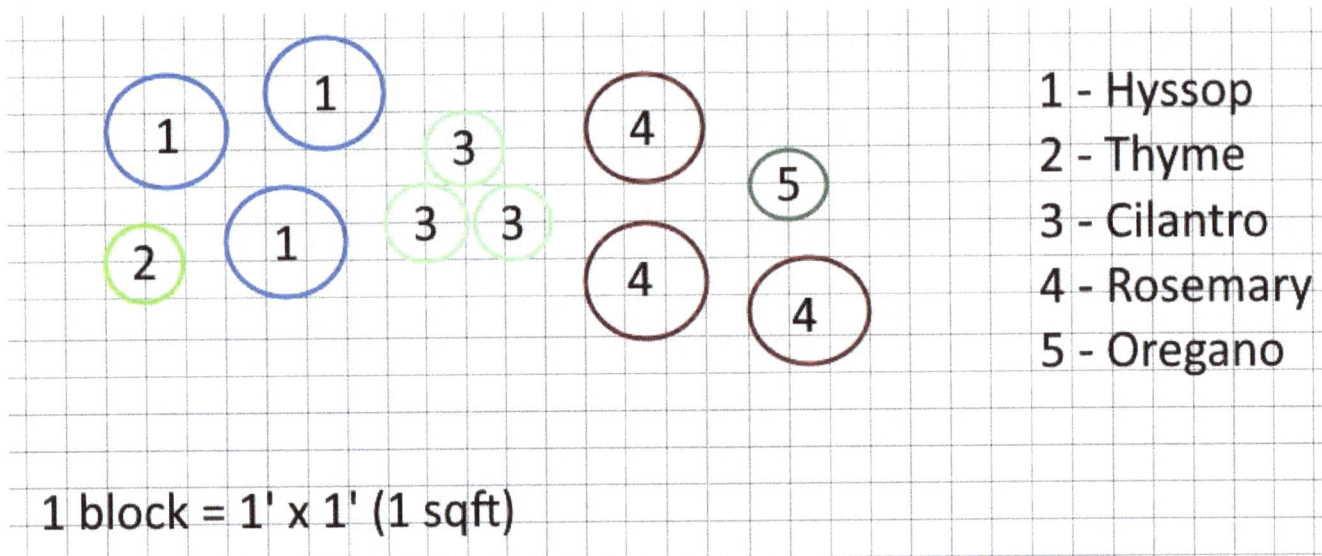

1 block = 1' x 1' (1 sqft)

1 - Hyssop
2 - Thyme
3 - Cilantro
4 - Rosemary
5 - Oregano

Assembly Instructions

Garden Size (Approximate):	19' L x 9'W
Pruning Category:	1
Watering Needs:	2
Sun Requirements:	4
Plant Zones:	3-11
Bloom Colors:	Blue, White, Purple
Bloom Time Range:	Summer
Average Time to Install:	6 hours
Approximate Bedding:	171sf
Mulch:	1 cuyds
Pine Straw:	4 bales
Rock:	2 tons at 3" thick
Other Cultivars Available to Sub:	Yes
Special Needs:	

Till garden and amend soil with composted material such as mulched leaves or shredded pine.

Using the planting diagram, measure for plant placement and sit each plant in its proper place. Adjust placement based on the shape of the actual bed.

Dig each hole twice as wide as the root ball. Sprinkle in starter fertilizer to the bottom of the hole (follow directions on package for proper application). Set plant in hole. Push soil back around plant, tamping in tight with the handle end of the shovel to remove all air pockets. Tamp soil tight at top of root ball.

Repeat for each plant.

Water in all plants thoroughly.

Top beds with mulch, pine straw or other bedding materials to hold moisture and keep roots warm in winter and cool in summer.

Common Name	Hyssop
Scientific Name	Hyssopus officinalis
Status	Perennial
Mature Size (H x W)	2x2
Pruning Category (1-5)	1
Watering Category (1-5)	2
Sun Category (1-5)	4
USDA Hardiness Zone:	4-9
Bloom Season	Summer

Common Name	Thyme
Scientific Name	Thymus vulgaris
Status	Perennial
Mature Size (H x W)	1x2
Pruning Category (1-5)	1
Watering Category (1-5)	2
Sun Category (1-5)	4
USDA Hardiness Zone:	5-10
Bloom Season	Summer

Common Name	Cilantro
Scientific Name	Coriandum sativum
Status	Perennial
Mature Size (H x W)	3x3
Pruning Category (1-5)	1
Watering Category (1-5)	2
Sun Category (1-5)	4
USDA Hardiness Zone:	3-11
Bloom Season	Summer

Common Name	Rosemary
Scientific Name	Rosmarinus officinalis
Status	Perennial
Mature Size (H x W)	3x4
Pruning Category (1-5)	1
Watering Category (1-5)	2
Sun Category (1-5)	4
USDA Hardiness Zone:	5-10
Bloom Season	Summer

Common Name	Oregano
Scientific Name	Origanum vulgare
Status	Perennial
Mature Size (H x W)	3x2
Pruning Category (1-5)	1
Watering Category (1-5)	2
Sun Category (1-5)	4
USDA Hardiness Zone:	5-10
Bloom Season	Summer

Granny's Pantry

Edible Gardens

Description

My grandma was always growing something. She was frugal and kept a garden to save money. Today, we have dried, frozen and pre-packaged everything, but it's still nice to eat clean and fresh. Switch out herbs with your favorites or add in vegetables for more variety.

Ingredients

(2) Dill
(1) Fothergilla
(1) Cilantro
(2) Marigold
(3) Borage
(3) Bee Balm

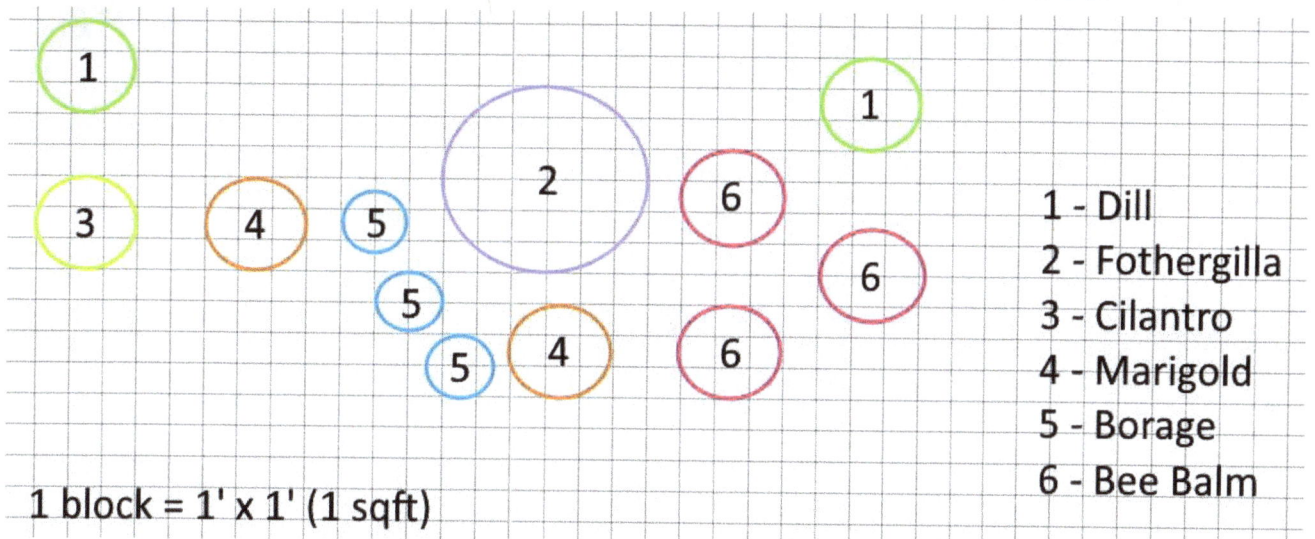

1 block = 1' x 1' (1 sqft)

1 - Dill
2 - Fothergilla
3 - Cilantro
4 - Marigold
5 - Borage
6 - Bee Balm

Assembly Instructions

Garden Size (Approximate):	26'L x 11'W
Pruning Category:	1
Watering Needs:	2
Sun Requirements:	4
Plant Zones:	2-11
Bloom Colors:	White, Yellow, Orange, Blue, Pink
Bloom Time Range:	Spring-Summer
Average Time to Install:	6 hours
Approximate Bedding:	286sf
Mulch:	1.75cuyds
Pine Straw:	7 bales
Rock:	3.5 tons at 3" thick
Other Cultivars Available to Sub:	Yes
Special Needs:	

Till garden and amend soil with composted material such as mulched leaves or shredded pine.

Using the planting diagram, measure for plant placement and sit each plant in its proper place. Adjust placement based on the shape of the actual bed.

Dig each hole twice as wide as the root ball. Sprinkle in starter fertilizer to the bottom of the hole (follow directions on package for proper application). Set plant in hole. Push soil back around plant, tamping in tight with the handle end of the shovel to remove all air pockets. Tamp soil tight at top of root ball.

Repeat for each plant.

Water in all plants thoroughly.

Top beds with mulch, pine straw or other bedding materials to hold moisture and keep roots warm in winter and cool in summer.

Common Name	Dill
Scientific Name	Anethum graveolens
Status	Perennial
Mature Size (H x W)	3x2
Pruning Category (1-5)	1
Watering Category (1-5)	1
Sun Category (1-5)	4
USDA Hardiness Zone:	3-11
Bloom Season	Summer

Common Name	Fothergilla
Scientific Name	Fothergilla gardenii
Status	Deciduous
Mature Size (H x W)	4x4
Pruning Category (1-5)	1
Watering Category (1-5)	2
Sun Category (1-5)	3
USDA Hardiness Zone:	4-9
Bloom Season	Spring

Common Name	Cilantro
Scientific Name	Coriandum sativum
Status	Perennial
Mature Size (H x W)	3x3
Pruning Category (1-5)	1
Watering Category (1-5)	2
Sun Category (1-5)	4
USDA Hardiness Zone:	3-11
Bloom Season	Summer

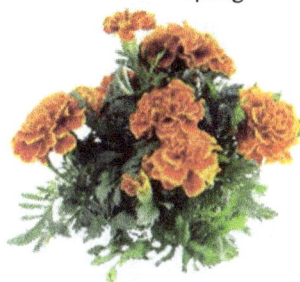

Common Name	Marigold
Scientific Name	Tagetes
Status	Perennial
Mature Size (H x W)	2x2
Pruning Category (1-5)	1
Watering Category (1-5)	2
Sun Category (1-5)	4
USDA Hardiness Zone:	2-11
Bloom Season	Summer

Common Name	Borage
Scientific Name	Borago officinalis
Status	Annual
Mature Size (H x W)	2x2
Pruning Category (1-5)	1
Watering Category (1-5)	2
Sun Category (1-5)	4
USDA Hardiness Zone:	NA
Bloom Season	Summer

Common Name	Bee Balm
Scientific Name	Monarda
Status	Perennial
Mature Size (H x W)	3x3
Pruning Category (1-5)	1
Watering Category (1-5)	2
Sun Category (1-5)	4
USDA Hardiness Zone:	2-10
Bloom Season	Summer

Tall Tales

Description

No one likes to prune. It's a necessary evil to keep the garden neat and clean and the plants in the right shapes and sizes. Unless, of course, you choose the right plants, the right shape, the right location. This garden will tend to itself. Plant with height to the back for a fabulous layered look. Mulch regularly to keep the roots cool in warmer zones.

Ingredients

(2) Teddy Bear Magnolia
(2) Spartan Juniper
(3) Green Giant Arborvitae
(4) Gold Thread Cypress
(3) Nana Globosa Dwarf Cryptomeria

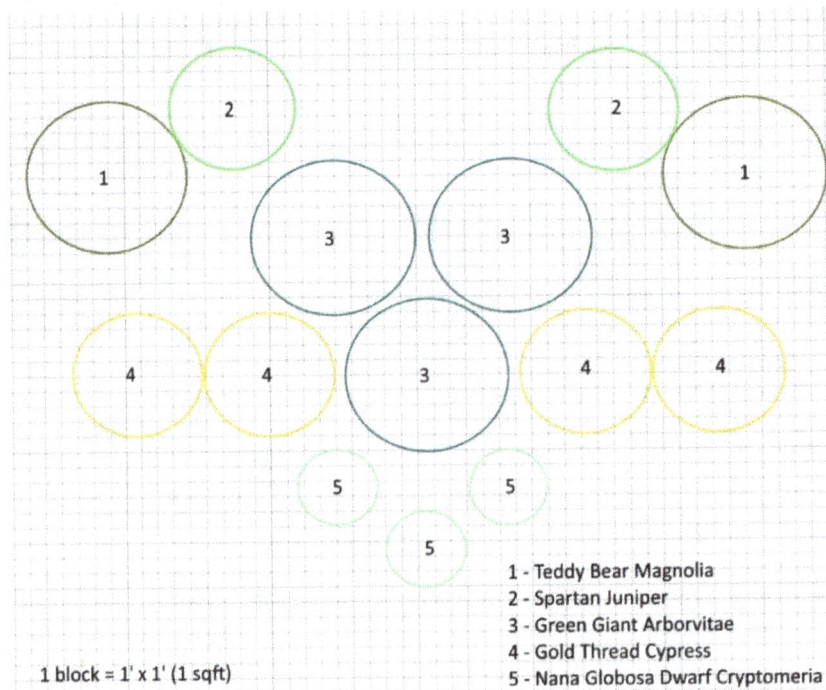

1 block = 1' x 1' (1 sqft)

1 - Teddy Bear Magnolia
2 - Spartan Juniper
3 - Green Giant Arborvitae
4 - Gold Thread Cypress
5 - Nana Globosa Dwarf Cryptomeria

Tall Tales

Evergreen Gardens

Assembly Instructions

Garden Size (Approximate):	50'L x 36'W
Pruning Category:	1
Watering Needs:	2
Sun Requirements:	3
Plant Zones:	4-9
Bloom Colors:	White
Bloom Time Range:	Spring
Average Time to Install:	18 hours
Approximate Bedding:	1,800sf
Mulch:	11 cuyds
Pine Straw:	43 bales
Rock:	22 tons at 3" thick
Other Cultivars Available to Sub:	Yes
Special Needs:	

Till garden and amend soil with composted material such as mulched leaves or shredded pine.

Using the planting diagram, measure for plant placement and sit each plant in its proper place. Adjust placement based on the shape of the actual bed.

Dig each hole twice as wide as the root ball. Sprinkle in starter fertilizer to the bottom of the hole (follow directions on package for proper application). Set plant in hole. Push soil back around plant, tamping in tight with the handle end of the shovel to remove all air pockets. Tamp soil tight at top of root ball.

Repeat for each plant.

Water in all plants thoroughly.

Top beds with mulch, pine straw or other bedding materials to hold moisture and keep roots warm in winter and cool in summer.

Tall Tales

Evergreen Gardens

Common Name	Teddy Bear Magnolia
Scientific Name	Magnolia grandiflora 'Southern Charm'
Status	Evergreen
Mature Size (H x W)	20x12
Pruning Category (1-5)	1
Watering Category (1-5)	2
Sun Category (1-5)	4
USDA Hardiness Zone:	7-9
Bloom Season	Spring

Common Name	Spartan Juniper
Scientific Name	Juniperus chinensis 'Spartan'
Status	Evergreen
Mature Size (H x W)	20x6
Pruning Category (1-5)	1
Watering Category (1-5)	1
Sun Category (1-5)	4
USDA Hardiness Zone:	6-9
Bloom Season	None

Common Name	Green Giant Arborvitae
Scientific Name	Thuja standishii × plicata 'Green Giant'
Status	Evergreen
Mature Size (H x W)	20x10
Pruning Category (1-5)	1
Watering Category (1-5)	3
Sun Category (1-5)	4
USDA Hardiness Zone:	4-8
Bloom Season	None

Common Name	Gold Thread Cypress
Scientific Name	Chamaecyparis pisifera 'Gold Thread'
Status	Evergreen
Mature Size (H x W)	12x10
Pruning Category (1-5)	1
Watering Category (1-5)	1
Sun Category (1-5)	4
USDA Hardiness Zone:	6-9
Bloom Season	None

Common Name	Nana Globosa Dwarf Cryptomeria
Scientific Name	Cryptomeria japonica 'Globosa Nana'
Status	Evergreen
Mature Size (H x W)	4x4
Pruning Category (1-5)	1
Watering Category (1-5)	1
Sun Category (1-5)	3
USDA Hardiness Zone:	6-9
Bloom Season	None

Brand New Do

Evergreen Gardens

Description

Everyone loves a fresh new look. Spruce up the curb with pure evergreen delight. This low maintenance foundation garden has a colorful base with plenty of blooms throughout the year to give it more style and character. Choose a bedding material which accentuates the home and blends in with the plants.

Ingredients

(3) Liriope
(9) Acorus Grass
(1) Zebra Grass
(1) Cleyera
(3) Autumn Moonlight Encore Azalea
(5) Mini Loropetalum
(3) Baby Gem Boxwood
(3) Nordic Inkberry Holly
(1) Blue Point Juniper

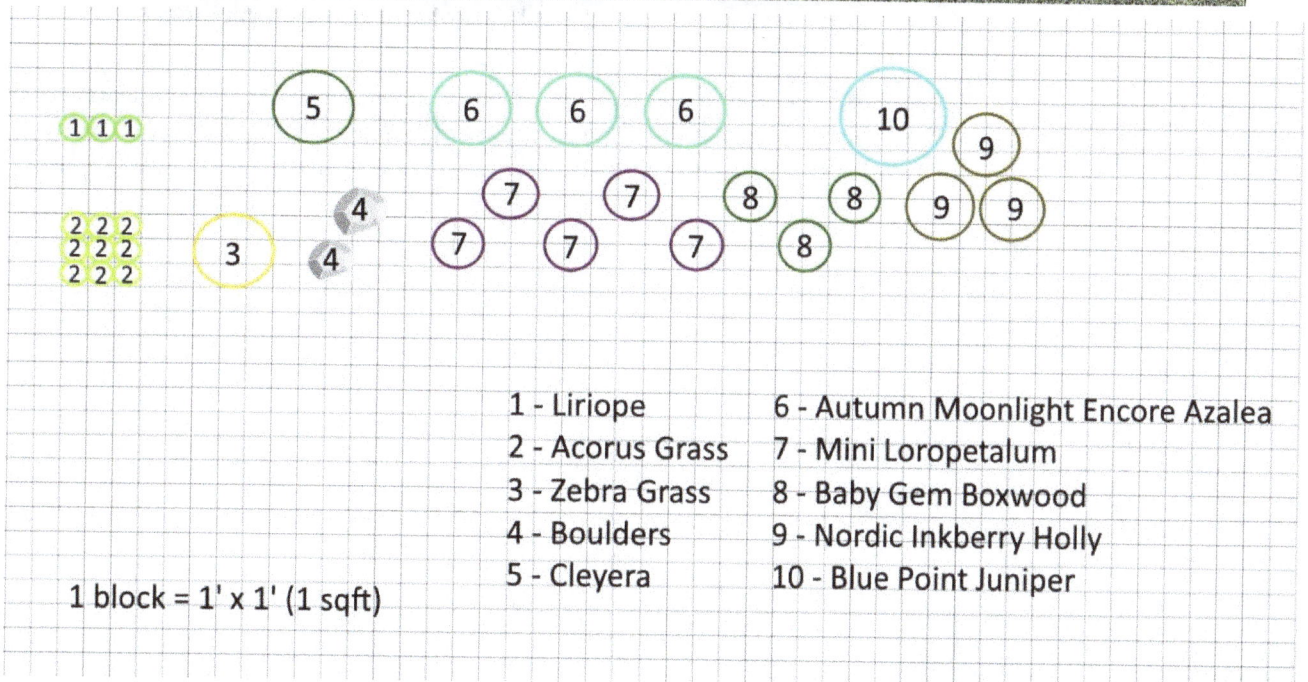

1 - Liriope
2 - Acorus Grass
3 - Zebra Grass
4 - Boulders
5 - Cleyera
6 - Autumn Moonlight Encore Azalea
7 - Mini Loropetalum
8 - Baby Gem Boxwood
9 - Nordic Inkberry Holly
10 - Blue Point Juniper

1 block = 1' x 1' (1 sqft)

Assembly Instructions

Garden Size (Approximate):	37'L x 10'W
Pruning Category:	2
Watering Needs:	2
Sun Requirements:	3
Plant Zones:	4-10
Bloom Colors:	White, Purple
Bloom Time Range:	Spring-Fall
Average Time to Install:	12 hours
Approximate Bedding:	370sf
Mulch:	2.25 cuyds
Pine Straw:	9 bales
Rock:	4.6 tons at 3" thick
Other Cultivars Available to Sub:	Yes
Special Needs:	

Till garden and amend soil with composted material such as mulched leaves or shredded pine.

Using the planting diagram, set boulders by digging into the soil several inches to create a foundation slightly below the grade of the garden. Set the boulder on to the foundation then spread the removed soil around the boulders to bring the soil height back up to grade level.

Measure for plant placement and sit each plant in its proper place. Adjust placement based on the shape of the actual bed.

Dig each hole twice as wide as the root ball. Sprinkle in starter fertilizer to the bottom of the hole (follow directions on package for proper application). Set plant in hole. Push soil back around plant, tamping in tight with the handle end of the shovel to remove all air pockets. Tamp soil tight at top of root ball.

Repeat for each plant.

Water in all plants thoroughly.

Top beds with mulch, pine straw or other bedding materials to hold moisture and keep roots warm in winter and cool in summer.

Brand New Do

Evergreen Gardens

Common Name	Liriope
Scientific Name	Liriope muscari
Status	Perennial
Mature Size (H x W)	2x2
Pruning Category (1-5)	1
Watering Category (1-5)	1
Sun Category (1-5)	4
USDA Hardiness Zone:	6-10
Bloom Season	Summer

Common Name	Acorus Grass
Scientific Name	Acorus gramineus
Status	Perennial
Mature Size (H x W)	1x1
Pruning Category (1-5)	1
Watering Category (1-5)	1
Sun Category (1-5)	2
USDA Hardiness Zone:	6-9
Bloom Season	None

Common Name	Zebra Grass
Scientific Name	Miscanthus sinensis 'Zebrinus'
Status	Perennial
Mature Size (H x W)	3x3
Pruning Category (1-5)	1
Watering Category (1-5)	1
Sun Category (1-5)	3
USDA Hardiness Zone:	5-9
Bloom Season	None

Common Name	Cleyera
Scientific Name	Ternstroemia gymnanthera
Status	Evergreen
Mature Size (H x W)	10x8
Pruning Category (1-5)	4
Watering Category (1-5)	2
Sun Category (1-5)	3
USDA Hardiness Zone:	7-10
Bloom Season	Spring

Common Name	Autumn Moonlight Encore Azalea
Scientific Name	Rhododendron 'Mootum' PP18416
Status	Evergreen
Mature Size (H x W)	3x3
Pruning Category (1-5)	2
Watering Category (1-5)	3
Sun Category (1-5)	4
USDA Hardiness Zone:	7-10
Bloom Season	Spring, Fall

Common Name	Mini Loropetalum
Scientific Name	Loropetalum chinense 'Beni-Hime'
Status	Evergreen
Mature Size (H x W)	3x3
Pruning Category (1-5)	2
Watering Category (1-5)	2
Sun Category (1-5)	3
USDA Hardiness Zone:	7-10
Bloom Season	Spring

Brand New Do

Evergreen Gardens

Common Name	Baby Gem Boxwood
Scientific Name	Buxus microphylla var. japonica 'Gregem'
Status	Evergreen
Mature Size (H x W)	2x2
Pruning Category (1-5)	4
Watering Category (1-5)	3
Sun Category (1-5)	4
USDA Hardiness Zone:	4-9
Bloom Season	None

Common Name	Nordic Inkberry Holly
Scientific Name	Ilex glabra
Status	Evergreen
Mature Size (H x W)	3x3
Pruning Category (1-5)	4
Watering Category (1-5)	2
Sun Category (1-5)	4
USDA Hardiness Zone:	5-8
Bloom Season	None-Inconspicuous

Common Name	Blue Point Juniper
Scientific Name	Juniperus chinensis 'Blue Point'
Status	Evergreen
Mature Size (H x W)	15x8
Pruning Category (1-5)	1
Watering Category (1-5)	1
Sun Category (1-5)	4
USDA Hardiness Zone:	6-9
Bloom Season	None

Enticing Entrances

Description

Simple and clean. This small garden is fully evergreen for varied texture and interest. The low maintenance shrubs are a snap to manage. The reblooming power of Encore Azaleas adds spring and fall color that dazzles and brightens up the landscape.

Ingredients

(1) Dwarf Alberta Spruce
(3) Carissa Holly
(1) Gold Cone Juniper
(8) Autumn Moonlight Encore Azalea

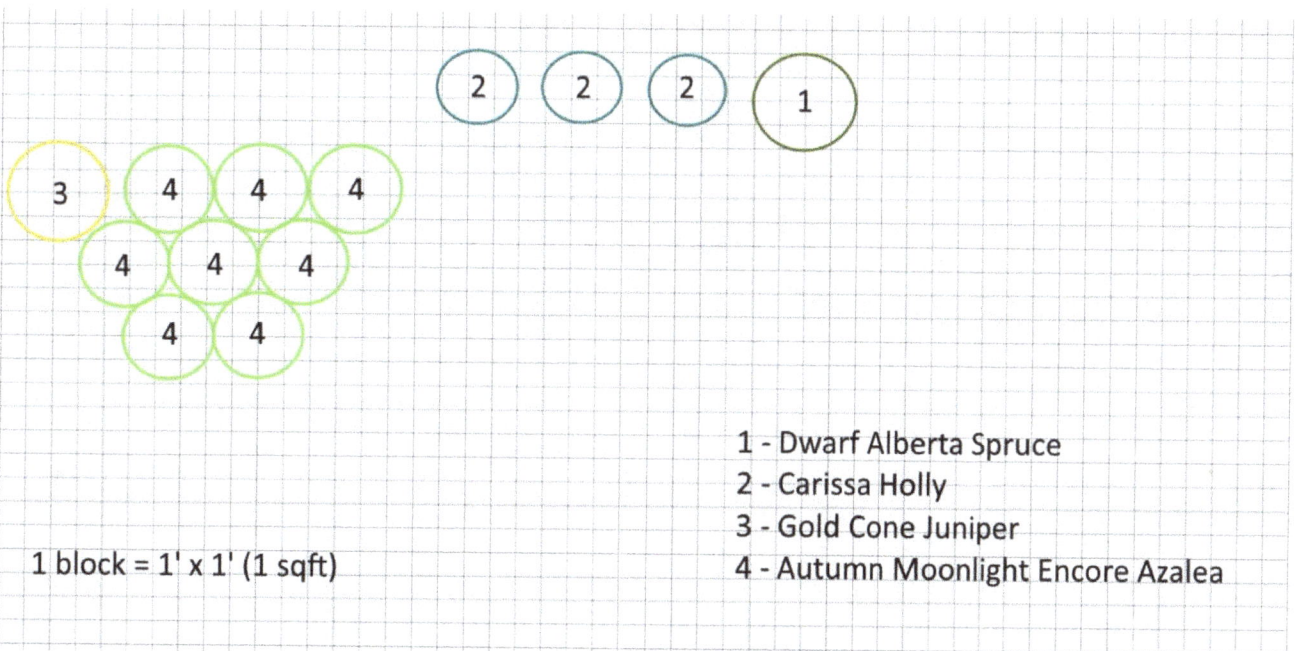

1 block = 1' x 1' (1 sqft)

1 - Dwarf Alberta Spruce
2 - Carissa Holly
3 - Gold Cone Juniper
4 - Autumn Moonlight Encore Azalea

Assembly Instructions

Garden Size (Approximate):	33'L x 14'W
Pruning Category:	2
Watering Needs:	2
Sun Requirements:	4
Plant Zones:	3-10
Bloom Colors:	White
Bloom Time Range:	Spring, Fall
Average Time to Install:	8 hours
Approximate Bedding:	462sf
Mulch:	2.85 cuyds
Pine Straw:	11 bales
Rock:	5.75 tons at 3" thick
Other Cultivars Available to Sub:	Yes
Special Needs:	

Till garden and amend soil with composted material such as mulched leaves or shredded pine.

Using the planting diagram, measure for plant placement and sit each plant in its proper place. Adjust placement based on the shape of the actual bed.

Dig each hole twice as wide as the root ball. Sprinkle in starter fertilizer to the bottom of the hole (follow directions on package for proper application). Set plant in hole. Push soil back around plant, tamping in tight with the handle end of the shovel to remove all air pockets. Tamp soil tight at top of root ball.

Repeat for each plant.

Water in all plants thoroughly.

Top beds with mulch, pine straw or other bedding materials to hold moisture and keep roots warm in winter and cool in summer.

Common Name	Dwarf Alberta Spruce
Scientific Name	Picea glauca
Status	Evergreen
Mature Size (H x W)	5x4
Pruning Category (1-5)	1
Watering Category (1-5)	2
Sun Category (1-5)	3
USDA Hardiness Zone:	3-8
Bloom Season	None

Common Name	Carissa Holly
Scientific Name	Ilex cornuta 'Carissa'
Status	Evergreen
Mature Size (H x W)	4x4
Pruning Category (1-5)	4
Watering Category (1-5)	2
Sun Category (1-5)	4
USDA Hardiness Zone:	7-9
Bloom Season	None-Inconspicuous

Common Name	Gold Cone Juniper
Scientific Name	Juniperus communis 'Gold Cone'
Status	Evergreen
Mature Size (H x W)	15x8
Pruning Category (1-5)	1
Watering Category (1-5)	1
Sun Category (1-5)	4
USDA Hardiness Zone:	6-9
Bloom Season	None

Common Name	Autumn Moonlight Encore Azalea
Scientific Name	Rhododendron 'Mootum' PP18416
Status	Evergreen
Mature Size (H x W)	3x3
Pruning Category (1-5)	2
Watering Category (1-5)	3
Sun Category (1-5)	4
USDA Hardiness Zone:	7-10
Bloom Season	Spring, Fall

Business Casual

Description

A little formal, a little casual. This evergreen foundation garden is virtually maintenance free, but has a lot of color to brighten up the straight lines of the house. Fat and fluffy Cypress don the corners to soften the hard lines while the low front shrubs allow light in to the home. The ever-changing color of Kaleidoscope Abelia adds interest throughout the year.

Ingredients

(2) Gold Thread Cypress
(3) Tea Olive (Osmanthus)
(5) Kaleidoscope Abelia
(1) Spiral Gold Cone Juniper

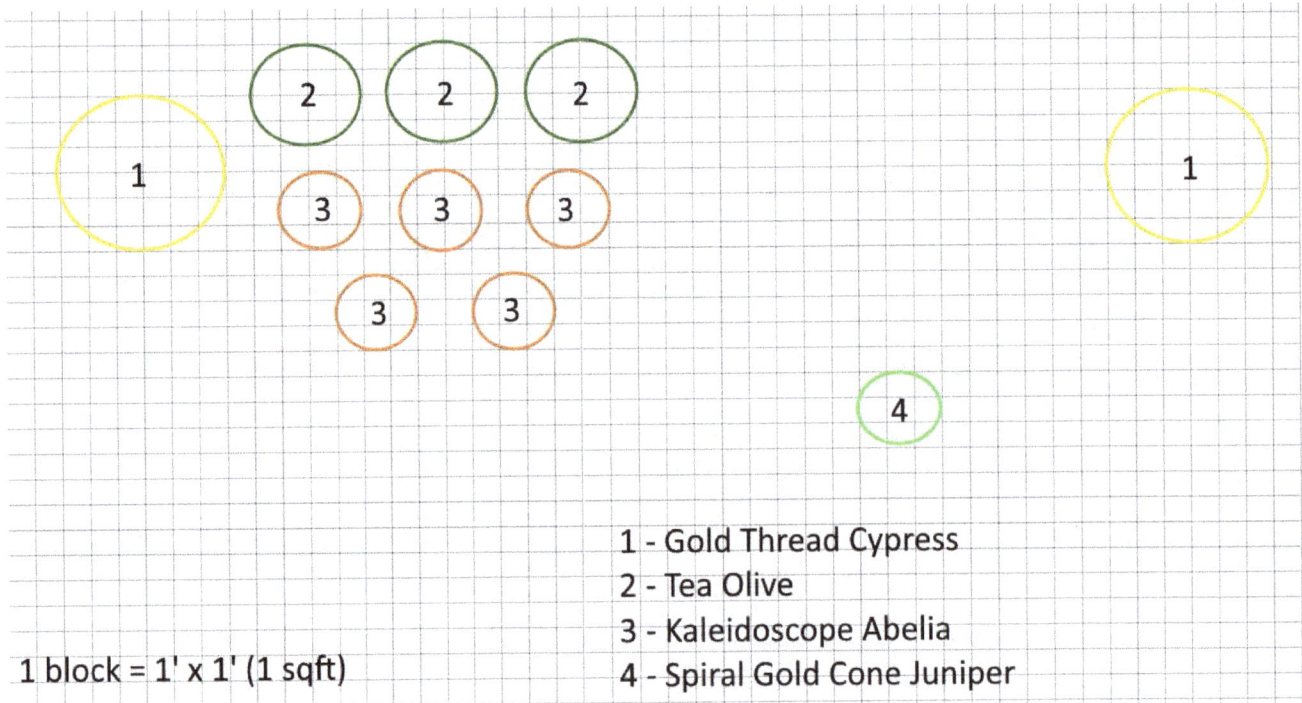

1 block = 1' x 1' (1 sqft)

1 - Gold Thread Cypress
2 - Tea Olive
3 - Kaleidoscope Abelia
4 - Spiral Gold Cone Juniper

Assembly Instructions

Garden Size (Approximate):	32'L x 15'W
Pruning Category:	2
Watering Needs:	2
Sun Requirements:	4
Plant Zones:	6-10
Bloom Colors:	Pink, White
Bloom Time Range:	Spring, Fall
Average Time to Install:	6 hours
Approximate Bedding:	480sf
Mulch:	3 cuyds
Pine Straw:	12 bales
Rock:	6 tons
Other Cultivars Available to Sub:	Yes
Special Needs:	

Till garden and amend soil with composted material such as mulched leaves or shredded pine.

Using the planting diagram, measure for plant placement and sit each plant in its proper place. Adjust placement based on the shape of the actual bed.

Dig each hole twice as wide as the root ball. Sprinkle in starter fertilizer to the bottom of the hole (follow directions on package for proper application). Set plant in hole. Push soil back around plant, tamping in tight with the handle end of the shovel to remove all air pockets. Tamp soil tight at top of root ball.

Repeat for each plant.

Water in all plants thoroughly.

Top beds with mulch, pine straw or other bedding materials to hold moisture and keep roots warm in winter and cool in summer.

Common Name	Gold Thread Cypress
Scientific Name	Chamaecyparis pisifera 'Gold Thread'
Status	Evergreen
Mature Size (H x W)	12x10
Pruning Category (1-5)	1
Watering Category (1-5)	1
Sun Category (1-5)	4
USDA Hardiness Zone:	6-9
Bloom Season	None

Common Name	Tea Olive
Scientific Name	Osmanthus fragrans
Status	Evergreen
Mature Size (H x W)	6x6
Pruning Category (1-5)	3
Watering Category (1-5)	2
Sun Category (1-5)	3
USDA Hardiness Zone:	8-10
Bloom Season	Spring

Common Name	Kaleidoscope Abelia
Scientific Name	Abelia x grandiflora 'Kaleidoscope'
Status	Semi Deciduous
Mature Size (H x W)	3x3
Pruning Category (1-5)	1
Watering Category (1-5)	2
Sun Category (1-5)	4
USDA Hardiness Zone:	6-9
Bloom Season	Fall

Common Name	Gold Cone Juniper
Scientific Name	Juniperus communis 'Gold Cone'
Status	Evergreen
Mature Size (H x W)	15x8
Pruning Category (1-5)	1
Watering Category (1-5)	1
Sun Category (1-5)	4
USDA Hardiness Zone:	6-9
Bloom Season	None

Home Sweet Home

Home Sweet Home

Evergreen Gardens

Description
Home evokes emotions of well-being, tranquility, safety and security. It's where we go after a long day, a great event, a sad happening or a happy reunion. We have holidays, stay-cations, gatherings and family under one roof we call home. It should be welcoming and warm from the curb to the door.

Ingredients
(2) Foster Holly
(6) Green Beauty Boxwood
(4) Blue Star Juniper Shrub
(2) Nellie R. Stevens Holly
(3) Purple Diamond Loropetalum

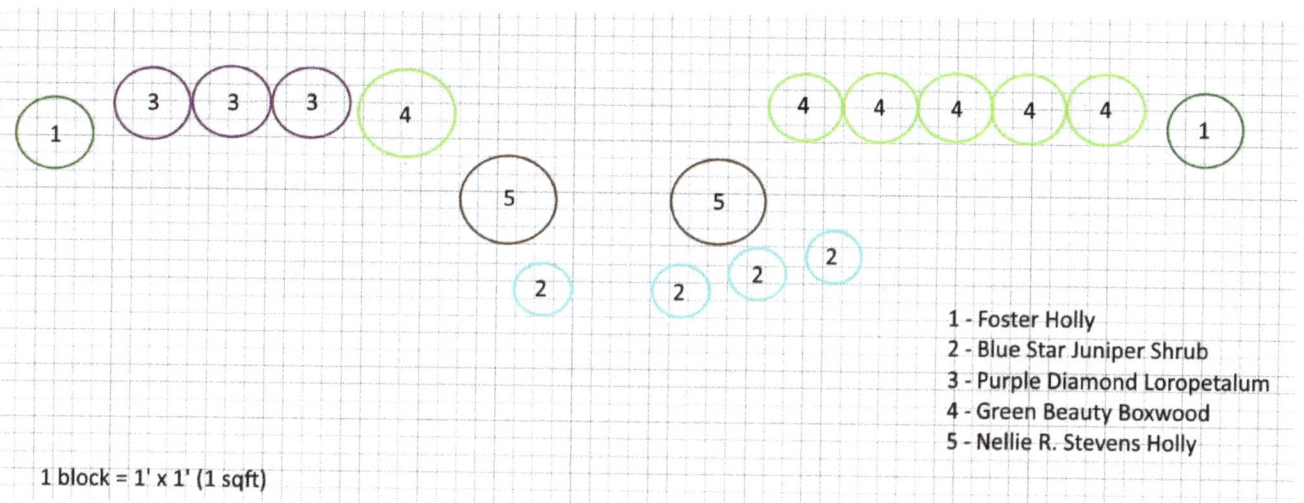

1 - Foster Holly
2 - Blue Star Juniper Shrub
3 - Purple Diamond Loropetalum
4 - Green Beauty Boxwood
5 - Nellie R. Stevens Holly

1 block = 1' x 1' (1 sqft)

Assembly Instructions

Garden Size (Approximate):	60'L x 14'W
Pruning Category:	3
Watering Needs:	2
Sun Requirements:	4
Plant Zones:	4-10
Bloom Colors:	Purple
Bloom Time Range:	Spring
Average Time to Install:	12 hours
Approximate Bedding:	840sf
Mulch:	5 cuyds
Pine Straw:	20 bales
Rock:	10.5 tons at 3" thick
Other Cultivars Available to Sub:	Yes
Special Needs:	

Till garden and amend soil with composted material such as mulched leaves or shredded pine.

Using the planting diagram, measure for plant placement and sit each plant in its proper place. Adjust placement based on the shape of the actual bed.

Dig each hole twice as wide as the root ball. Sprinkle in starter fertilizer to the bottom of the hole (follow directions on package for proper application). Set plant in hole. Push soil back around plant, tamping in tight with the handle end of the shovel to remove all air pockets. Tamp soil tight at top of root ball.

Repeat for each plant.

Water in all plants thoroughly.

Top beds with mulch, pine straw or other bedding materials to hold moisture and keep roots warm in winter and cool in summer.

Common Name	Foster Holly
Scientific Name	Ilex x attenuata 'Fosteri'
Status	Evergreen
Mature Size (H x W)	20x7
Pruning Category (1-5)	5
Watering Category (1-5)	2
Sun Category (1-5)	4
USDA Hardiness Zone:	7-9
Bloom Season	None-Inconspicuous

Common Name	Blue Star Juniper Shrub
Scientific Name	Juniperus squamata 'Blue Star'
Status	Evergreen
Mature Size (H x W)	3x4
Pruning Category (1-5)	1
Watering Category (1-5)	1
Sun Category (1-5)	3
USDA Hardiness Zone:	6-9
Bloom Season	None

Common Name	Purple Diamond Loropetalum
Scientific Name	Loropetalum chinense 'Shang-hi' PP18331
Status	Evergreen
Mature Size (H x W)	5x5
Pruning Category (1-5)	2
Watering Category (1-5)	2
Sun Category (1-5)	3
USDA Hardiness Zone:	7-10
Bloom Season	Spring

Common Name	Green Beauty Boxwood
Scientific Name	Buxus microphylla var. japonica 'Green Beauty'
Status	Evergreen
Mature Size (H x W)	4x4
Pruning Category (1-5)	4
Watering Category (1-5)	3
Sun Category (1-5)	4
USDA Hardiness Zone:	4-9
Bloom Season	None

Common Name	Nellie R. Stevens Holly
Scientific Name	Ilex x 'Nellie R. Stevens'
Status	Evergreen
Mature Size (H x W)	25x15
Pruning Category (1-5)	5
Watering Category (1-5)	2
Sun Category (1-5)	4
USDA Hardiness Zone:	7-9
Bloom Season	None-Inconspicuous

Executive Privilege

Description

The repeating theme of this garden with white crape myrtles and red azaleas ties together a long garden bed. Gardenias near the door will provide weeks of sweet blooms for welcome homes and welcoming guests. Low maintenance blue point junipers add height at the entry to match the columns and color throughout adds interest and beauty.

Ingredients

(2) Natchez Crape Myrtle
(3) Dwarf Cryptomeria
(5) Kaleidoscope Abelia
(5) Hardy Daisy Gardenia
(8) Autumn Embers Encore Azalea

(42) 4" Annual Flowers
(3) Gold Mop Cypress
(3) Stella d'Oro Daylily
(2) Blue Point Juniper

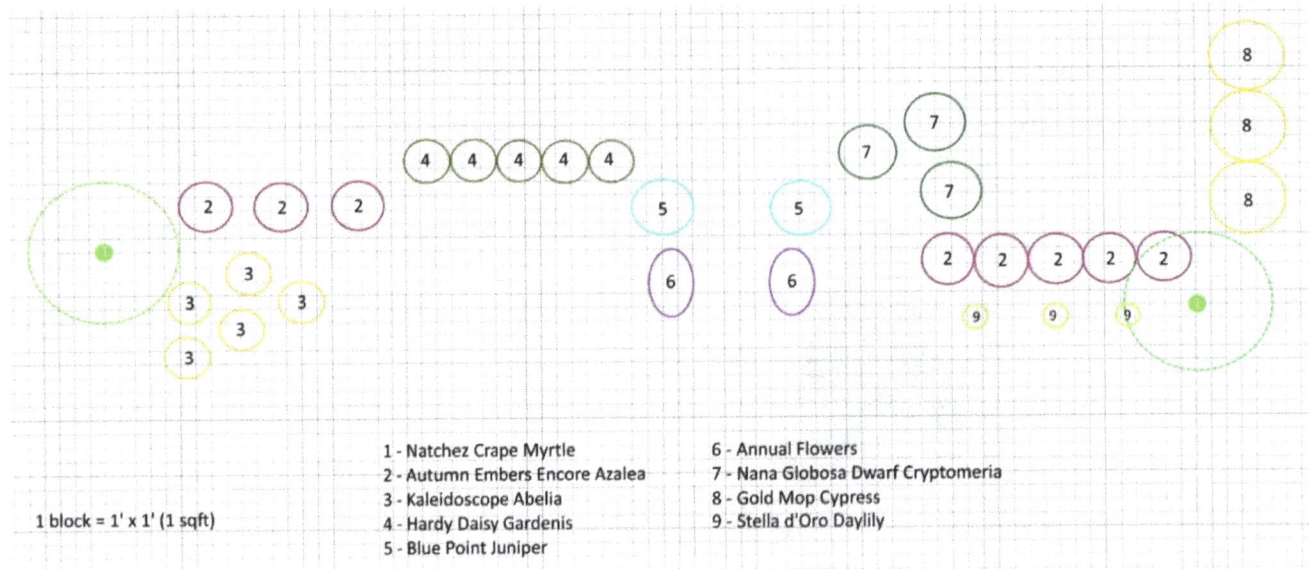

1 block = 1' x 1' (1 sqft)

1 - Natchez Crape Myrtle
2 - Autumn Embers Encore Azalea
3 - Kaleidoscope Abelia
4 - Hardy Daisy Gardenis
5 - Blue Point Juniper
6 - Annual Flowers
7 - Nana Globosa Dwarf Cryptomeria
8 - Gold Mop Cypress
9 - Stella d'Oro Daylily

Assembly Instructions

Garden Size (Approximate):	83'L x 22'W
Pruning Category:	1
Watering Needs:	2
Sun Requirements:	4
Plant Zones:	3-11
Bloom Colors:	White, Red, Yellow, Pink
Bloom Time Range:	Spring-Fall
Average Time to Install:	22 hours
Approximate Bedding:	1,826sf
Mulch:	11.25 cuyds
Pine Straw:	44 bales
Rock:	23 tons
Other Cultivars Available to Sub:	Yes
Special Needs:	This cultivar of crape myrtle is considered dwarf. There is no need to cut back every year (also called "knuckling").

Till garden and amend soil with composted material such as mulched leaves or shredded pine.

Using the planting diagram, measure for plant placement and sit each plant in its proper place. Adjust placement based on the shape of the actual bed.

Dig each hole twice as wide as the root ball. Sprinkle in starter fertilizer to the bottom of the hole (follow directions on package for proper application). Set plant in hole. Push soil back around plant, tamping in tight with the handle end of the shovel to remove all air pockets. Tamp soil tight at top of root ball.

Repeat for each plant.

Water in all plants thoroughly.

Top beds with mulch, pine straw or other bedding materials to hold moisture and keep roots warm in winter and cool in summer.

Executive Privilege

Common Name	Natchez Crape Myrtle
Scientific Name	Lagerstroemia indica x fauriei 'Natchez'
Status	Deciduous
Mature Size (H x W)	30x10
Pruning Category (1-5)	1
Watering Category (1-5)	2
Sun Category (1-5)	4
USDA Hardiness Zone:	6-11
Bloom Season	Summer

Common Name	Kaleidoscope Abelia
Scientific Name	Abelia x grandiflora 'Kaleidoscope'
Status	Semi Deciduous
Mature Size (H x W)	3x3
Pruning Category (1-5)	1
Watering Category (1-5)	2
Sun Category (1-5)	4
USDA Hardiness Zone:	6-9
Bloom Season	Fall

Common Name	Blue Point Juniper
Scientific Name	Juniperus chinensis 'Blue Point'
Status	Evergreen
Mature Size (H x W)	15x8
Pruning Category (1-5)	1
Watering Category (1-5)	1
Sun Category (1-5)	4
USDA Hardiness Zone:	6-9
Bloom Season	None

Foundation Beds

Common Name	Autumn Embers Encore Azalea
Scientific Name	Rhododendron 'Conleb'
Status	Evergreen
Mature Size (H x W)	4x4.5
Pruning Category (1-5)	2
Watering Category (1-5)	3
Sun Category (1-5)	4
USDA Hardiness Zone:	7-10
Bloom Season	Spring, Fall

Common Name	Hardy Daisy Gardenia
Scientific Name	Gardenia jasminoides 'Kleim's Hardy'
Status	Evergreen
Mature Size (H x W)	4x4
Pruning Category (1-5)	2
Watering Category (1-5)	3
Sun Category (1-5)	4
USDA Hardiness Zone:	7-11
Bloom Season	Summer, Fall

Common Name	Nana Globosa Dwarf Cryptomeria
Scientific Name	Cryptomeria japonica 'Globosa Nana'
Status	Evergreen
Mature Size (H x W)	4x4
Pruning Category (1-5)	1
Watering Category (1-5)	1
Sun Category (1-5)	3
USDA Hardiness Zone:	6-9
Bloom Season	None

Executive Privilege

Common Name	Vinca
Scientific Name	Catharanthus roseus
Status	Annual
Mature Size (H x W)	1.5x1.5
Pruning Category (1-5)	1
Watering Category (1-5)	1
Sun Category (1-5)	5
USDA Hardiness Zone:	4-8
Bloom Season	Summer

Common Name	Gold Mop Cypress
Scientific Name	Chamaecyparis
Status	Evergreen
Mature Size (H x W)	6x6
Pruning Category (1-5)	1
Watering Category (1-5)	1
Sun Category (1-5)	4
USDA Hardiness Zone:	6-9
Bloom Season	None

Common Name	Stella d'Oro Daylily
Scientific Name	Hemerocallis 'Stella d'Oro'
Status	Perennial
Mature Size (H x W)	2x2
Pruning Category (1-5)	1
Watering Category (1-5)	2
Sun Category (1-5)	4
USDA Hardiness Zone:	3-9
Bloom Season	Summer

That's Amore

Description

You'll get your weekends back with this low maintenance front landscape. Very little pruning means maintenance is quick. Blooms along the walk to the front door greet guests and offer sweet scents. The bold red of the Japanese Maple offsets the corner of the house to soften the lines. The pinks and purples accent the Japanese Maple and add interest to the corner. A repeating smaller Japanese Maple in the center ties it all together.

Ingredients

(3) Autumn Chiffon Encore Azaleas
(11) Mini Loropetalum
(1) Bloodgood Japanese Maple
(3) Color Guard Yucca
(4) American Boxwood
(15) Acorus Grass
(1) Dissectum Japanese Maple
(1) Japonica Camellia

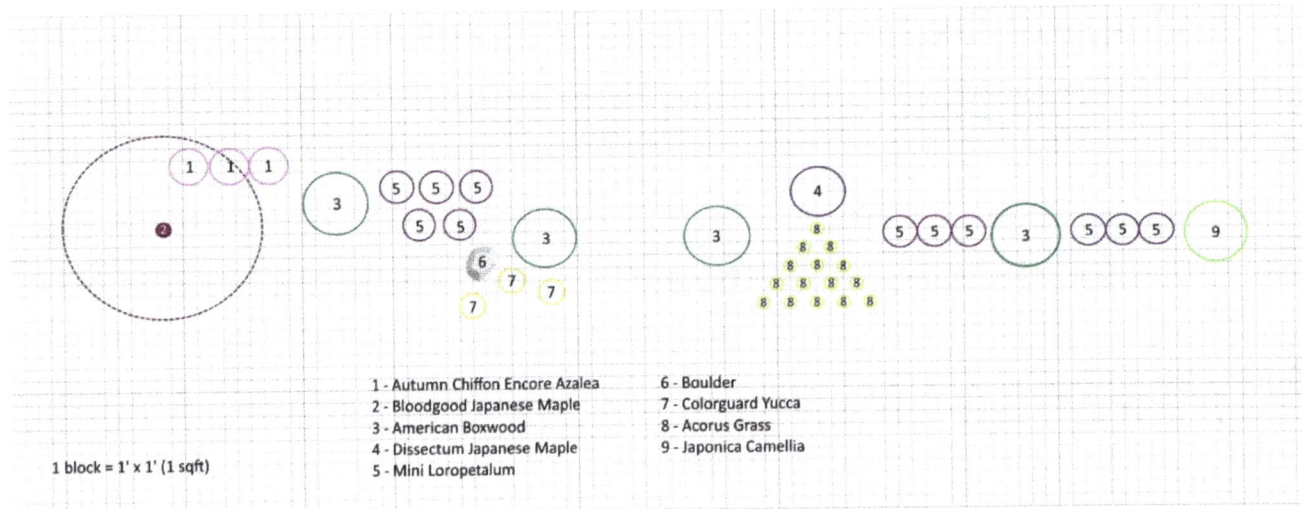

1 - Autumn Chiffon Encore Azalea
2 - Bloodgood Japanese Maple
3 - American Boxwood
4 - Dissectum Japanese Maple
5 - Mini Loropetalum
6 - Boulder
7 - Colorguard Yucca
8 - Acorus Grass
9 - Japonica Camellia

1 block = 1' x 1' (1 sqft)

Assembly Instructions

Garden Size (Approximate):	90'L x 15'W
Pruning Category:	2
Watering Needs:	2
Sun Requirements:	4
Plant Zones:	4-11
Bloom Colors:	Pink, Purple, White
Bloom Time Range:	Four Seasons
Average Time to Install:	18 hours
Approximate Bedding:	1,350sf
Mulch:	8.3 cuyds
Pine Straw:	32 bales
Rock:	17 tons at 3" thick
Other Cultivars Available to Sub:	Yes
Special Needs:	

Till garden and amend soil with composted material such as mulched leaves or shredded pine.

Using the planting diagram, set boulders by digging into the soil several inches to create a foundation slightly below the grade of the garden. Set the boulder on to the foundation then spread the removed soil around the boulders to bring the soil height back up to grade level.

Measure for plant placement and sit each plant in its proper place. Adjust placement based on the shape of the actual bed.

Dig each hole twice as wide as the root ball. Sprinkle in starter fertilizer to the bottom of the hole (follow directions on package for proper application). Set plant in hole. Push soil back around plant, tamping in tight with the handle end of the shovel to remove all air pockets. Tamp soil tight at top of root ball.

Repeat for each plant.

Water in all plants thoroughly.

Top beds with mulch, pine straw or other bedding materials to hold moisture and keep roots warm in winter and cool in summer.

Common Name	Autumn Chiffon Encore Azalea
Scientific Name	Rhododendron 'Robled' PP15862
Status	Evergreen
Mature Size (H x W)	3.5x3.5
Pruning Category (1-5)	2
Watering Category (1-5)	3
Sun Category (1-5)	4
USDA Hardiness Zone:	7-10
Bloom Season	Spring, Fall

Common Name	Bloodgood Japanese Maple
Scientific Name	Acer palmatum 'Bloodgood'
Status	Deciduous
Mature Size (H x W)	15x10
Pruning Category (1-5)	1
Watering Category (1-5)	2
Sun Category (1-5)	4
USDA Hardiness Zone:	5-8
Bloom Season	None

Common Name	American Boxwood
Scientific Name	Buxus sempervirens
Status	Evergreen
Mature Size (H x W)	5x5
Pruning Category (1-5)	4
Watering Category (1-5)	3
Sun Category (1-5)	4
USDA Hardiness Zone:	4-9
Bloom Season	None

Common Name	Dissectum Japanese Maple
Scientific Name	Acer palmatum var dissectum
Status	Deciduous
Mature Size (H x W)	6x9
Pruning Category (1-5)	2
Watering Category (1-5)	2
Sun Category (1-5)	3
USDA Hardiness Zone:	5-8
Bloom Season	None

Common Name	Mini Loropetalum
Scientific Name	Loropetalum chinense 'Beni-Hime'
Status	Evergreen
Mature Size (H x W)	3x3
Pruning Category (1-5)	2
Watering Category (1-5)	2
Sun Category (1-5)	3
USDA Hardiness Zone:	7-10
Bloom Season	Spring

Common Name	Color Guard Yucca
Scientific Name	Yucca filamentosa 'Color Guard'
Status	Succulent
Mature Size (H x W)	2x2
Pruning Category (1-5)	1
Watering Category (1-5)	1
Sun Category (1-5)	5
USDA Hardiness Zone:	5-11
Bloom Season	Summer

That's Amore

Foundation Beds

Common Name	Acorus Grass
Scientific Name	Acorus gramineus
Status	Perennial
Mature Size (H x W)	1x1
Pruning Category (1-5)	1
Watering Category (1-5)	1
Sun Category (1-5)	2
USDA Hardiness Zone:	6-9
Bloom Season	None

Common Name	Camellia Japonica
Scientific Name	Camellia japonica
Status	Evergreen
Mature Size (H x W)	12x6
Pruning Category (1-5)	1
Watering Category (1-5)	2
Sun Category (1-5)	3
USDA Hardiness Zone:	7-10
Bloom Season	Winter

Fabuloso

Description

This lovely and simple landscape design brings consistent color and texture to a small space. The Japanese maple softens the corner and shades the small front porch. The Loropetalum carry the color over toward the door and the junipers, with their blue hue, add interest to the corner and entry walk.

Ingredients

(2) Spartan Juniper
(1) Emperor Japanese Maple
(3) Purple Diamond Loropetalum
(5) Mardi Gras Abelia

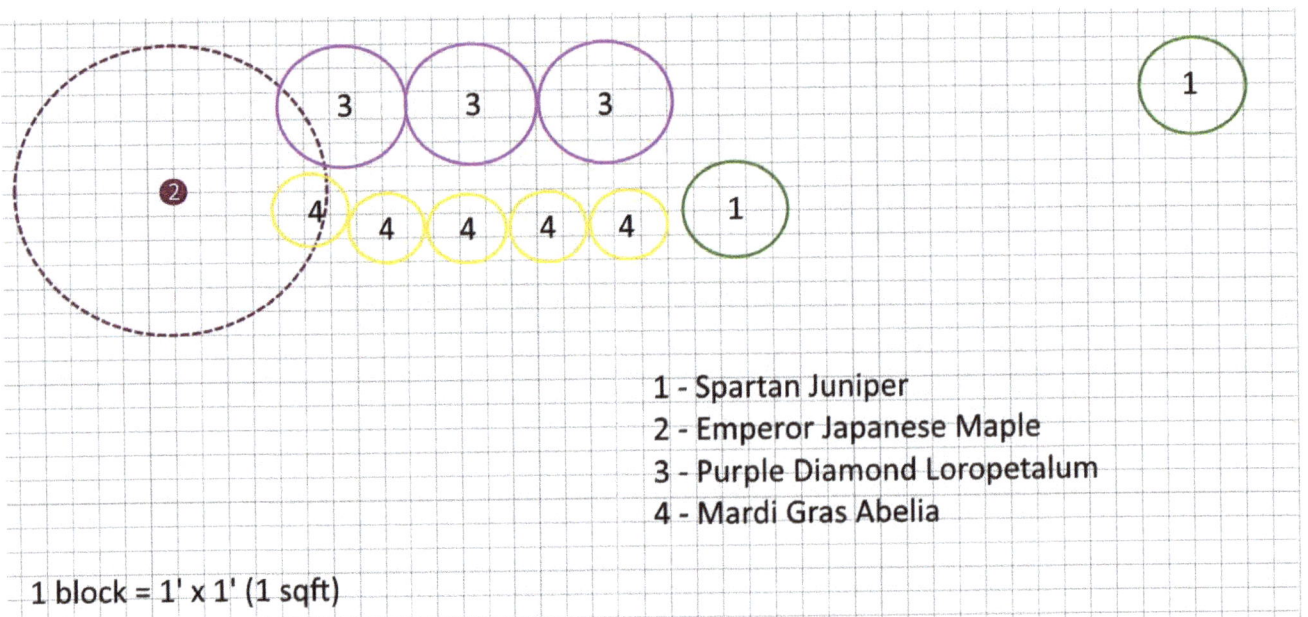

1 - Spartan Juniper
2 - Emperor Japanese Maple
3 - Purple Diamond Loropetalum
4 - Mardi Gras Abelia

1 block = 1' x 1' (1 sqft)

Fabuloso

Assembly Instructions

Garden Size (Approximate):	35'L x 12'W
Pruning Category:	1
Watering Needs:	2
Sun Requirements:	4
Plant Zones:	5-10
Bloom Colors:	Pink
Bloom Time Range:	Spring, Fall
Average Time to Install:	7 hours
Approximate Bedding:	420sf
Mulch:	2.6 cuyds
Pine Straw:	10 bales
Rock:	5.25 tons at 3" thick
Other Cultivars Available to Sub:	Yes
Special Needs:	

Till garden and amend soil with composted material such as mulched leaves or shredded pine.

Using the planting diagram, measure for plant placement and sit each plant in its proper place. Adjust placement based on the shape of the actual bed.

Dig each hole twice as wide as the root ball. Sprinkle in starter fertilizer to the bottom of the hole (follow directions on package for proper application). Set plant in hole. Push soil back around plant, tamping in tight with the handle end of the shovel to remove all air pockets. Tamp soil tight at top of root ball.

Repeat for each plant.

Water in all plants thoroughly.

Top beds with mulch, pine straw or other bedding materials to hold moisture and keep roots warm in winter and cool in summer.

Common Name	Spartan Juniper
Scientific Name	Juniperus chinensis 'Spartan'
Status	Evergreen
Mature Size (H x W)	20x6
Pruning Category (1-5)	1
Watering Category (1-5)	1
Sun Category (1-5)	4
USDA Hardiness Zone:	6-9
Bloom Season	None

Common Name	Emperor Japanese Maple
Scientific Name	Acer palmatum 'Emperor I'
Status	Deciduous
Mature Size (H x W)	15x10
Pruning Category (1-5)	1
Watering Category (1-5)	2
Sun Category (1-5)	4
USDA Hardiness Zone:	5-8
Bloom Season	None

Common Name	Purple Diamond Loropetalum
Scientific Name	Loropetalum chinense 'Shang-hi' PP18331
Status	Evergreen
Mature Size (H x W)	5x5
Pruning Category (1-5)	2
Watering Category (1-5)	2
Sun Category (1-5)	3
USDA Hardiness Zone:	7-10
Bloom Season	Spring

Common Name	Mardi Gras Abelia
Scientific Name	Abelia x grandiflora 'Mardi Gras'
Status	Semi Deciduous
Mature Size (H x W)	3x3
Pruning Category (1-5)	1
Watering Category (1-5)	2
Sun Category (1-5)	4
USDA Hardiness Zone:	6-9
Bloom Season	Fall

Jacket and Tie

Description

This neat and tidy landscape keeps everything in order. The corners are softened with smaller arborvitae while the consistent height and shape of the hedges adds order and a sense of grace and style. The front walk is lined with four season plants to provide returning blooms in the warmer months with consistent color throughout the winter.

Ingredients

(2) Emerald Green Arborvitae
(16) Baby Gem Boxwood
(2) Globosa Nana Dwarf Cryptomeria
(18) Liriope
(5) Sunshine Ligustrum
(16) Stella d'Oro Daylily
(7) Wintergreen Boxwood

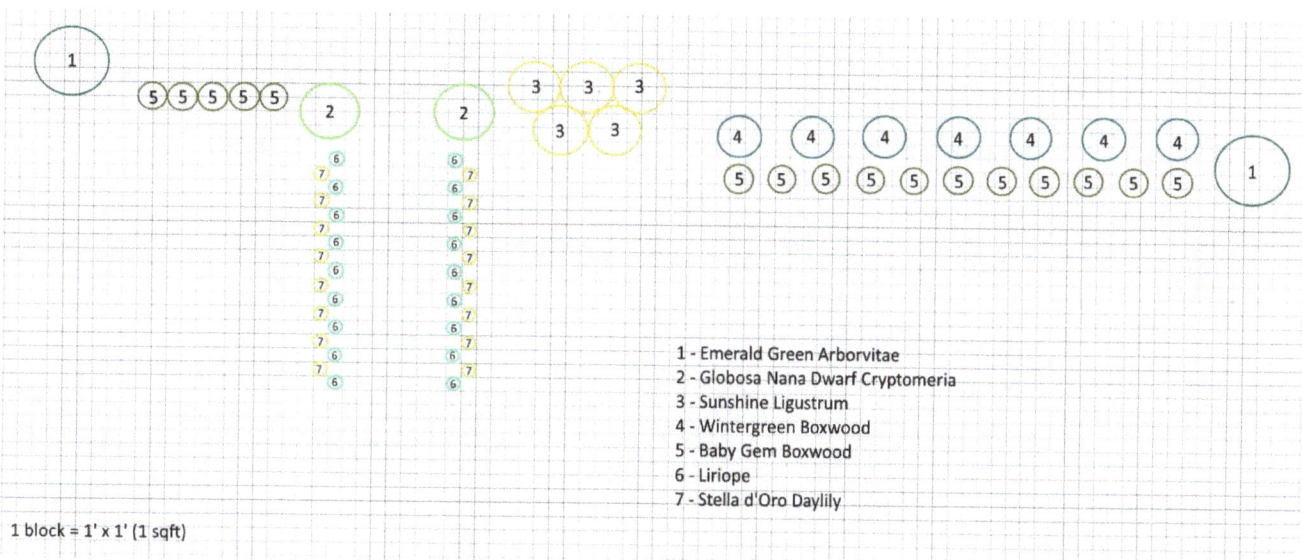

1 - Emerald Green Arborvitae
2 - Globosa Nana Dwarf Cryptomeria
3 - Sunshine Ligustrum
4 - Wintergreen Boxwood
5 - Baby Gem Boxwood
6 - Liriope
7 - Stella d'Oro Daylily

1 block = 1' x 1' (1 sqft)

Assembly Instructions

Garden Size (Approximate):	77'L x 26'W
Pruning Category:	2
Watering Needs:	2
Sun Requirements:	4
Plant Zones:	3-10
Bloom Colors:	White, Yellow
Bloom Time Range:	Summer
Average Time to Install:	24 hours
Approximate Bedding:	2,002sf
Mulch:	12.3 cuyds
Pine Straw:	48 bales
Rock:	25 tons at 3" thick
Other Cultivars Available to Sub:	Yes
Special Needs:	

Till garden and amend soil with composted material such as mulched leaves or shredded pine.

Using the planting diagram, measure for plant placement and sit each plant in its proper place. Adjust placement based on the shape of the actual bed.

Dig each hole twice as wide as the root ball. Sprinkle in starter fertilizer to the bottom of the hole (follow directions on package for proper application). Set plant in hole. Push soil back around plant, tamping in tight with the handle end of the shovel to remove all air pockets. Tamp soil tight at top of root ball.

Repeat for each plant.

Water in all plants thoroughly.

Top beds with mulch, pine straw or other bedding materials to hold moisture and keep roots warm in winter and cool in summer.

Jacket and Tie

Foundation Beds

Common Name	Emerald Green Arborvitae
Scientific Name	Thuja occidentalis
Status	Evergreen
Mature Size (H x W)	15x5
Pruning Category (1-5)	1
Watering Category (1-5)	3
Sun Category (1-5)	4
USDA Hardiness Zone:	4-8
Bloom Season	None

Common Name	Nana Globosa Dwarf Cryptomeria
Scientific Name	Cryptomeria japonica 'Globosa Nana'
Status	Evergreen
Mature Size (H x W)	4x4
Pruning Category (1-5)	1
Watering Category (1-5)	1
Sun Category (1-5)	3
USDA Hardiness Zone:	6-9
Bloom Season	None

Common Name	Sunshine Ligustrum
Scientific Name	Ligustrum sinense 'Sunshine'
Status	Evergreen
Mature Size (H x W)	4x4
Pruning Category (1-5)	4
Watering Category (1-5)	2
Sun Category (1-5)	5
USDA Hardiness Zone:	7-10
Bloom Season	None-Inconspicuous

Common Name	Wintergreen Boxwood
Scientific Name	Buxus microphylla 'Wintergreen'
Status	Evergreen
Mature Size (H x W)	3x4
Pruning Category (1-5)	4
Watering Category (1-5)	3
Sun Category (1-5)	4
USDA Hardiness Zone:	4-9
Bloom Season	None

Common Name	Liriope
Scientific Name	Liriope muscari
Status	Perennial
Mature Size (H x W)	2x2
Pruning Category (1-5)	1
Watering Category (1-5)	1
Sun Category (1-5)	4
USDA Hardiness Zone:	6-10
Bloom Season	Summer

Common Name	Stella d'Oro Daylily
Scientific Name	Hemerocallis 'Stella d'Oro'
Status	Perennial
Mature Size (H x W)	2x2
Pruning Category (1-5)	1
Watering Category (1-5)	2
Sun Category (1-5)	4
USDA Hardiness Zone:	3-9
Bloom Season	Summer

Description

Small house or large, if being the best on the block is your thing, a great landscape is the best place to start. Neat and clean is always the best design. This compact and colorful landscape will certainly get you noticed. Brilliant pink in the shrub form crape myrtle highlights the corner while beautiful and fragrant blooms brighten up the walk.

Ingredients

(1) Cleyera
(1) Dwarf Crape Myrtle
(3) Mini Loropetalum
(3) Hardy Daisy Gardenia
(3) Drift Roses
(1) Degroots Spire Arborvitae

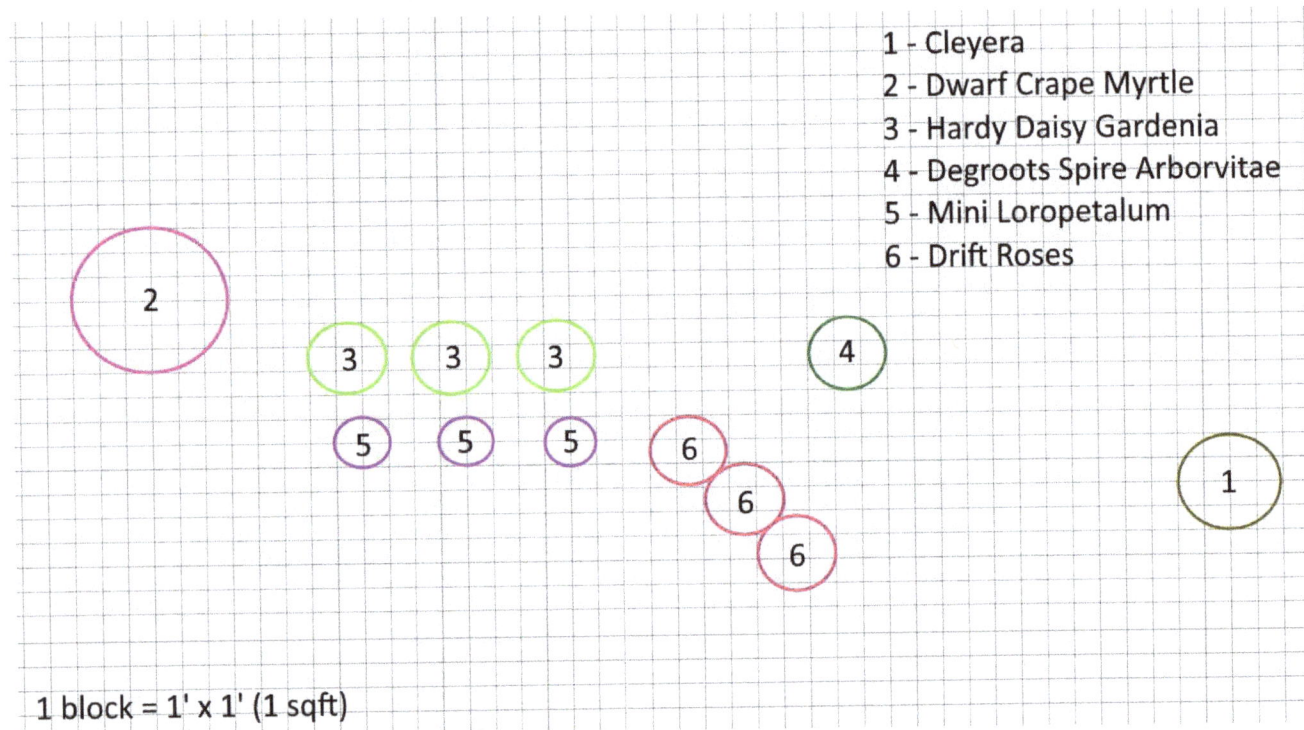

1 - Cleyera
2 - Dwarf Crape Myrtle
3 - Hardy Daisy Gardenia
4 - Degroots Spire Arborvitae
5 - Mini Loropetalum
6 - Drift Roses

1 block = 1' x 1' (1 sqft)

Assembly Instructions

Garden Size (Approximate):	36L x 16'W
Pruning Category:	2
Watering Needs:	2
Sun Requirements:	4
Plant Zones:	4-11
Bloom Colors:	White, Pink, Purple, Peach
Bloom Time Range:	Spring-Fall
Average Time to Install:	7 hours
Approximate Bedding:	576sf
Mulch:	3.5 cuyds
Pine Straw:	14 bales
Rock:	7.2 tons at 3" thick
Other Cultivars Available to Sub:	Yes
Special Needs:	Dead head roses throughout the season to get more blooms.

Till garden and amend soil with composted material such as mulched leaves or shredded pine.

Using the planting diagram, measure for plant placement and sit each plant in its proper place. Adjust placement based on the shape of the actual bed.

Dig each hole twice as wide as the root ball. Sprinkle in starter fertilizer to the bottom of the hole (follow directions on package for proper application). Set plant in hole. Push soil back around plant, tamping in tight with the handle end of the shovel to remove all air pockets. Tamp soil tight at top of root ball.

Repeat for each plant.

Water in all plants thoroughly.

Top beds with mulch, pine straw or other bedding materials to hold moisture and keep roots warm in winter and cool in summer.

Gravitas

Foundation Beds

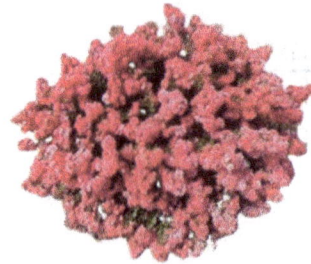

Common Name	Cleyera
Scientific Name	Ternstroemia gymnanthera
Status	Evergreen
Mature Size (H x W)	10x8
Pruning Category (1-5)	4
Watering Category (1-5)	2
Sun Category (1-5)	3
USDA Hardiness Zone:	7-10
Bloom Season	Spring

Common Name	Dwarf Crape Myrtle (Shrub Form)
Scientific Name	Lagerstroemia 'Gamad I' Razzle Dazzle Cherry
Status	Deciduous
Mature Size (H x W)	6x6
Pruning Category (1-5)	1
Watering Category (1-5)	2
Sun Category (1-5)	4
USDA Hardiness Zone:	6-11
Bloom Season	Summer

Common Name	Hardy Daisy Gardenia
Scientific Name	Gardenia jasminoides 'Kleim's Hardy'
Status	Evergreen
Mature Size (H x W)	4x4
Pruning Category (1-5)	2
Watering Category (1-5)	3
Sun Category (1-5)	4
USDA Hardiness Zone:	7-11
Bloom Season	Summer, Fall

Common Name	Degroots Spire Arborvitae
Scientific Name	Thuja occidentalis 'Degroot's Spire'
Status	Evergreen
Mature Size (H x W)	20x3
Pruning Category (1-5)	1
Watering Category (1-5)	3
Sun Category (1-5)	4
USDA Hardiness Zone:	4-8
Bloom Season	None

Common Name	Mini Loropetalum
Scientific Name	Loropetalum chinense 'Beni-Hime'
Status	Evergreen
Mature Size (H x W)	3x3
Pruning Category (1-5)	2
Watering Category (1-5)	2
Sun Category (1-5)	3
USDA Hardiness Zone:	7-10
Bloom Season	Spring

Common Name	Drift Rose
Scientific Name	Rosa 'Meijocos'
Status	Deciduous
Mature Size (H x W)	3x3
Pruning Category (1-5)	2
Watering Category (1-5)	2
Sun Category (1-5)	5
USDA Hardiness Zone:	5-10
Bloom Season	Summer

Rocky Top Retreat

Description

Bring a little mountain retreat home. The natural cedars and pines will evoke feelings of being at a mountain cabin. Touches of color and variety add a personal touch to this sloping hill. The natural boulder steps make it feel like it has always been there.

Ingredients

(1) Twist & Shout Hydrangea
(1) Teddy Bear Magnolia
(2) George Tabor Azalea
(3) Tea Olive (Osmanthus)
(1) Dwarf Blue Spruce
(1) Blue Point Juniper
(3) Dwarf Cryptomeria
(3) Japanese Painted Fern
(1) Gold Thread Cypress

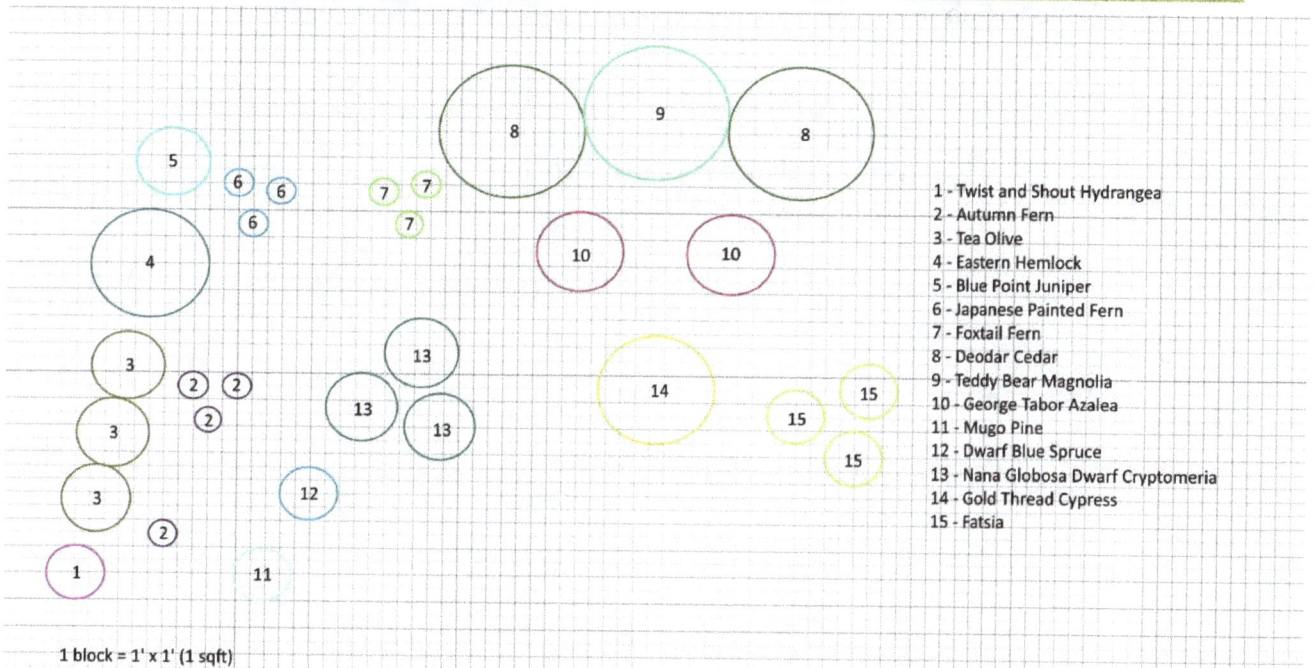

(4) Autumn Fern
(1) Mugo Pine
(1) Eastern Hemlock
(3) Fatsia
(3) Foxtail Fern
(2) Deodar Cedar

1 - Twist and Shout Hydrangea
2 - Autumn Fern
3 - Tea Olive
4 - Eastern Hemlock
5 - Blue Point Juniper
6 - Japanese Painted Fern
7 - Foxtail Fern
8 - Deodar Cedar
9 - Teddy Bear Magnolia
10 - George Tabor Azalea
11 - Mugo Pine
12 - Dwarf Blue Spruce
13 - Nana Globosa Dwarf Cryptomeria
14 - Gold Thread Cypress
15 - Fatsia

1 block = 1' x 1' (1 sqft)

Assembly Instructions

Garden Size (Approximate):	58'L x 41'W
Pruning Category:	1
Watering Needs:	2
Sun Requirements:	3
Plant Zones:	3-11
Bloom Colors:	Purple, White, Pink
Bloom Time Range:	Spring-Fall
Average Time to Install:	16 hours
Approximate Bedding:	2,378 sf
Mulch:	15 cuyds
Pine Straw:	57 bales
Rock:	30 tons at 3" thick
Other Cultivars Available to Sub:	Yes
Special Needs:	Mulch dwarf blue spruce heavily in summer in warmer climates to protect it from heat.

Till garden and amend soil with composted material such as mulched leaves or shredded pine.

Using the planting diagram, measure for plant placement and sit each plant in its proper place. Adjust placement based on the shape of the actual bed.

Dig each hole twice as wide as the root ball. Sprinkle in starter fertilizer to the bottom of the hole (follow directions on package for proper application). Set plant in hole. Push soil back around plant, tamping in tight with the handle end of the shovel to remove all air pockets. Tamp soil tight at top of root ball.

Repeat for each plant.

Water in all plants thoroughly.

Top beds with mulch, pine straw or other bedding materials to hold moisture and keep roots warm in winter and cool in summer.

Common Name	Twist and Shout Hydrangea
Scientific Name	Hydrangea macrophylla 'PIIHM-I'
Status	Deciduous
Mature Size (H x W)	4x4
Pruning Category (1-5)	1
Watering Category (1-5)	3
Sun Category (1-5)	3
USDA Hardiness Zone:	4-9
Bloom Season	Summer

Common Name	Autumn Fern
Scientific Name	Dryopteris erythrosora
Status	Perennial
Mature Size (H x W)	2x2
Pruning Category (1-5)	1
Watering Category (1-5)	3
Sun Category (1-5)	2
USDA Hardiness Zone:	4-8
Bloom Season	None

Common Name	Tea Olive
Scientific Name	Osmanthus fragrans
Status	Evergreen
Mature Size (H x W)	6x6
Pruning Category (1-5)	3
Watering Category (1-5)	2
Sun Category (1-5)	3
USDA Hardiness Zone:	8-10
Bloom Season	Spring

Common Name	Eastern Hemlock
Scientific Name	Tsuga canadensis
Status	Evergreen
Mature Size (H x W)	6x6
Pruning Category (1-5)	1
Watering Category (1-5)	3
Sun Category (1-5)	2
USDA Hardiness Zone:	5-7
Bloom Season	None

Common Name	Blue Point Juniper
Scientific Name	Juniperus chinensis 'Blue Point'
Status	Evergreen
Mature Size (H x W)	15x8
Pruning Category (1-5)	1
Watering Category (1-5)	1
Sun Category (1-5)	4
USDA Hardiness Zone:	6-9
Bloom Season	None

Common Name	Japanese Painted Fern
Scientific Name	Athyrium niponicum
Status	Perennial
Mature Size (H x W)	2x2
Pruning Category (1-5)	1
Watering Category (1-5)	3
Sun Category (1-5)	2
USDA Hardiness Zone:	4-8
Bloom Season	None

Common Name	Foxtail Fern
Scientific Name	Asparagus aethiopicus
Status	Perennial
Mature Size (H x W)	2x2
Pruning Category (1-5)	1
Watering Category (1-5)	3
Sun Category (1-5)	2
USDA Hardiness Zone:	4-8
Bloom Season	None

Common Name	Deodar Cedar
Scientific Name	Cedrus deodara
Status	Evergreen
Mature Size (H x W)	50x30
Pruning Category (1-5)	1
Watering Category (1-5)	2
Sun Category (1-5)	3
USDA Hardiness Zone:	6-7
Bloom Season	None

Common Name	Teddy Bear Magnolia
Scientific Name	Magnolia grandiflora 'Southern Charm'
Status	Evergreen
Mature Size (H x W)	20x12
Pruning Category (1-5)	1
Watering Category (1-5)	2
Sun Category (1-5)	4
USDA Hardiness Zone:	7-9
Bloom Season	Spring

Common Name	George Tabor Azalea
Scientific Name	Rhododendron x 'George Tabor'
Status	Evergreen
Mature Size (H x W)	5x5
Pruning Category (1-5)	2
Watering Category (1-5)	3
Sun Category (1-5)	3
USDA Hardiness Zone:	7-9
Bloom Season	Spring

Common Name	Dwarf Mugo Pine
Scientific Name	Pinus mugo
Status	Evergreen
Mature Size (H x W)	4x3
Pruning Category (1-5)	1
Watering Category (1-5)	1
Sun Category (1-5)	3
USDA Hardiness Zone:	3-7
Bloom Season	None-Inconspicuous

Common Name	Dwarf Blue Spruce
Scientific Name	Picea pungens 'Globosa'
Status	Evergreen
Mature Size (H x W)	2x2
Pruning Category (1-5)	1
Watering Category (1-5)	2
Sun Category (1-5)	3
USDA Hardiness Zone:	3-8
Bloom Season	None

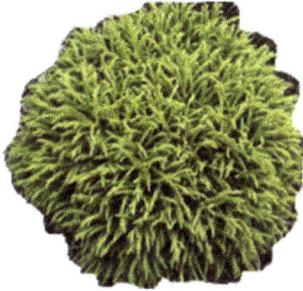

Common Name	Nana Globosa Dwarf Cryptomeria
Scientific Name	Cryptomeria japonica 'Globosa Nana'
Status	Evergreen
Mature Size (H x W)	4x4
Pruning Category (1-5)	1
Watering Category (1-5)	1
Sun Category (1-5)	3
USDA Hardiness Zone:	6-9
Bloom Season	None

Common Name	Gold Thread Cypress
Scientific Name	Chamaecyparis pisifera 'Gold Thread'
Status	Evergreen
Mature Size (H x W)	12x10
Pruning Category (1-5)	1
Watering Category (1-5)	1
Sun Category (1-5)	4
USDA Hardiness Zone:	6-9
Bloom Season	None

Common Name	Fatsia
Scientific Name	Fatsia japonica
Status	Evergreen
Mature Size (H x W)	5x5
Pruning Category (1-5)	1
Watering Category (1-5)	3
Sun Category (1-5)	3
USDA Hardiness Zone:	7-11
Bloom Season	Fall

Description

Indeed, an easy landscape install with few plants but plenty of interest. Junipers will eventually spread to touch and fill the hill while the height of the dwarf spruce and juniper shrubs will hold interest.

Ingredients

(1) Dwarf Weeping Norway Spruce
(3) Sea Green Juniper
(3) Blue Star Juniper Shrub
(9) Gold Lace Juniper

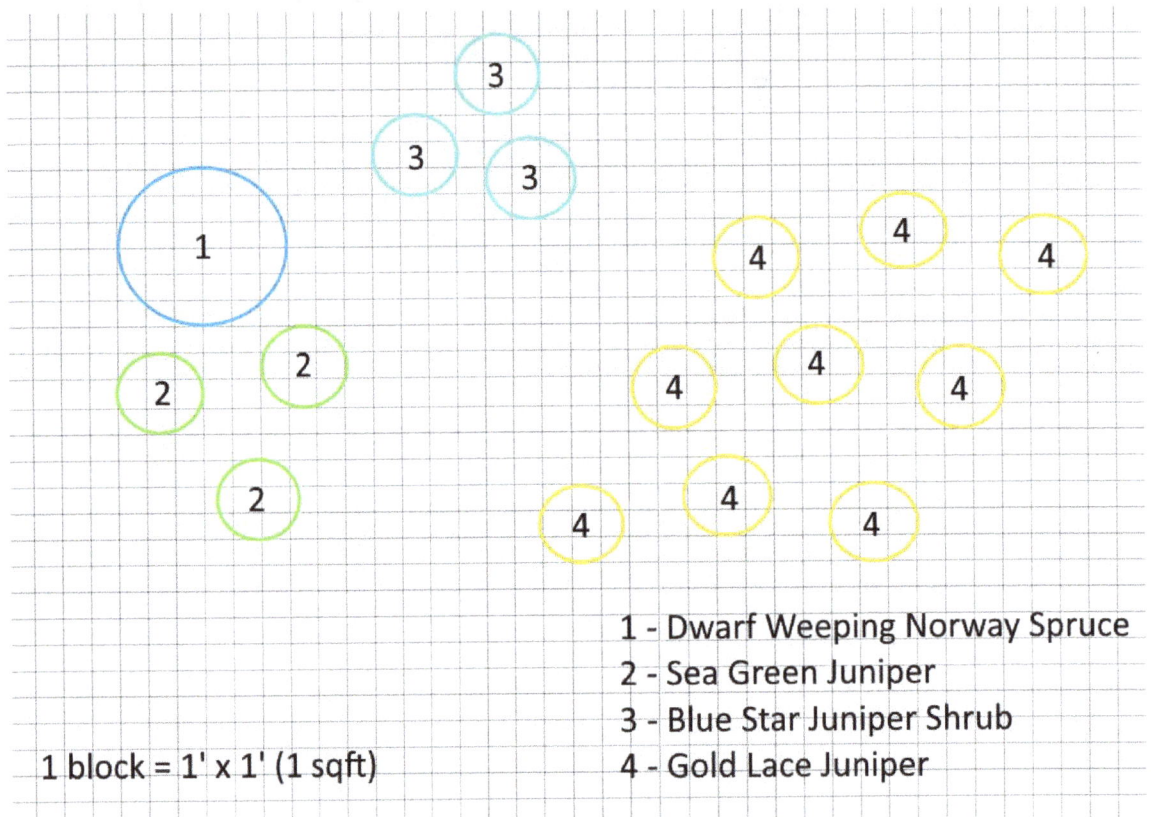

1 block = 1' x 1' (1 sqft)

1 - Dwarf Weeping Norway Spruce
2 - Sea Green Juniper
3 - Blue Star Juniper Shrub
4 - Gold Lace Juniper

Easy Peesy

Hillside Gardens

Assembly Instructions

Garden Size (Approximate):	34'L x 20'W
Pruning Category:	1
Watering Needs:	1
Sun Requirements:	3
Plant Zones:	3-9
Bloom Colors:	None
Bloom Time Range:	N/A
Average Time to Install:	7 hours
Approximate Bedding:	680sf
Mulch:	4 cuyds
Pine Straw:	16 bales
Rock:	8.5 tons at 3" thick
Other Cultivars Available to Sub:	Yes
Special Needs:	

Till garden and amend soil with composted material such as mulched leaves or shredded pine.

Using the planting diagram, measure for plant placement and sit each plant in its proper place. Adjust placement based on the shape of the actual bed.

Dig each hole twice as wide as the root ball. Sprinkle in starter fertilizer to the bottom of the hole (follow directions on package for proper application). Set plant in hole. Push soil back around plant, tamping in tight with the handle end of the shovel to remove all air pockets. Tamp soil tight at top of root ball.

Repeat for each plant.

Water in all plants thoroughly.

Top beds with mulch, pine straw or other bedding materials to hold moisture and keep roots warm in winter and cool in summer.

Common Name	Dwarf Weeping Norway Spruce
Scientific Name	Picea abies 'Pendula'
Status	Evergreen
Mature Size (H x W)	5x5
Pruning Category (1-5)	1
Watering Category (1-5)	2
Sun Category (1-5)	3
USDA Hardiness Zone:	3-8
Bloom Season	None

Common Name	Sea Green Juniper
Scientific Name	Juniperus chinensis 'Sea Green'
Status	Evergreen
Mature Size (H x W)	2x5
Pruning Category (1-5)	1
Watering Category (1-5)	1
Sun Category (1-5)	4
USDA Hardiness Zone:	6-9
Bloom Season	None

Common Name	Blue Star Juniper Shrub
Scientific Name	Juniperus squamata 'Blue Star'
Status	Evergreen
Mature Size (H x W)	3x4
Pruning Category (1-5)	1
Watering Category (1-5)	1
Sun Category (1-5)	3
USDA Hardiness Zone:	6-9
Bloom Season	None

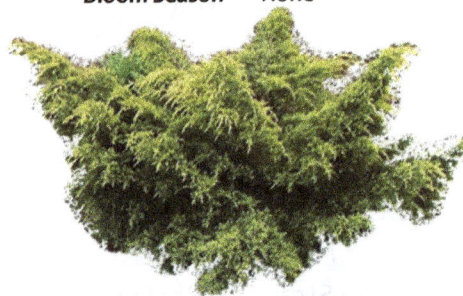

Common Name	Gold Lace Juniper
Scientific Name	Juniperus chinensis 'Gold Lace'
Status	Evergreen
Mature Size (H x W)	2.5x6
Pruning Category (1-5)	1
Watering Category (1-5)	1
Sun Category (1-5)	4
USDA Hardiness Zone:	6-9
Bloom Season	None

Jack and Jill

Hillside Gardens

Description

When your landscape hands you hilly slopes, dress them up with color and texture. Boulders protruding from the hill bring a natural feel to the garden but planned and planted perennials and evergreens give it classic style. Contrasting colors from white to red to purple provide something for everyone to enjoy.

Ingredients

(5) Limelight Hydrangea   (3) Lantana
(6) Mini Loropetalum   (1) Rosemary
(3) Shasta Daisy   (94) 4" Vinca
(3) Veronica Spicata
(5) Blackeyed Susan
(3) Knock Out Rose (Red)

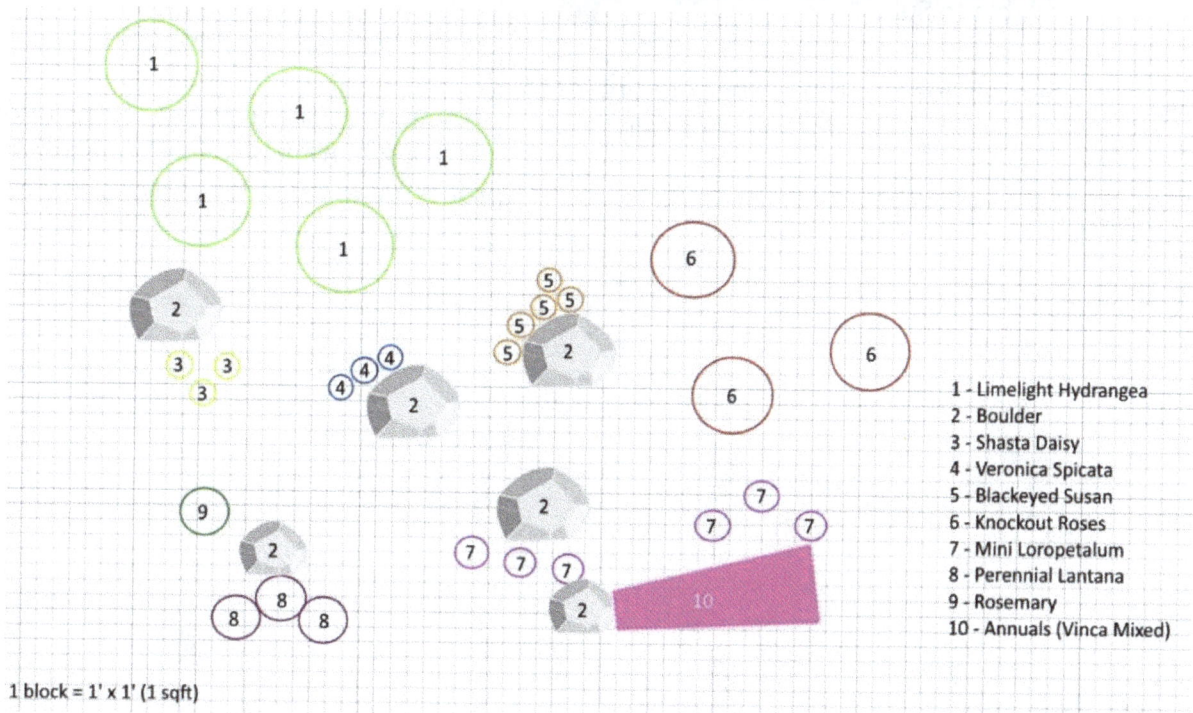

1 - Limelight Hydrangea
2 - Boulder
3 - Shasta Daisy
4 - Veronica Spicata
5 - Blackeyed Susan
6 - Knockout Roses
7 - Mini Loropetalum
8 - Perennial Lantana
9 - Rosemary
10 - Annuals (Vinca Mixed)

1 block = 1' x 1' (1 sqft)

Assembly Instructions

Garden Size (Approximate):	51'L x 41'W
Pruning Category:	1
Watering Needs:	2
Sun Requirements:	4
Plant Zones:	3-11
Bloom Colors:	White, Yellow, Blue, Red, Purple, Orange, Pink
Bloom Time Range:	Spring-Summer
Average Time to Install:	15 hours
Approximate Bedding:	2,091sf
Mulch:	13 cuyds
Pine Straw:	50 bales
Rock:	26 tons at 3" thick
Other Cultivars Available to Sub:	Yes
Special Needs:	Prune knock out roses to 18" at end of Fall

Till garden and amend soil with composted material such as mulched leaves or shredded pine.

Using the planting diagram, set boulders by digging into the soil several inches to create a foundation slightly below the grade of the garden. Set the boulder on to the foundation then spread the removed soil around the boulders to bring the soil height back up to grade level.

Measure for plant placement and sit each plant in its proper place. Adjust placement based on the shape of the actual bed.

Dig each hole twice as wide as the root ball. Sprinkle in starter fertilizer to the bottom of the hole (follow directions on package for proper application). Set plant in hole. Push soil back around plant, tamping in tight with the handle end of the shovel to remove all air pockets. Tamp soil tight at top of root ball.

Repeat for each plant.

Water in all plants thoroughly.

Top beds with mulch, pine straw or other bedding materials to hold moisture and keep roots warm in winter and cool in summer.

Common Name	Limelight Hydrangea
Scientific Name	Hydrangea paniculala 'Limelight'
Status	Deciduous
Mature Size (H x W)	6x6
Pruning Category (1-5)	1
Watering Category (1-5)	3
Sun Category (1-5)	4
USDA Hardiness Zone:	4-9
Bloom Season	Summer

Common Name	Shasta Daisy
Scientific Name	Leucanthemum x superbum
Status	Perennial
Mature Size (H x W)	2.5x2.5
Pruning Category (1-5)	1
Watering Category (1-5)	2
Sun Category (1-5)	4
USDA Hardiness Zone:	4-10
Bloom Season	Summer

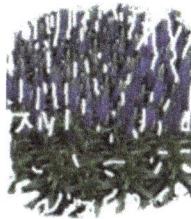

Common Name	Veronica Spicata
Scientific Name	Veronica spicata
Status	Perennial
Mature Size (H x W)	2.5x2.5
Pruning Category (1-5)	1
Watering Category (1-5)	2
Sun Category (1-5)	4
USDA Hardiness Zone:	4-8
Bloom Season	Summer

Common Name	Blackeyed Susan
Scientific Name	Rudbeckia hirta
Status	Perennial
Mature Size (H x W)	2x2
Pruning Category (1-5)	1
Watering Category (1-5)	2
Sun Category (1-5)	4
USDA Hardiness Zone:	3-9
Bloom Season	Summer

Common Name	Knock Out Rose
Scientific Name	Rosa Radrazz
Status	Deciduous
Mature Size (H x W)	4x4
Pruning Category (1-5)	2
Watering Category (1-5)	2
Sun Category (1-5)	5
USDA Hardiness Zone:	5-10
Bloom Season	Summer

Common Name	Mini Loropetalum
Scientific Name	Loropetalum chinense 'Beni-Hime'
Status	Evergreen
Mature Size (H x W)	3x3
Pruning Category (1-5)	2
Watering Category (1-5)	2
Sun Category (1-5)	3
USDA Hardiness Zone:	7-10
Bloom Season	Spring

Common Name	Lantana
Scientific Name	Lantana
Status	Perennial
Mature Size (H x W)	3x5
Pruning Category (1-5)	1
Watering Category (1-5)	2
Sun Category (1-5)	5
USDA Hardiness Zone:	7-11
Bloom Season	Summer

Common Name	Rosemary
Scientific Name	Rosmarinus officinalis
Status	Perennial
Mature Size (H x W)	3x4
Pruning Category (1-5)	1
Watering Category (1-5)	2
Sun Category (1-5)	4
USDA Hardiness Zone:	5-10
Bloom Season	Summer

Common Name	Vinca
Scientific Name	Catharanthus roseus
Status	Annual
Mature Size (H x W)	1.5x1.5
Pruning Category (1-5)	1
Watering Category (1-5)	1
Sun Category (1-5)	5
USDA Hardiness Zone:	4-8
Bloom Season	Summer

Frankly My Dear

Hillside Gardens

Description

Bright colors, seasonal blooms and natural rocks create a wonderful hill side garden. The Rose of Sharon blooms will bring hummingbirds and butterflies to visit and draw the eye to the peak of the hill. The lovely flowering quince will welcome spring with some of the earliest blooms in the garden. The drift roses keep the blooms coming all through summer to first frost.

Ingredients

(3) Flowering Quince
(1) Rose of Sharon
(10) Peach Drift Roses

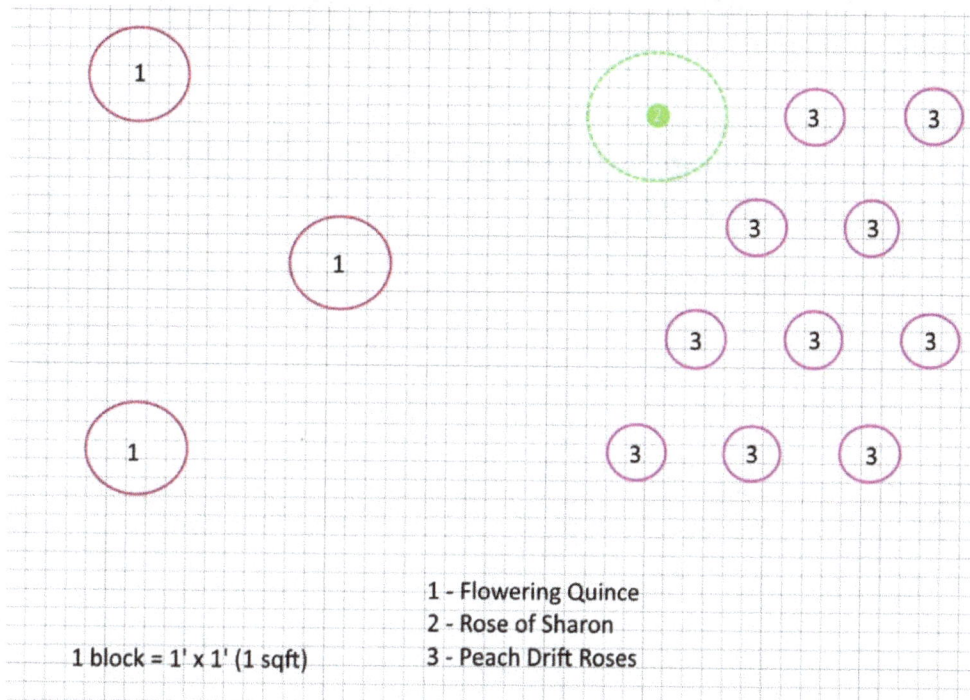

1 - Flowering Quince
2 - Rose of Sharon
3 - Peach Drift Roses

1 block = 1' x 1' (1 sqft)

Frankly My Dear

Assembly Instructions

Garden Size (Approximate):	34'L x 25'W
Pruning Category:	2
Watering Needs:	3
Sun Requirements:	5
Plant Zones:	4-10
Bloom Colors:	Pink, Purple, Peach
Bloom Time Range:	Spring-Summer
Average Time to Install:	9 hours
Approximate Bedding:	850sf
Mulch:	5.25cuyds
Pine Straw:	20 bales
Rock:	11 tons at 3" thick
Other Cultivars Available to Sub:	Yes
Special Needs:	Dead head roses throughout the season to get more blooms.

Till garden and amend soil with composted material such as mulched leaves or shredded pine.

Using the planting diagram, measure for plant placement and sit each plant in its proper place. Adjust placement based on the shape of the actual bed.

Dig each hole twice as wide as the root ball. Sprinkle in starter fertilizer to the bottom of the hole (follow directions on package for proper application). Set plant in hole. Push soil back around plant, tamping in tight with the handle end of the shovel to remove all air pockets. Tamp soil tight at top of root ball.

Repeat for each plant.

Water in all plants thoroughly.

Top beds with mulch, pine straw or other bedding materials to hold moisture and keep roots warm in winter and cool in summer.

Frankly My Dear

Hillside Gardens

Common Name	Flowering Quince
Scientific Name	Chaenomeles
Status	Deciduous
Mature Size (H x W)	6x5
Pruning Category (1-5)	2
Watering Category (1-5)	2
Sun Category (1-5)	4
USDA Hardiness Zone:	4-10
Bloom Season	Spring

Common Name	Rose of Sharon
Scientific Name	Hibiscus syriacus
Status	Deciduous
Mature Size (H x W)	18x12
Pruning Category (1-5)	1
Watering Category (1-5)	3
Sun Category (1-5)	5
USDA Hardiness Zone:	5-10
Bloom Season	Summer

Common Name	Drift Rose
Scientific Name	Rosa 'Meijocos'
Status	Deciduous
Mature Size (H x W)	3x3
Pruning Category (1-5)	2
Watering Category (1-5)	2
Sun Category (1-5)	5
USDA Hardiness Zone:	5-10
Bloom Season	Summer

Description

The party will always be at your house at the plateau of this beautiful boulder hillside walkup. Colors, smells, textures and blooms will welcome friends, family and neighbors to the upper sitting area. Fluffy grasses line the path up to the big beautiful hydrangea blooms.

Ingredients

(2) Hardy Daisy Gardenia   (5) Bee Balm
(3) Harbor Dwarf Nandina
(15) Stella d'Oro Daylily
(3) Peach Drift Roses
(2) White Drift Roses
(42) Liriope
(2) Knock Out Rose
(3) Autumn Chiffon Encore Azalea
(3) Endless Summer Hydrangea

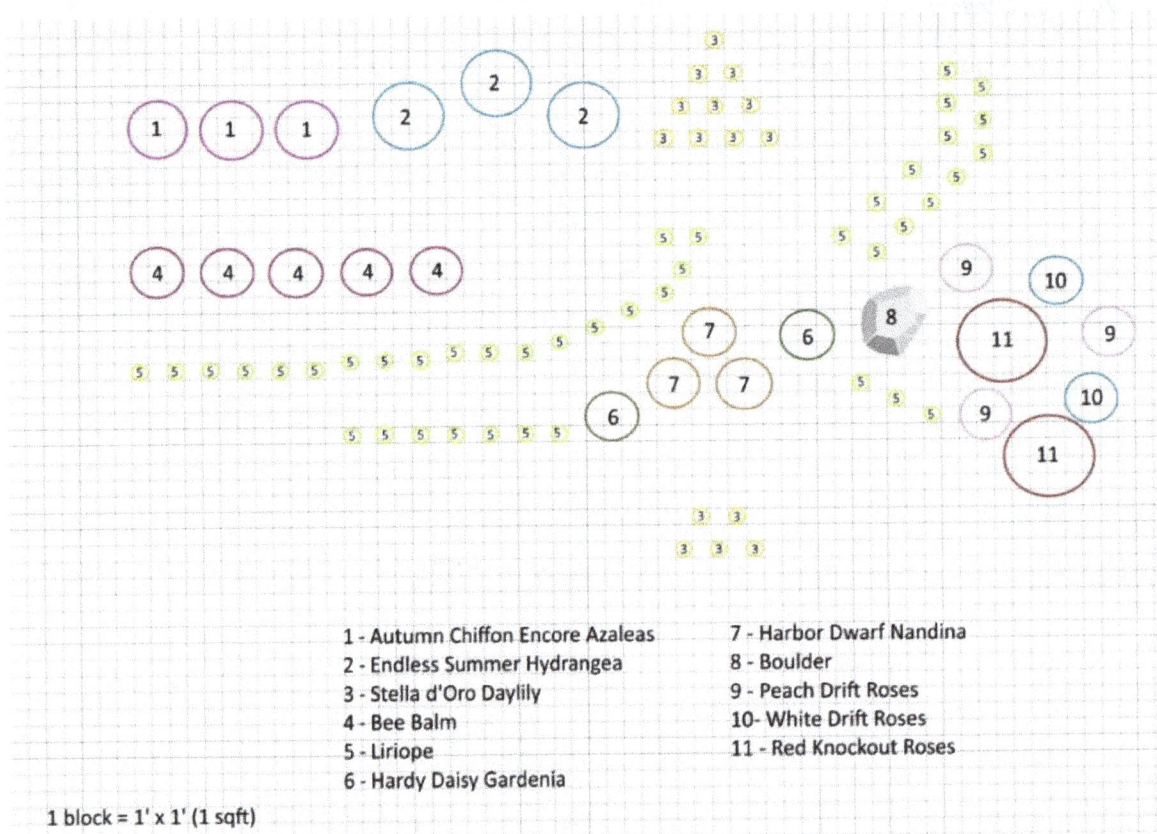

1 - Autumn Chiffon Encore Azaleas
2 - Endless Summer Hydrangea
3 - Stella d'Oro Daylily
4 - Bee Balm
5 - Liriope
6 - Hardy Daisy Gardenia

7 - Harbor Dwarf Nandina
8 - Boulder
9 - Peach Drift Roses
10- White Drift Roses
11 - Red Knockout Roses

1 block = 1' x 1' (1 sqft)

Assembly Instructions

Garden Size (Approximate):	58'L x 32'W
Pruning Category:	2
Watering Needs:	2
Sun Requirements:	4
Plant Zones:	2-11
Bloom Colors:	Pink, Blue, Purple, Yellow, White, Peach, Red
Bloom Time Range:	Spring-Fall
Average Time to Install:	20 hours
Approximate Bedding:	1,856sf
Mulch:	11.5 cuyds
Pine Straw:	44 bales
Rock:	23 tons at 3" thick
Other Cultivars Available to Sub:	Yes
Special Needs:	Prune knock out roses to 18" at end of Fall Dead head roses throughout the season to get more blooms.

Till garden and amend soil with composted material such as mulched leaves or shredded pine.

Using the planting diagram, set boulders by digging into the soil several inches to create a foundation slightly below the grade of the garden. Set the boulder on to the foundation then spread the removed soil around the boulders to bring the soil height back up to grade level.

Measure for plant placement and sit each plant in its proper place. Adjust placement based on the shape of the actual bed.

Dig each hole twice as wide as the root ball. Sprinkle in starter fertilizer to the bottom of the hole (follow directions on package for proper application). Set plant in hole. Push soil back around plant, tamping in tight with the handle end of the shovel to remove all air pockets. Tamp soil tight at top of root ball.

Repeat for each plant.

Water in all plants thoroughly.

Top beds with mulch, pine straw or other bedding materials to hold moisture and keep roots warm in winter and cool in summer.

Common Name	Autumn Chiffon Encore Azalea
Scientific Name	Rhododendron 'Robled' PP15862
Status	Evergreen
Mature Size (H x W)	3.5x3.5
Pruning Category (1-5)	2
Watering Category (1-5)	3
Sun Category (1-5)	4
USDA Hardiness Zone:	7-10
Bloom Season	Spring, Fall

Common Name	Endless Summer Hydrangea
Scientific Name	Hydrangea macrophylla 'Bailmacfive' PPAF
Status	Deciduous
Mature Size (H x W)	3x3
Pruning Category (1-5)	1
Watering Category (1-5)	3
Sun Category (1-5)	3
USDA Hardiness Zone:	4-9
Bloom Season	Summer

Common Name	Stella d'Oro Daylily
Scientific Name	Hemerocallis 'Stella d'Oro'
Status	Perennial
Mature Size (H x W)	2x2
Pruning Category (1-5)	1
Watering Category (1-5)	2
Sun Category (1-5)	4
USDA Hardiness Zone:	3-9
Bloom Season	Summer

Common Name	Bee Balm
Scientific Name	Monarda
Status	Perennial
Mature Size (H x W)	3x3
Pruning Category (1-5)	1
Watering Category (1-5)	2
Sun Category (1-5)	4
USDA Hardiness Zone:	2-10
Bloom Season	Summer

Common Name	Liriope
Scientific Name	Liriope muscari
Status	Perennial
Mature Size (H x W)	2x2
Pruning Category (1-5)	1
Watering Category (1-5)	1
Sun Category (1-5)	4
USDA Hardiness Zone:	6-10
Bloom Season	Summer

Common Name	Hardy Daisy Gardenia
Scientific Name	Gardenia jasminoides 'Kleim's Hardy'
Status	Evergreen
Mature Size (H x W)	4x4
Pruning Category (1-5)	2
Watering Category (1-5)	3
Sun Category (1-5)	4
USDA Hardiness Zone:	7-11
Bloom Season	Summer, Fall

Common Name	Harbor Dwarf Nandina
Scientific Name	Nandina domestica 'Harbour Dwarf'
Status	Evergreen
Mature Size (H x W)	3x3
Pruning Category (1-5)	2
Watering Category (1-5)	2
Sun Category (1-5)	3
USDA Hardiness Zone:	5-10
Bloom Season	Summer

Common Name	Drift Rose
Scientific Name	Rosa 'Meijocos'
Status	Deciduous
Mature Size (H x W)	3x3
Pruning Category (1-5)	2
Watering Category (1-5)	2
Sun Category (1-5)	5
USDA Hardiness Zone:	5-10
Bloom Season	Summer

Common Name	Knock Out Rose
Scientific Name	Rosa Radrazz
Status	Deciduous
Mature Size (H x W)	4x4
Pruning Category (1-5)	2
Watering Category (1-5)	2
Sun Category (1-5)	5
USDA Hardiness Zone:	5-10
Bloom Season	Summer

Description

A mailbox bed doesn't have to be complicated. Keep it simple with seasonal blooms and cool shade. The blooms of the dogwood will bring a cheery disposition to any mail carrier while the heavenly scent of the Daphne makes your box a carrier favorite.

Ingredients

(6) Daphne Odora
(1) White Dogwood

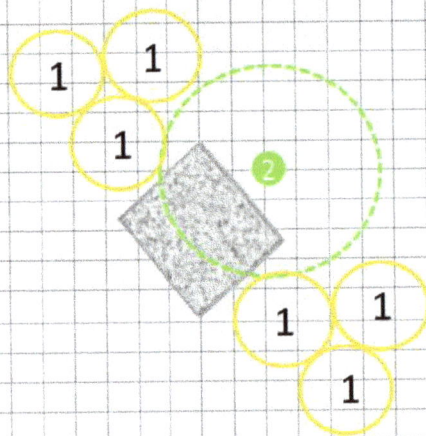

1 - Daphne Odora
2 - White Dogwood

1 block = 1' x 1' (1 sqft)

Assembly Instructions

Garden Size (Approximate):	14'L x 6'W
Pruning Category:	1
Watering Needs:	2
Sun Requirements:	2
Plant Zones:	3-9
Bloom Colors:	White
Bloom Time Range:	Spring
Average Time to Install:	4 hours
Approximate Bedding:	84sf
Mulch:	0.50 cuyds
Pine Straw:	2 bales
Rock:	1 ton at 3" thick
Other Cultivars Available to Sub:	Yes
Special Needs:	

Till garden and amend soil with composted material such as mulched leaves or shredded pine.

Using the planting diagram, measure for plant placement and sit each plant in its proper place. Adjust placement based on the shape of the actual bed.

Dig each hole twice as wide as the root ball. Sprinkle in starter fertilizer to the bottom of the hole (follow directions on package for proper application). Set plant in hole. Push soil back around plant, tamping in tight with the handle end of the shovel to remove all air pockets. Tamp soil tight at top of root ball.

Repeat for each plant.

Water in all plants thoroughly.

Top beds with mulch, pine straw or other bedding materials to hold moisture and keep roots warm in winter and cool in summer.

Common Name	Daphne Odora
Scientific Name	Daphne Odora
Status	Evergreen
Mature Size (H x W)	4x4
Pruning Category (1-5)	2
Watering Category (1-5)	2
Sun Category (1-5)	3
USDA Hardiness Zone:	4-9
Bloom Season	Spring

Common Name	White Dogwood
Scientific Name	Cornus florida
Status	Deciduous
Mature Size (H x W)	20x15
Pruning Category (1-5)	1
Watering Category (1-5)	2
Sun Category (1-5)	2
USDA Hardiness Zone:	3-8
Bloom Season	Spring

Fall Festival

Description

The show on your street will be at your mailbox every October as this Japanese Maple turns a blazing red. The seasonal color is spectacular as well. The evergreen boxwoods hold color through the cold winter months.

Ingredients

(2) American Boxwood
(6) Carissa Holly
(1) Bloodgood Japanese Maple

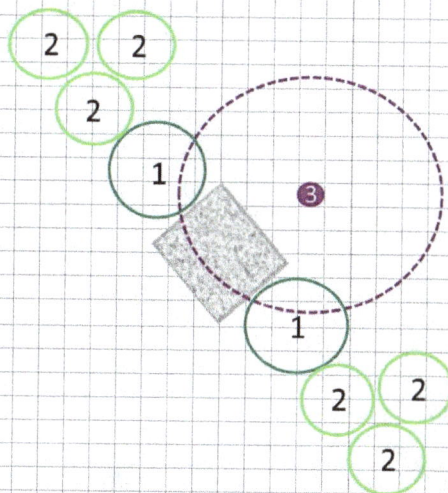

1 block = 1'x 1' (1 sqft)

1 - American Boxwood
2 - Carissa Holly
3 - Bloodgood Japanese Maple

Assembly Instructions

Garden Size (Approximate):	20'L x 10'W
Pruning Category:	3
Watering Needs:	2
Sun Requirements:	4
Plant Zones:	4-9
Bloom Colors:	None
Bloom Time Range:	N/A
Average Time to Install:	5 hours
Approximate Bedding:	200sf
Mulch:	1.25 cuyds
Pine Straw:	5 bales
Rock:	2.5 tons at 3" thick
Other Cultivars Available to Sub:	Yes
Special Needs:	

Till garden and amend soil with composted material such as mulched leaves or shredded pine.

Using the planting diagram, measure for plant placement and sit each plant in its proper place. Adjust placement based on the shape of the actual bed.

Dig each hole twice as wide as the root ball. Sprinkle in starter fertilizer to the bottom of the hole (follow directions on package for proper application). Set plant in hole. Push soil back around plant, tamping in tight with the handle end of the shovel to remove all air pockets. Tamp soil tight at top of root ball.

Repeat for each plant.

Water in all plants thoroughly.

Top beds with mulch, pine straw or other bedding materials to hold moisture and keep roots warm in winter and cool in summer.

Common Name	American Boxwood
Scientific Name	Buxus sempervirens
Status	Evergreen
Mature Size (H x W)	5x5
Pruning Category (1-5)	4
Watering Category (1-5)	3
Sun Category (1-5)	4
USDA Hardiness Zone:	4-9
Bloom Season	None

Common Name	Carissa Holly
Scientific Name	Ilex cornuta 'Carissa'
Status	Evergreen
Mature Size (H x W)	4x4
Pruning Category (1-5)	4
Watering Category (1-5)	2
Sun Category (1-5)	4
USDA Hardiness Zone:	7-9
Bloom Season	None-Inconspicuous

Common Name	Bloodgood Japanese Maple
Scientific Name	Acer palmatum 'Bloodgood'
Status	Deciduous
Mature Size (H x W)	15x10
Pruning Category (1-5)	1
Watering Category (1-5)	2
Sun Category (1-5)	4
USDA Hardiness Zone:	5-8
Bloom Season	None

Description

Greet summer with these seemingly endless blooms. The beautiful combination of red and yellow adds a cheery vibe to the mailbox. Cut back the rose late fall each year to keep a consistent size. Daylilies can be mulched each winter to protect the roots.

Ingredients

(6) Stella d'Oro Daylily

(1) Knock Out Rose (Red)

1 - Stella d'Oro Daylily
2 - Red Knockout Rose

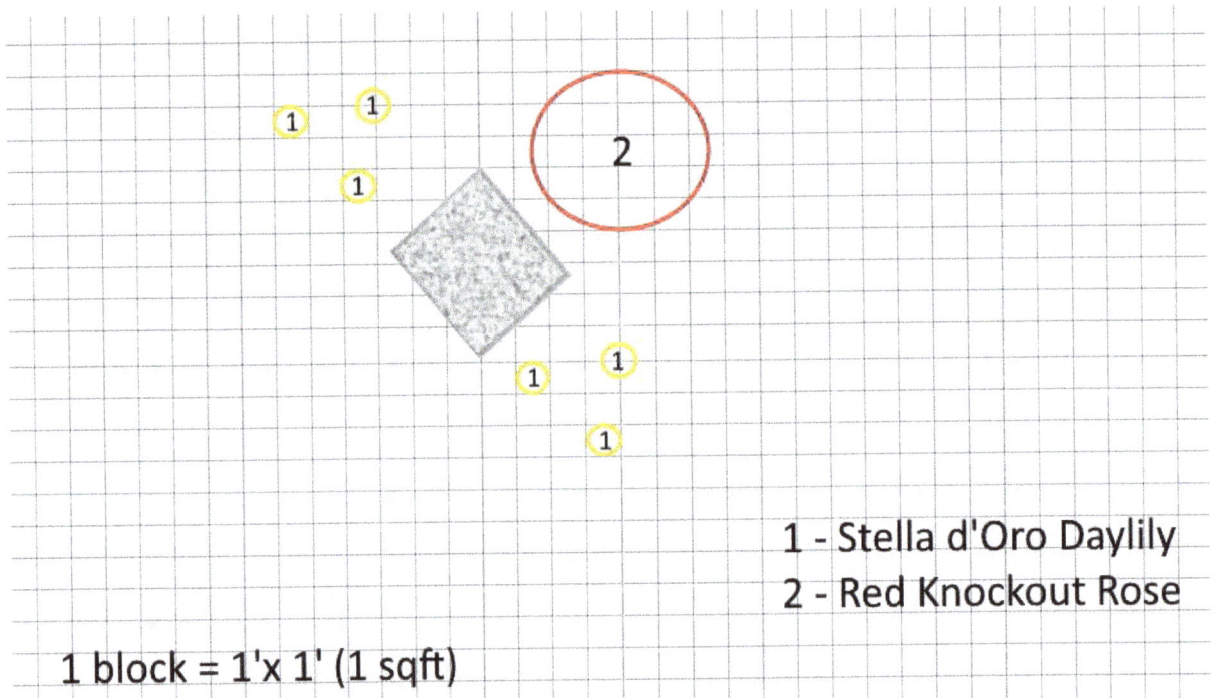

1 block = 1'x 1' (1 sqft)

Season's Greetings

Mailbox Landscapes

Garden Size (Approximate):	14'L x 8'W
Pruning Category:	1
Watering Needs:	2
Sun Requirements:	4
Plant Zones:	3-10
Bloom Colors:	Yellow, Red
Bloom Time Range:	Spring-Fall
Average Time to Install:	3 hours
Approximate Bedding:	112sf
Mulch:	0.70 cuyds
Pine Straw:	3 bales
Rock:	1.4 tons at 3" thick
Other Cultivars Available to Sub:	Yes
Special Needs:	Prune knock out roses to 18" at end of Fall

Till garden and amend soil with composted material such as mulched leaves or shredded pine.

Using the planting diagram, measure for plant placement and sit each plant in its proper place. Adjust placement based on the shape of the actual bed.

Dig each hole twice as wide as the root ball. Sprinkle in starter fertilizer to the bottom of the hole (follow directions on package for proper application). Set plant in hole. Push soil back around plant, tamping in tight with the handle end of the shovel to remove all air pockets. Tamp soil tight at top of root ball.

Repeat for each plant.

Water in all plants thoroughly.

Top beds with mulch, pine straw or other bedding materials to hold moisture and keep roots warm in winter and cool in summer.

Season's Greetings

Common Name	Knock Out Rose
Scientific Name	Rosa Radrazz
Status	Deciduous
Mature Size (H x W)	4x4
Pruning Category (1-5)	2
Watering Category (1-5)	2
Sun Category (1-5)	5
USDA Hardiness Zone:	5-10
Bloom Season	Summer

Common Name	Stella d'Oro Daylily
Scientific Name	Hemerocallis 'Stella d'Oro'
Status	Perennial
Mature Size (H x W)	2x2
Pruning Category (1-5)	1
Watering Category (1-5)	2
Sun Category (1-5)	4
USDA Hardiness Zone:	3-9
Bloom Season	Summer

De-Vine-Ly Simple

Description

Butterflies and hummingbirds will love to perch on your mail box with the sweet scent of jasmine luring them in. Annual flowers bring a clean and neat feel to the bed and keep it simple to install and maintain year after year. Start the jasmine on a wood trellis and train it over the mailbox for the greatest impact.

Ingredients

(1) Star Jasmine
(42) 4" Annuals (Vinca Mixed Color)

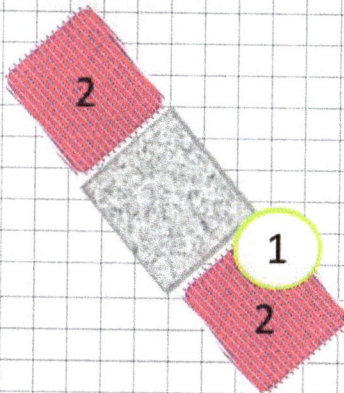

1 - Star Jasmine (vine)
2 - Annuals (Vinca Mixed Colors)

1 block = 1' x 1' (1 sqft)

Assembly Instructions

Garden Size (Approximate):	12'L x 4'W
Pruning Category:	2
Watering Needs:	1
Sun Requirements:	4
Plant Zones:	4-10
Bloom Colors:	White, Pink
Bloom Time Range:	Summer
Average Time to Install:	4 hours
Approximate Bedding:	48sf
Mulch:	0.25 cuyds
Pine Straw:	2 bales
Rock:	0.50 tons at 3" thick
Other Cultivars Available to Sub:	Yes
Special Needs:	

Till garden and amend soil with composted material such as mulched leaves or shredded pine.

Using the planting diagram, measure for plant placement and sit each plant in its proper place. Adjust placement based on the shape of the actual bed.

Dig each hole twice as wide as the root ball. Sprinkle in starter fertilizer to the bottom of the hole (follow directions on package for proper application). Set plant in hole. Push soil back around plant, tamping in tight with the handle end of the shovel to remove all air pockets. Tamp soil tight at top of root ball.

Repeat for each plant.

Water in all plants thoroughly.

Top beds with mulch, pine straw or other bedding materials to hold moisture and keep roots warm in winter and cool in summer.

De-Vine-Ly Simple

Mailbox Landscapes

Common Name	Star Jasmine
Scientific Name	Trachelospermum jasminoides
Status	Perennial
Mature Size (H x W)	vine
Pruning Category (1-5)	3
Watering Category (1-5)	2
Sun Category (1-5)	5
USDA Hardiness Zone:	7-10
Bloom Season	Summer

Common Name	Vinca
Scientific Name	Catharanthus roseus
Status	Annual
Mature Size (H x W)	1.5x1.5
Pruning Category (1-5)	1
Watering Category (1-5)	1
Sun Category (1-5)	5
USDA Hardiness Zone:	4-8
Bloom Season	Summer

Easy Like Sunday Morning

Description

This easy going, full growing bed will keep you strolling out to the box. Fluffy dwarf crape myrtles mean there's no need to trim each year and the autumn ferns will benefit from their shade. Cut back the ferns in the winter for the best foliage next spring.

Ingredients

(3) Natchez Crape Myrtle
(10) Autumn Fern

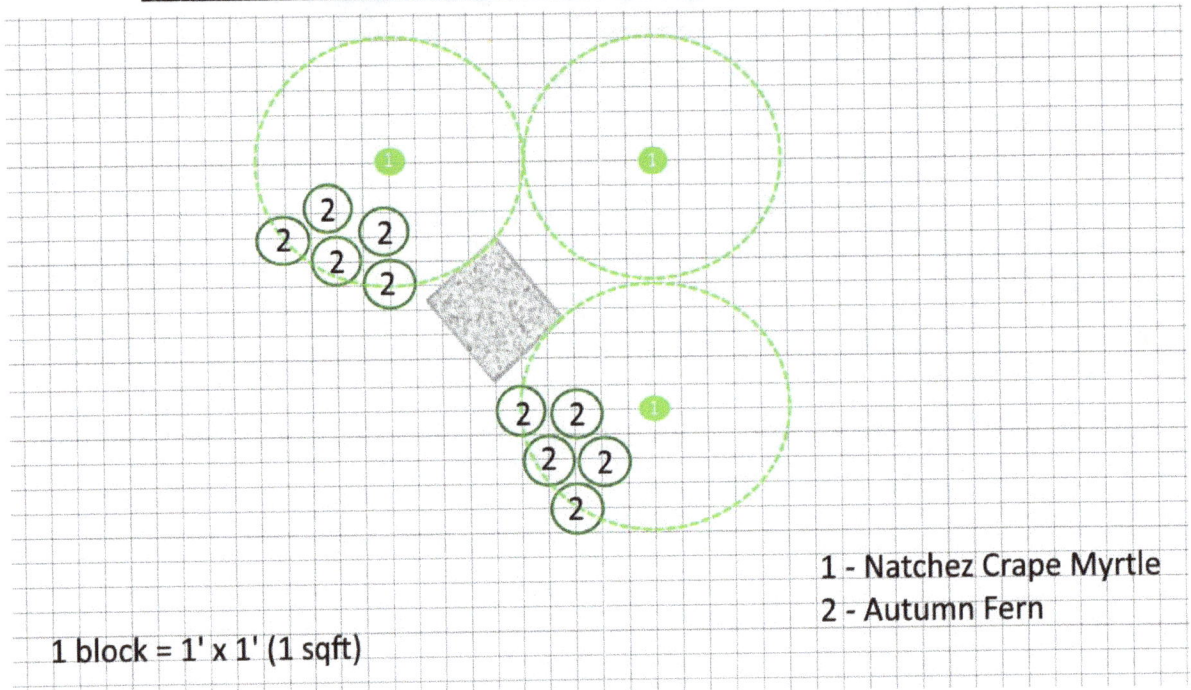

1 - Natchez Crape Myrtle
2 - Autumn Fern

1 block = 1' x 1' (1 sqft)

Assembly Instructions

Garden Size (Approximate):	20'L x 19'W
Pruning Category:	1
Watering Needs:	2
Sun Requirements:	3
Plant Zones:	4-11
Bloom Colors:	White
Bloom Time Range:	Summer
Average Time to Install:	5 hours
Approximate Bedding:	380sf
Mulch:	2.3 cuyds
Pine Straw:	9 bales
Rock:	4.75 tons
Other Cultivars Available to Sub:	Yes
Special Needs:	This cultivar of crape myrtle is considered dwarf. There is no need to cut back every year (also called "knuckling").

Till garden and amend soil with composted material such as mulched leaves or shredded pine.

Using the planting diagram, measure for plant placement and sit each plant in its proper place. Adjust placement based on the shape of the actual bed.

Dig each hole twice as wide as the root ball. Sprinkle in starter fertilizer to the bottom of the hole (follow directions on package for proper application). Set plant in hole. Push soil back around plant, tamping in tight with the handle end of the shovel to remove all air pockets. Tamp soil tight at top of root ball.

Repeat for each plant.

Water in all plants thoroughly.

Top beds with mulch, pine straw or other bedding materials to hold moisture and keep roots warm in winter and cool in summer.

Common Name	Natchez Crape Myrtle
Scientific Name	Lagerstroemia indica x fauriei 'Natchez'
Status	Deciduous
Mature Size (H x W)	30x10
Pruning Category (1-5)	1
Watering Category (1-5)	2
Sun Category (1-5)	4
USDA Hardiness Zone:	6-11
Bloom Season	Summer

Common Name	Autumn Fern
Scientific Name	Dryopteris erythrosora
Status	Perennial
Mature Size (H x W)	2x2
Pruning Category (1-5)	1
Watering Category (1-5)	3
Sun Category (1-5)	2
USDA Hardiness Zone:	4-8
Bloom Season	None

Homecoming Queen

Description

Take home the title of "Queen" with this beautiful fully perennial flower bed. Bold yellows contrast the purples and blues of the hydrangea and it's all tied together with the tri color lantana in the front. Frilly coreopsis always adds a touch of whimsy and is balanced with the upright and serious Heliopsis to the right. Mulch bed heavily during the winter to protect perennial roots, tubers and bulbs.

Ingredients

(3) Yellow Canna Lily   (1) Heliopsis
(3) Liatris   (3) Shasta Daisy
(3) Coreopsis
(3) Perennial Lantana (Tri Color)
(2) Endless Summer Hydrangea

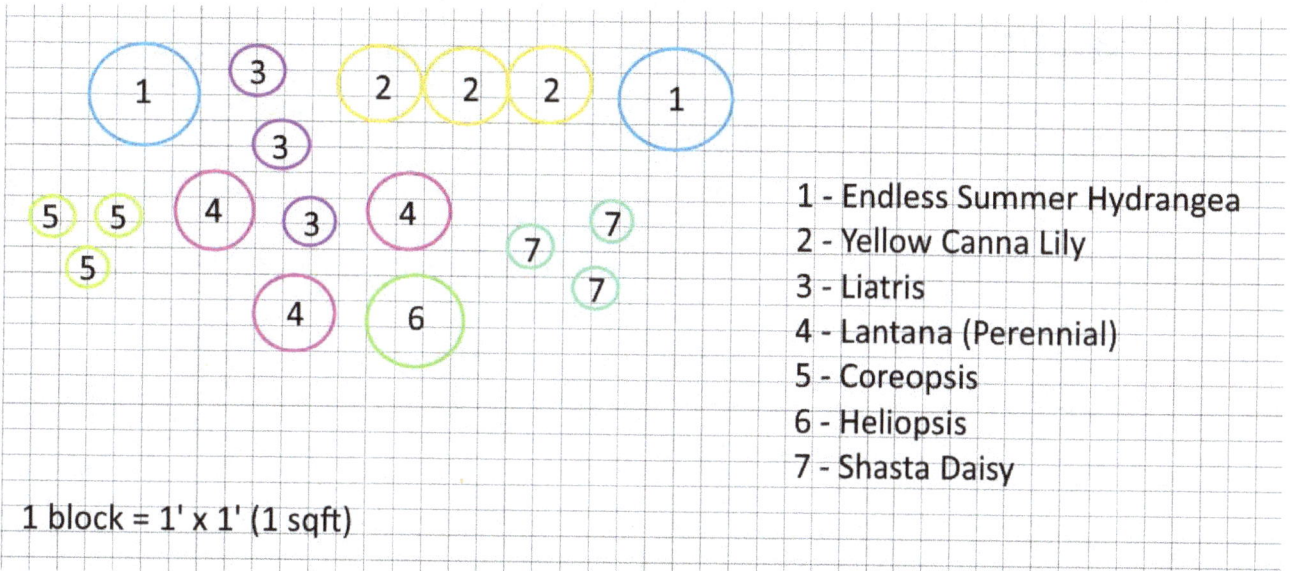

1 - Endless Summer Hydrangea
2 - Yellow Canna Lily
3 - Liatris
4 - Lantana (Perennial)
5 - Coreopsis
6 - Heliopsis
7 - Shasta Daisy

1 block = 1' x 1' (1 sqft)

Assembly Instructions

Garden Size (Approximate):	25'L x 13'W
Pruning Category:	1
Watering Needs:	2
Sun Requirements:	4
Plant Zones:	3-11
Bloom Colors:	Purple, Yellow, Orange, Red, White
Bloom Time Range:	Summer
Average Time to Install:	7 hours
Approximate Bedding:	325sf
Mulch:	2 cuyds
Pine Straw:	8 bales
Rock:	4 tons at 3" thick
Other Cultivars Available to Sub:	Yes
Special Needs:	

Till garden and amend soil with composted material such as mulched leaves or shredded pine.

Using the planting diagram, measure for plant placement and sit each plant in its proper place. Adjust placement based on the shape of the actual bed.

Dig each hole twice as wide as the root ball. Sprinkle in starter fertilizer to the bottom of the hole (follow directions on package for proper application). Set plant in hole. Push soil back around plant, tamping in tight with the handle end of the shovel to remove all air pockets. Tamp soil tight at top of root ball.

Repeat for each plant.

Water in all plants thoroughly.

Top beds with mulch, pine straw or other bedding materials to hold moisture and keep roots warm in winter and cool in summer.

Common Name	Endless Summer Hydrangea
Scientific Name	Hydrangea macrophylla 'Bailmacfive' PPAF
Status	Deciduous
Mature Size (H x W)	3x3
Pruning Category (1-5)	1
Watering Category (1-5)	3
Sun Category (1-5)	3
USDA Hardiness Zone:	4-9
Bloom Season	Summer

Common Name	Canna Lily
Scientific Name	Canna indica
Status	Perennial
Mature Size (H x W)	6x4
Pruning Category (1-5)	1
Watering Category (1-5)	3
Sun Category (1-5)	4
USDA Hardiness Zone:	4-9
Bloom Season	Summer

Common Name	Liatris
Scientific Name	Liatris spicata
Status	Perennial
Mature Size (H x W)	3x2
Pruning Category (1-5)	1
Watering Category (1-5)	2
Sun Category (1-5)	4
USDA Hardiness Zone:	5-9
Bloom Season	Summer

Common Name	Lantana
Scientific Name	Lantana
Status	Perennial
Mature Size (H x W)	3x5
Pruning Category (1-5)	1
Watering Category (1-5)	2
Sun Category (1-5)	5
USDA Hardiness Zone:	7-11
Bloom Season	Summer

Common Name	Coreopsis
Scientific Name	Selleophutum Urb. Tuckermannia Nutt.
Status	Perennial
Mature Size (H x W)	2.5x1
Pruning Category (1-5)	1
Watering Category (1-5)	2
Sun Category (1-5)	4
USDA Hardiness Zone:	3-9
Bloom Season	Summer

Common Name	Heliopsis
Scientific Name	Heliopsis helianthoides
Status	Perennial
Mature Size (H x W)	2x2
Pruning Category (1-5)	1
Watering Category (1-5)	2
Sun Category (1-5)	4
USDA Hardiness Zone:	3-9
Bloom Season	Summer

Common Name	Shasta Daisy
Scientific Name	Leucanthemum x superbum
Status	Perennial
Mature Size (H x W)	2.5x2.5
Pruning Category (1-5)	1
Watering Category (1-5)	2
Sun Category (1-5)	4
USDA Hardiness Zone:	4-10
Bloom Season	Summer

Description

This bed is unapologetically beautiful. Brilliant reds burst with color surrounding the full season of white blooms from the roses. Cheery daylily brightens up the front. Trim roses in the fall to maintain a consistent height and shape. Heavily mulch the bed to protect perennial roots during the winter months.

Ingredients

(2) Red Canna Lily
(3) White Drift Roses
(7) Red Daylily (Reblooming)

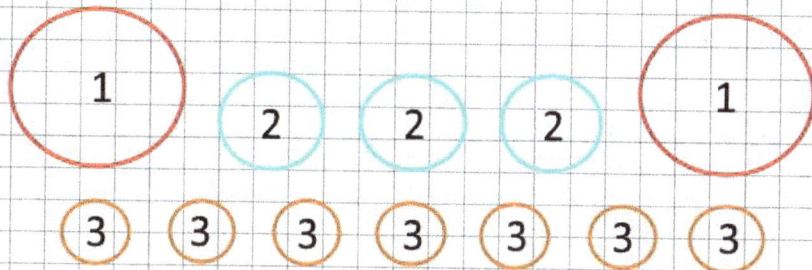

1 - Red Canna Lily
2 - White Drift Roses
3 - Red Daylily

1 block = 1' x 1' (1 sqft)

Assembly Instructions

Garden Size (Approximate):	23'L x 8'W
Pruning Category:	1
Watering Needs:	2
Sun Requirements:	4
Plant Zones:	3-10
Bloom Colors:	Red, White
Bloom Time Range:	Summer
Average Time to Install:	5 hours
Approximate Bedding:	184sf
Mulch:	1 cuyds
Pine Straw:	4 bales
Rock:	2.3 tons at 3" thick
Other Cultivars Available to Sub:	Yes
Special Needs:	Dead head roses throughout the season to get more blooms.

Till garden and amend soil with composted material such as mulched leaves or shredded pine.

Using the planting diagram, measure for plant placement and sit each plant in its proper place. Adjust placement based on the shape of the actual bed.

Dig each hole twice as wide as the root ball. Sprinkle in starter fertilizer to the bottom of the hole (follow directions on package for proper application). Set plant in hole. Push soil back around plant, tamping in tight with the handle end of the shovel to remove all air pockets. Tamp soil tight at top of root ball.

Repeat for each plant.

Water in all plants thoroughly.

Top beds with mulch, pine straw or other bedding materials to hold moisture and keep roots warm in winter and cool in summer.

Common Name	Canna Lily
Scientific Name	Canna indica
Status	Perennial
Mature Size (H x W)	6x4
Pruning Category (1-5)	1
Watering Category (1-5)	3
Sun Category (1-5)	4
USDA Hardiness Zone:	4-9
Bloom Season	Summer

Common Name	Drift Rose
Scientific Name	Rosa 'Meijocos'
Status	Deciduous
Mature Size (H x W)	3x3
Pruning Category (1-5)	2
Watering Category (1-5)	2
Sun Category (1-5)	5
USDA Hardiness Zone:	5-10
Bloom Season	Summer

Common Name	Red Daylily
Scientific Name	Hemerocallis 'Red Hot Returns'
Status	Perennial
Mature Size (H x W)	2x2
Pruning Category (1-5)	1
Watering Category (1-5)	2
Sun Category (1-5)	4
USDA Hardiness Zone:	3-9
Bloom Season	Summer

Description

You'll want to keep coming back for the non-stop summer blooms of this perennial bed. Iris fill the bed throughout early spring with a back drop of a flowy miscanthus grass. The bees and butterflies will frequently visit the blooms of the Blackeyed Susan and peony. Mulch the bed heavily after first frost to protect roots, tubers and bulbs for the winter.

Ingredients

(1) Miscanthus Grass
(3) Siberian Iris
(3) Blue Flag Iris
(3) Yellow Flag Iris
(1) Peony
(5) Blackeyed Susan

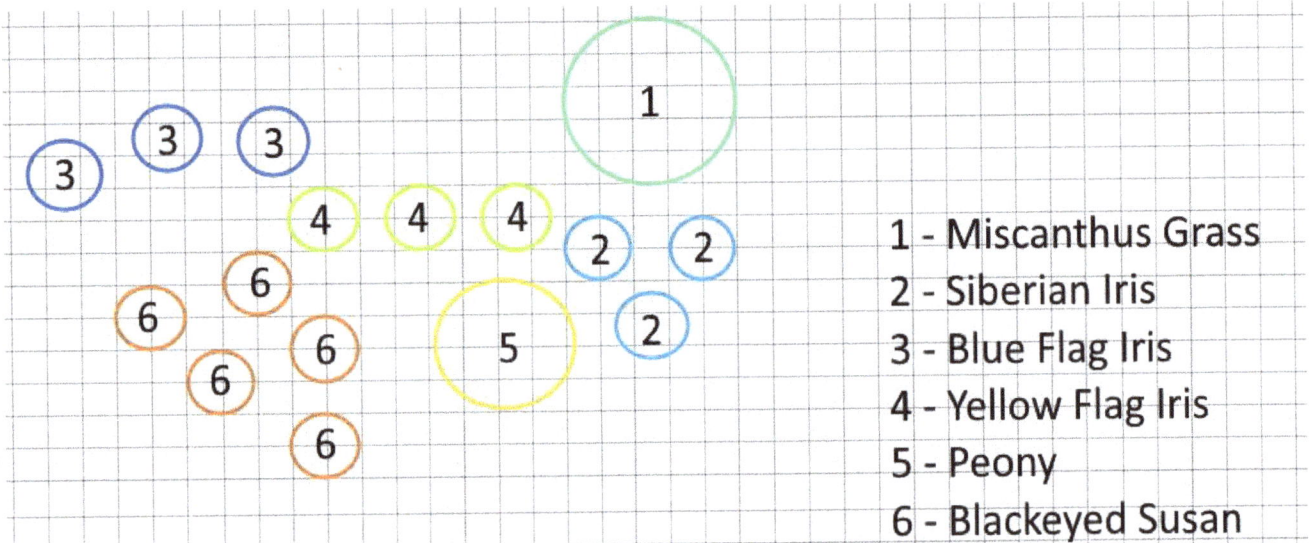

1 - Miscanthus Grass
2 - Siberian Iris
3 - Blue Flag Iris
4 - Yellow Flag Iris
5 - Peony
6 - Blackeyed Susan

1 block = 1' x 1' (1 sqft)

Assembly Instructions

Garden Size (Approximate):	20'L x 14'W
Pruning Category:	1
Watering Needs:	3
Sun Requirements:	3
Plant Zones:	3-10
Bloom Colors:	White, Blue, Yellow
Bloom Time Range:	Spring-Summer
Average Time to Install:	8 hours
Approximate Bedding:	280sf
Mulch:	1.75 cuyds
Pine Straw:	7 bales
Rock:	3.5 tons at 3" thick
Other Cultivars Available to Sub:	Yes
Special Needs:	

Till garden and amend soil with composted material such as mulched leaves or shredded pine.

Using the planting diagram, measure for plant placement and sit each plant in its proper place. Adjust placement based on the shape of the actual bed.

Dig each hole twice as wide as the root ball. Sprinkle in starter fertilizer to the bottom of the hole (follow directions on package for proper application). Set plant in hole. Push soil back around plant, tamping in tight with the handle end of the shovel to remove all air pockets. Tamp soil tight at top of root ball.

Repeat for each plant.

Water in all plants thoroughly.

Top beds with mulch, pine straw or other bedding materials to hold moisture and keep roots warm in winter and cool in summer.

Common Name	Adagio Miscanthus Grass
Scientific Name	Miscanthus sinensis 'Adagio'
Status	Perennial
Mature Size (H x W)	5x5
Pruning Category (1-5)	1
Watering Category (1-5)	1
Sun Category (1-5)	4
USDA Hardiness Zone:	6-10
Bloom Season	Summer

Common Name	Siberian Iris
Scientific Name	Iris sibirica
Status	Perennial
Mature Size (H x W)	2x2
Pruning Category (1-5)	1
Watering Category (1-5)	4
Sun Category (1-5)	3
USDA Hardiness Zone:	3-8
Bloom Season	Spring

Common Name	Blue Flag Iris
Scientific Name	Iris versicolor
Status	Perennial
Mature Size (H x W)	2x2
Pruning Category (1-5)	1
Watering Category (1-5)	4
Sun Category (1-5)	2
USDA Hardiness Zone:	3-8
Bloom Season	Spring

Common Name	Yellow Flag Iris
Scientific Name	Iris pseudacorus
Status	Perennial
Mature Size (H x W)	2x2
Pruning Category (1-5)	1
Watering Category (1-5)	4
Sun Category (1-5)	2
USDA Hardiness Zone:	3-8
Bloom Season	Spring

Common Name	Peony
Scientific Name	Paeonia
Status	Perennial
Mature Size (H x W)	2.5x4
Pruning Category (1-5)	1
Watering Category (1-5)	3
Sun Category (1-5)	3
USDA Hardiness Zone:	3-8
Bloom Season	Spring

Common Name	Blackeyed Susan
Scientific Name	Rudbeckia hirta
Status	Perennial
Mature Size (H x W)	2x2
Pruning Category (1-5)	1
Watering Category (1-5)	2
Sun Category (1-5)	4
USDA Hardiness Zone:	3-9
Bloom Season	Summer

Southern Belle

Perennial Beds

Description

This bed puts on a show all summer and on into the fall and first frost. The natural hillside is accent with boulders while the rising blooms from roses, asters and yarrow lead you up the stairs to the show stopping giant bloom of the hydrangea. Mulch the bed heavily in the winter to protect perennial roots.

Ingredients

(6) Limelight Hydrangea
(3) Autumn Joy Sedum
(3) White Drift Roses
(5) Fernleaf Yarrow
(3) Gold Lace Juniper

(2) Thyme
(3) Stokes Aster
(3) Obedient Plant
(5) Drift Roses

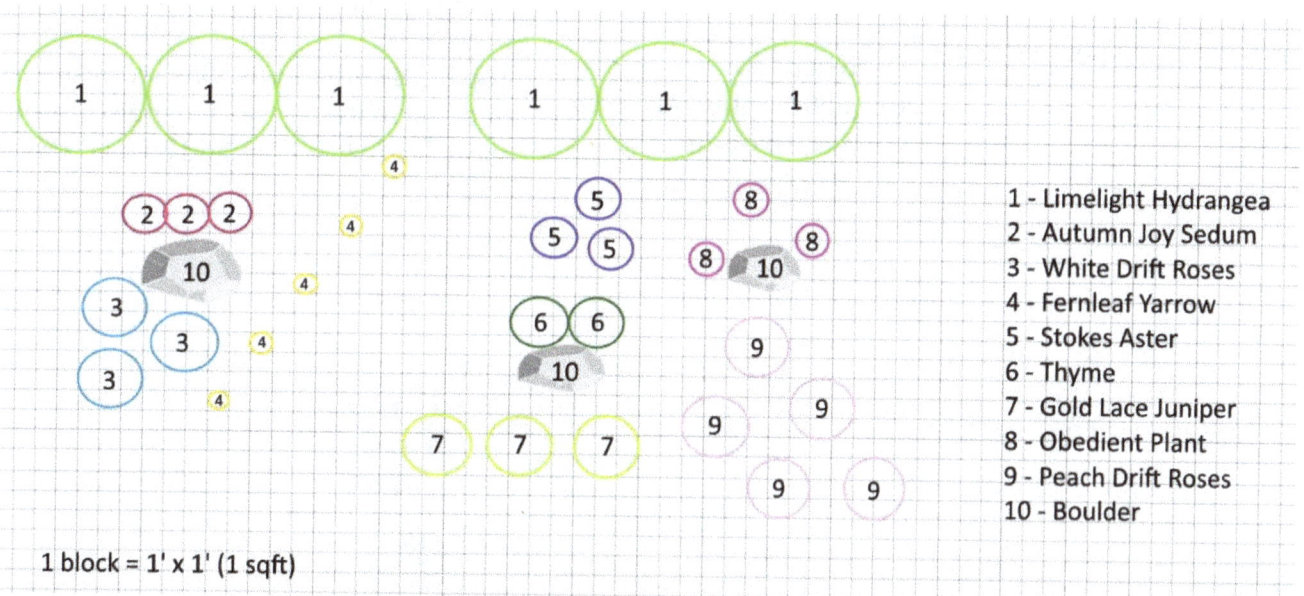

1 - Limelight Hydrangea
2 - Autumn Joy Sedum
3 - White Drift Roses
4 - Fernleaf Yarrow
5 - Stokes Aster
6 - Thyme
7 - Gold Lace Juniper
8 - Obedient Plant
9 - Peach Drift Roses
10 - Boulder

1 block = 1' x 1' (1 sqft)

Assembly Instructions

Garden Size (Approximate):	42'L x 23'W
Pruning Category:	1
Watering Needs:	2
Sun Requirements:	4
Plant Zones:	3-10
Bloom Colors:	White, Pink, Yellow, Blue, Purple, Peach
Bloom Time Range:	Spring-Fall
Average Time to Install:	16 hours
Approximate Bedding:	966sf
Mulch:	6 cuyds
Pine Straw:	23 bales
Rock:	12 tons at 3" thick
Other Cultivars Available to Sub:	Yes
Special Needs:	Dead head roses throughout the season to get more blooms.

Till garden and amend soil with composted material such as mulched leaves or shredded pine.

Using the planting diagram, set boulders by digging into the soil several inches to create a foundation slightly below the grade of the garden. Set the boulder on to the foundation then spread the removed soil around the boulders to bring the soil height back up to grade level.

Measure for plant placement and sit each plant in its proper place. Adjust placement based on the shape of the actual bed.

Dig each hole twice as wide as the root ball. Sprinkle in starter fertilizer to the bottom of the hole (follow directions on package for proper application). Set plant in hole. Push soil back around plant, tamping in tight with the handle end of the shovel to remove all air pockets. Tamp soil tight at top of root ball.

Repeat for each plant.

Water in all plants thoroughly.

Top beds with mulch, pine straw or other bedding materials to hold moisture and keep roots warm in winter and cool in summer.

Common Name	Limelight Hydrangea
Scientific Name	Hydrangea paniculala 'Limelight'
Status	Deciduous
Mature Size (H x W)	6x6
Pruning Category (1-5)	1
Watering Category (1-5)	3
Sun Category (1-5)	4
USDA Hardiness Zone:	4-9
Bloom Season	Summer

Common Name	Autumn Joy Sedum
Scientific Name	Hylotelephium telephium 'Autumn Joy'
Status	Perennial
Mature Size (H x W)	2x2
Pruning Category (1-5)	1
Watering Category (1-5)	1
Sun Category (1-5)	5
USDA Hardiness Zone:	3-8
Bloom Season	Fall

Common Name	Drift Rose
Scientific Name	Rosa 'Meijocos'
Status	Deciduous
Mature Size (H x W)	3x3
Pruning Category (1-5)	2
Watering Category (1-5)	2
Sun Category (1-5)	5
USDA Hardiness Zone:	5-10
Bloom Season	Summer

Common Name	Fernleaf Yarrow
Scientific Name	Achillea filipendulina
Status	Perennial
Mature Size (H x W)	2x2
Pruning Category (1-5)	1
Watering Category (1-5)	1
Sun Category (1-5)	3
USDA Hardiness Zone:	3-7
Bloom Season	Spring

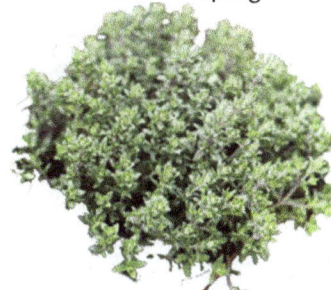

Common Name	Stokes Aster
Scientific Name	Stokesia laeis
Status	Perennial
Mature Size (H x W)	2x2
Pruning Category (1-5)	1
Watering Category (1-5)	2
Sun Category (1-5)	4
USDA Hardiness Zone:	8-9a
Bloom Season	Summer

Common Name	Thyme
Scientific Name	Thymus vulgaris
Status	Perennial
Mature Size (H x W)	1x2
Pruning Category (1-5)	1
Watering Category (1-5)	2
Sun Category (1-5)	4
USDA Hardiness Zone:	5-10
Bloom Season	Summer

Southern Belle

Common Name	Gold Lace Juniper
Scientific Name	Juniperus chinensis 'Gold Lace'
Status	Evergreen
Mature Size (H x W)	2.5x6
Pruning Category (1-5)	1
Watering Category (1-5)	1
Sun Category (1-5)	4
USDA Hardiness Zone:	6-9
Bloom Season	None

Perennial Beds

Common Name	Obedient Plant
Scientific Name	Physostegia virginia
Status	Perennial
Mature Size (H x W)	2x1
Pruning Category (1-5)	1
Watering Category (1-5)	2
Sun Category (1-5)	4
USDA Hardiness Zone:	3-10
Bloom Season	Fall

Sugar Daddy

Description

Bold crape myrtles are the backdrop for this simple yet beautiful garden bed. Shrub form crape myrtles accentuate the back and contrast the bold reds. Showy clethra with its white blooms takes center stage. The bed is a mix of deciduous shrubs and trees and perennial shrubs and requires little ongoing maintenance.

Ingredients

(3) Dynamite Crape Myrtle
(2) Dwarf Crape Myrtle (shrub form)
(1) Clethra Alnifolia

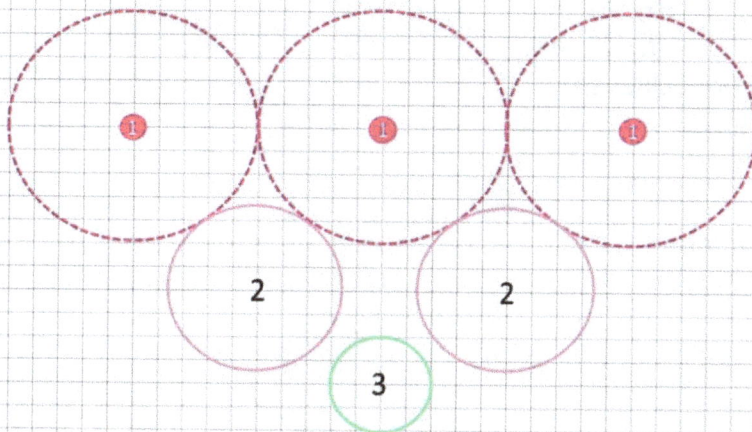

1 - Dynamite Crape Myrtle
2 - Dwarf Crape Myrtle (shrub form)
3 - Clethra Alnifolia

1 block = 1' x 1' (1 sqft)

Sugar Daddy

Perennial Beds

Assembly Instructions

Garden Size (Approximate):	30'L x 18'W
Pruning Category:	1
Watering Needs:	2
Sun Requirements:	3
Plant Zones:	3-11
Bloom Colors:	Red, Pink, White
Bloom Time Range:	Summer
Average Time to Install:	6 hours
Approximate Bedding:	540sf
Mulch:	3.3 cuyds
Pine Straw:	13 bales
Rock:	6.75 tons
Other Cultivars Available to Sub:	Yes
Special Needs:	This cultivar of crape myrtle is considered dwarf. There is no need to cut back every year (also called "knuckling").
	Clethra can tolerate salt spray in coastal areas.

Till garden and amend soil with composted material such as mulched leaves or shredded pine.

Using the planting diagram, measure for plant placement and sit each plant in its proper place. Adjust placement based on the shape of the actual bed.

Dig each hole twice as wide as the root ball. Sprinkle in starter fertilizer to the bottom of the hole (follow directions on package for proper application). Set plant in hole. Push soil back around plant, tamping in tight with the handle end of the shovel to remove all air pockets. Tamp soil tight at top of root ball.

Repeat for each plant.

Water in all plants thoroughly.

Top beds with mulch, pine straw or other bedding materials to hold moisture and keep roots warm in winter and cool in summer.

Common Name	Dynamite Crape Myrtle
Scientific Name	Lagerstroemia indica 'Whit II' Dynamite
Status	Deciduous
Mature Size (H x W)	15x10
Pruning Category (1-5)	1
Watering Category (1-5)	2
Sun Category (1-5)	4
USDA Hardiness Zone:	6-11
Bloom Season	Summer

Common Name	Dwarf Crape Myrtle (Shrub Form)
Scientific Name	Lagerstroemia 'Gamad I' Razzle Dazzle Cherry
Status	Deciduous
Mature Size (H x W)	6x6
Pruning Category (1-5)	1
Watering Category (1-5)	2
Sun Category (1-5)	4
USDA Hardiness Zone:	6-11
Bloom Season	Summer

Common Name	Clethra Alnifolia
Scientific Name	Clethra Alnifolia
Status	Deciduous
Mature Size (H x W)	5x4
Pruning Category (1-5)	1
Watering Category (1-5)	3
Sun Category (1-5)	2
USDA Hardiness Zone:	3-9
Bloom Season	Summer

Description

Larges spaces at the back side of properties are usually exposed to traffic, other properties or unwanted vistas. Close that gap with large cryptomeria as a back drop and more delicate shrubs in front. The tropical feel of the fatsia will accent the garden and give it a less closed-in vibe. Lower ground covering juniper and a focal point Hinoki cypress finish off the look.

Ingredients

(3) Cryptomeria
(3) Fatsia
(1) Hinoki Cypress
(3) Illicium Parviflorum (Anise)
(6) Gold Lace Juniper

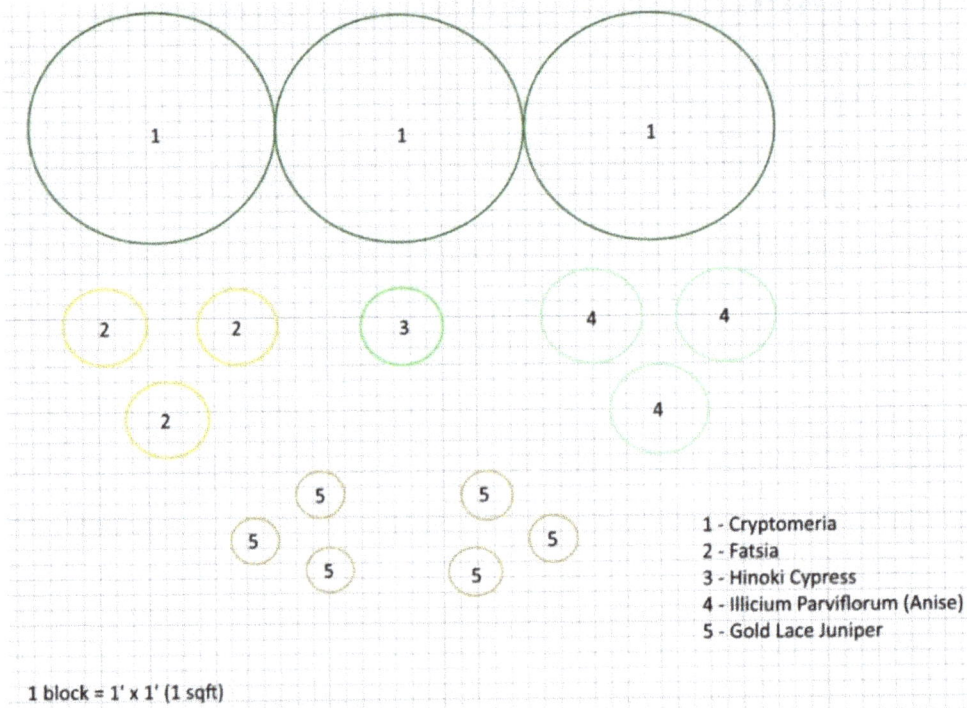

1 - Cryptomeria
2 - Fatsia
3 - Hinoki Cypress
4 - Illicium Parviflorum (Anise)
5 - Gold Lace Juniper

1 block = 1' x 1' (1 sqft)

Assembly Instructions

Garden Size (Approximate):	45'L x 38'W
Pruning Category:	1
Watering Needs:	2
Sun Requirements:	3
Plant Zones:	6-11
Bloom Colors:	White
Bloom Time Range:	Spring, Fall
Average Time to Install:	8 hours
Approximate Bedding:	1,710sf
Mulch:	10.5 cuyds
Pine Straw:	41 bales
Rock:	21 tons at 3" thick
Other Cultivars Available to Sub:	Yes
Special Needs:	

Till garden and amend soil with composted material such as mulched leaves or shredded pine.

Using the planting diagram, measure for plant placement and sit each plant in its proper place. Adjust placement based on the shape of the actual bed.

Dig each hole twice as wide as the root ball. Sprinkle in starter fertilizer to the bottom of the hole (follow directions on package for proper application). Set plant in hole. Push soil back around plant, tamping in tight with the handle end of the shovel to remove all air pockets. Tamp soil tight at top of root ball.

Repeat for each plant.

Water in all plants thoroughly.

Top beds with mulch, pine straw or other bedding materials to hold moisture and keep roots warm in winter and cool in summer.

Common Name	Cryptomeria
Scientific Name	Cryptomeria japonica
Status	Evergreen
Mature Size (H x W)	50x30
Pruning Category (1-5)	1
Watering Category (1-5)	1
Sun Category (1-5)	4
USDA Hardiness Zone:	6-9
Bloom Season	None

Common Name	Fatsia
Scientific Name	Fatsia japonica
Status	Evergreen
Mature Size (H x W)	5x5
Pruning Category (1-5)	1
Watering Category (1-5)	3
Sun Category (1-5)	3
USDA Hardiness Zone:	7-11
Bloom Season	Fall

Common Name	Hinoki Cypress
Scientific Name	Chamaecyparis obtusa
Status	Evergreen
Mature Size (H x W)	5x4
Pruning Category (1-5)	1
Watering Category (1-5)	1
Sun Category (1-5)	4
USDA Hardiness Zone:	6-9
Bloom Season	None

Common Name	Illicium
Scientific Name	Illicium Parviflorum
Status	Evergreen
Mature Size (H x W)	5x5
Pruning Category (1-5)	2
Watering Category (1-5)	1
Sun Category (1-5)	3
USDA Hardiness Zone:	7-10
Bloom Season	Spring

Common Name	Gold Lace Juniper
Scientific Name	Juniperus chinensis 'Gold Lace'
Status	Evergreen
Mature Size (H x W)	2.5x6
Pruning Category (1-5)	1
Watering Category (1-5)	1
Sun Category (1-5)	4
USDA Hardiness Zone:	6-9
Bloom Season	None

Description

Even cantankerous neighbors will have to appreciate the beauty of this bed, with or without the fence. The delicate branches of the butterfly shrub will grace the garden all summer as bees and hummingbirds delight in the fragrant blooms and opportunity to pollinate. Dry the rosemary leaves for a fragrant addition to an indoor arrangement. Allow the gardenias to grow to their natural height and shape for the most impact from their blooms.

Ingredients

(1) Butterfly Shrub
(6) August Beauty Gardenia
(1) Rosemary
(3) Blackeyed Susan
(3) Autumn Joy Sedum
(3) Shasta Daisy
(28) Ice Plant

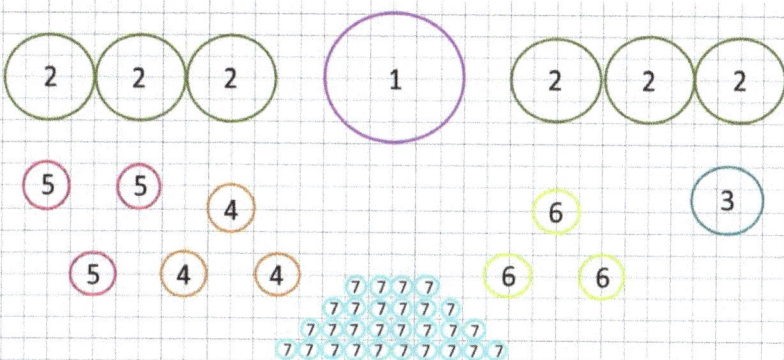

1 - Butterfly Shrub
2 - August Beauty Gardenia
3 - Rosemary
4 - Blackeyed Susan
5 - Autumn Joy Sedum
6 - Shasta Daisy
7 - Ice Plant

1 block = 1' x 1' (1 sqft)

Spectacular Debut

Assembly Instructions

Garden Size (Approximate):	34'L x 16'W
Pruning Category:	1
Watering Needs:	2
Sun Requirements:	4
Plant Zones:	3-11
Bloom Colors:	Purple, White, Blue, Yellow, Pink
Bloom Time Range:	Summer-Fall
Average Time to Install:	12 hours
Approximate Bedding:	544sf
Mulch:	3.3 cuyds
Pine Straw:	13 bales
Rock:	7 tons
Other Cultivars Available to Sub:	Yes
Special Needs:	

Till garden and amend soil with composted material such as mulched leaves or shredded pine.

Using the planting diagram, measure for plant placement and sit each plant in its proper place. Adjust placement based on the shape of the actual bed.

Dig each hole twice as wide as the root ball. Sprinkle in starter fertilizer to the bottom of the hole (follow directions on package for proper application). Set plant in hole. Push soil back around plant, tamping in tight with the handle end of the shovel to remove all air pockets. Tamp soil tight at top of root ball.

Repeat for each plant.

Water in all plants thoroughly.

Top beds with mulch, pine straw or other bedding materials to hold moisture and keep roots warm in winter and cool in summer.

Common Name	Butterfly Shrub
Scientific Name	Buddleia
Status	Deciduous
Mature Size (H x W)	6x4
Pruning Category (1-5)	2
Watering Category (1-5)	2
Sun Category (1-5)	5
USDA Hardiness Zone:	5-11
Bloom Season	Summer

Common Name	August Beauty Gardenia
Scientific Name	Gardenia jasminoides 'August Beauty'
Status	Evergreen
Mature Size (H x W)	5x5
Pruning Category (1-5)	2
Watering Category (1-5)	3
Sun Category (1-5)	4
USDA Hardiness Zone:	7-11
Bloom Season	Summer, Fall

Common Name	Rosemary
Scientific Name	Rosmarinus officinalis
Status	Perennial
Mature Size (H x W)	3x4
Pruning Category (1-5)	1
Watering Category (1-5)	2
Sun Category (1-5)	4
USDA Hardiness Zone:	5-10
Bloom Season	Summer

Common Name	Blackeyed Susan
Scientific Name	Rudbeckia hirta
Status	Perennial
Mature Size (H x W)	2x2
Pruning Category (1-5)	1
Watering Category (1-5)	2
Sun Category (1-5)	4
USDA Hardiness Zone:	3-9
Bloom Season	Summer

Common Name	Autumn Joy Sedum
Scientific Name	Hylotelephium telephium 'Autumn Joy'
Status	Perennial
Mature Size (H x W)	2x2
Pruning Category (1-5)	1
Watering Category (1-5)	1
Sun Category (1-5)	5
USDA Hardiness Zone:	3-8
Bloom Season	Fall

Common Name	Shasta Daisy
Scientific Name	Leucanthemum x superbum
Status	Perennial
Mature Size (H x W)	2.5x2.5
Pruning Category (1-5)	1
Watering Category (1-5)	2
Sun Category (1-5)	4
USDA Hardiness Zone:	4-10
Bloom Season	Summer

Common Name	Ice Plant
Scientific Name	Aizoaceae
Status	Perennial
Mature Size (H x W)	1X1
Pruning Category (1-5)	1
Watering Category (1-5)	2
Sun Category (1-5)	3
USDA Hardiness Zone:	6-8
Bloom Season	Summer

Description

Fences might make good neighbors, but they can also be an eyesore in the garden. Soften an unsightly fence with fluffy illicium and colorful Loropetalum. These evergreen beauties will hold color all year for a nice perennial garden back drop or stand alone to provide needed privacy. Repeat the pattern for longer beds.

Ingredients

(3) Illicium Parviflorum (Anise)
(5) Crimson Fire Loropetalum

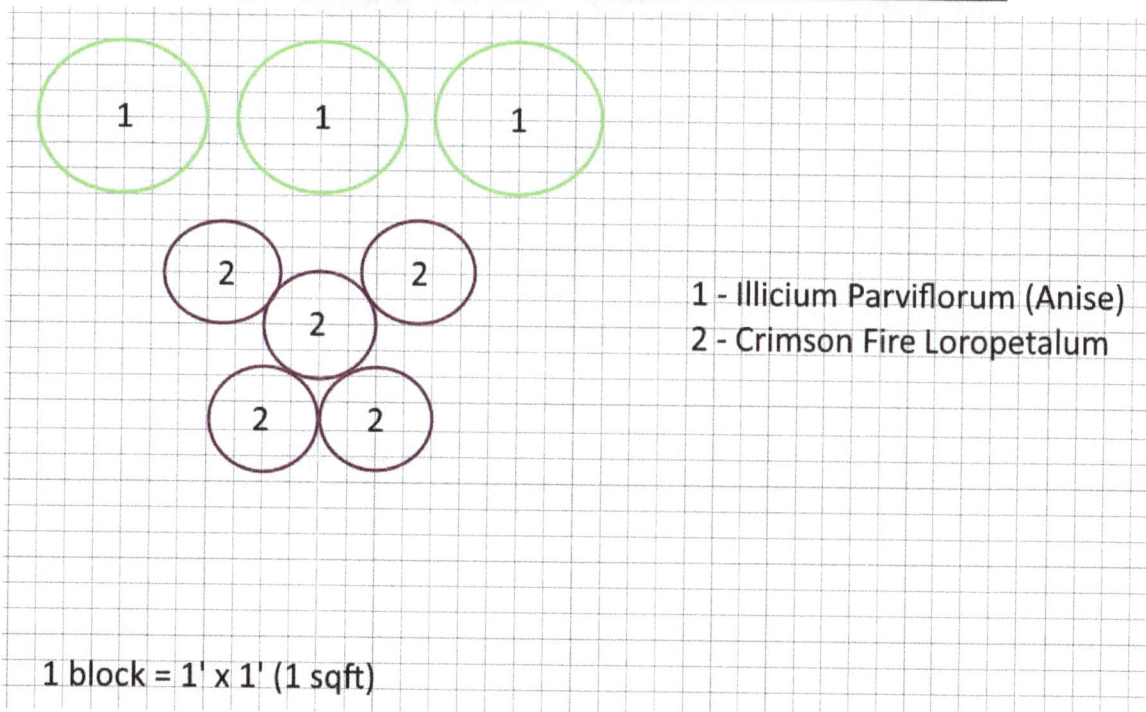

1 - Illicium Parviflorum (Anise)
2 - Crimson Fire Loropetalum

1 block = 1' x 1' (1 sqft)

Assembly Instructions

Garden Size (Approximate):	20'L x 17'W
Pruning Category:	2
Watering Needs:	2
Sun Requirements:	3
Plant Zones:	7-10
Bloom Colors:	Purple, White
Bloom Time Range:	Spring
Average Time to Install:	4 hours
Approximate Bedding:	340sf
Mulch:	2 cuyds
Pine Straw:	8 bales
Rock:	4.25 tons at 3" thick
Other Cultivars Available to Sub:	Yes
Special Needs:	

Till garden and amend soil with composted material such as mulched leaves or shredded pine.

Using the planting diagram, measure for plant placement and sit each plant in its proper place. Adjust placement based on the shape of the actual bed.

Dig each hole twice as wide as the root ball. Sprinkle in starter fertilizer to the bottom of the hole (follow directions on package for proper application). Set plant in hole. Push soil back around plant, tamping in tight with the handle end of the shovel to remove all air pockets. Tamp soil tight at top of root ball.

Repeat for each plant.

Water in all plants thoroughly.

Top beds with mulch, pine straw or other bedding materials to hold moisture and keep roots warm in winter and cool in summer.

Common Name	Illicium
Scientific Name	Illicium Parviflorum
Status	Evergreen
Mature Size (H x W)	5x5
Pruning Category (1-5)	2
Watering Category (1-5)	1
Sun Category (1-5)	3
USDA Hardiness Zone:	7-10
Bloom Season	Spring

Common Name	Crimson Fire Loropetalum
Scientific Name	Loropetalum chinense var. rubrum 'Crimson Fire'
Status	Evergreen
Mature Size (H x W)	4x4
Pruning Category (1-5)	2
Watering Category (1-5)	2
Sun Category (1-5)	3
USDA Hardiness Zone:	7-10
Bloom Season	Spring

Height of Excellence

Description

This garden maintains itself and maintains a need for privacy. The cone shaped arborvitae will hold their shape year after year with no pruning required and are smaller than traditional Leyland cypress or cryptomeria which end up taking over the entire landscape. Follow spacing guides for best results when plants are mature.

Ingredients

(3) Green Giant Arborvitae
(5) Emerald Green Arborvitae

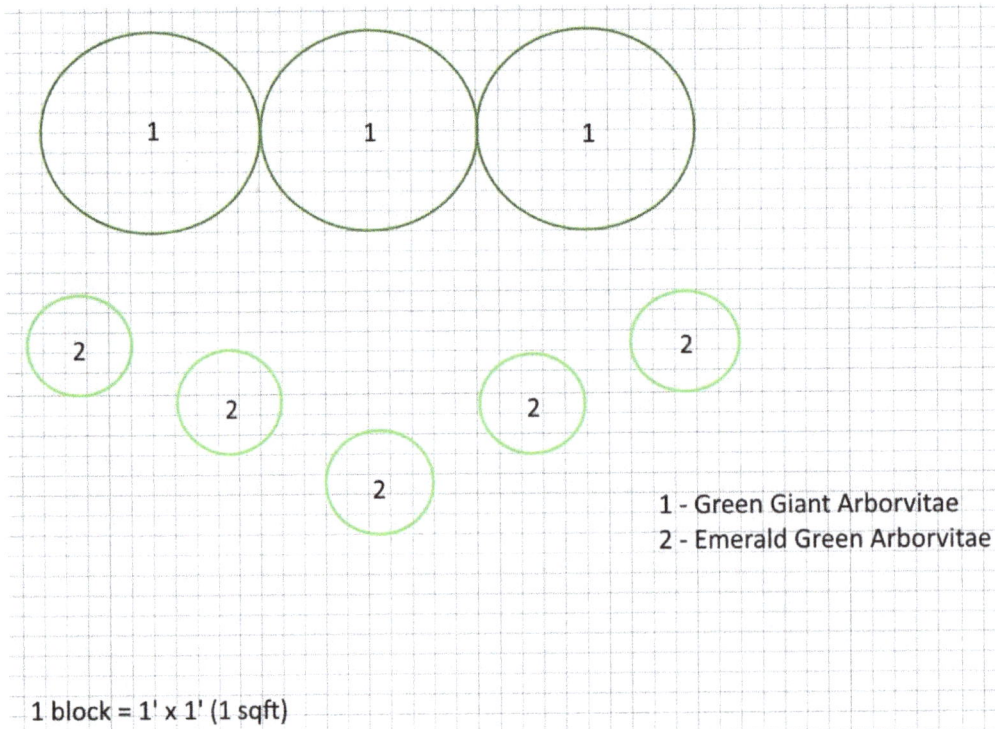

1 - Green Giant Arborvitae
2 - Emerald Green Arborvitae

1 block = 1' x 1' (1 sqft)

Assembly Instructions

Garden Size (Approximate):	34'L x 25'W
Pruning Category:	1
Watering Needs:	3
Sun Requirements:	4
Plant Zones:	4-8
Bloom Colors:	None
Bloom Time Range:	N/A
Average Time to Install:	8 hours
Approximate Bedding:	850sf
Mulch:	5.25 cuyds
Pine Straw:	20 bales
Rock:	10.6 tons at 3" thick
Other Cultivars Available to Sub:	Yes
Special Needs:	

Till garden and amend soil with composted material such as mulched leaves or shredded pine.

Using the planting diagram, measure for plant placement and sit each plant in its proper place. Adjust placement based on the shape of the actual bed.

Dig each hole twice as wide as the root ball. Sprinkle in starter fertilizer to the bottom of the hole (follow directions on package for proper application). Set plant in hole. Push soil back around plant, tamping in tight with the handle end of the shovel to remove all air pockets. Tamp soil tight at top of root ball.

Repeat for each plant.

Water in all plants thoroughly.

Top beds with mulch, pine straw or other bedding materials to hold moisture and keep roots warm in winter and cool in summer.

Common Name	Green Giant Arborvitae
Scientific Name	Thuja standishii × plicata 'Green Giant'
Status	Evergreen
Mature Size (H x W)	20x10
Pruning Category (1-5)	1
Watering Category (1-5)	3
Sun Category (1-5)	4
USDA Hardiness Zone:	4-8
Bloom Season	None

Common Name	Emerald Green Arborvitae
Scientific Name	Thuja occidentalis
Status	Evergreen
Mature Size (H x W)	15x5
Pruning Category (1-5)	1
Watering Category (1-5)	3
Sun Category (1-5)	4
USDA Hardiness Zone:	4-8
Bloom Season	None

Raising the Bar

Description

Privacy doesn't have to come at the cost of installing a green living wall. These staggered hollies will make for a great back drop to any landscape. Space based on guidelines for best results when plants are mature. The pokey nature of some of the hollies will deter unwanted deer from trespassing on your garden as well.

Ingredients

(2) Emily Brunner Holly
(3) Foster Holly
(3) Nellie R. Stevens Holly
(3) Mary Nell Holly

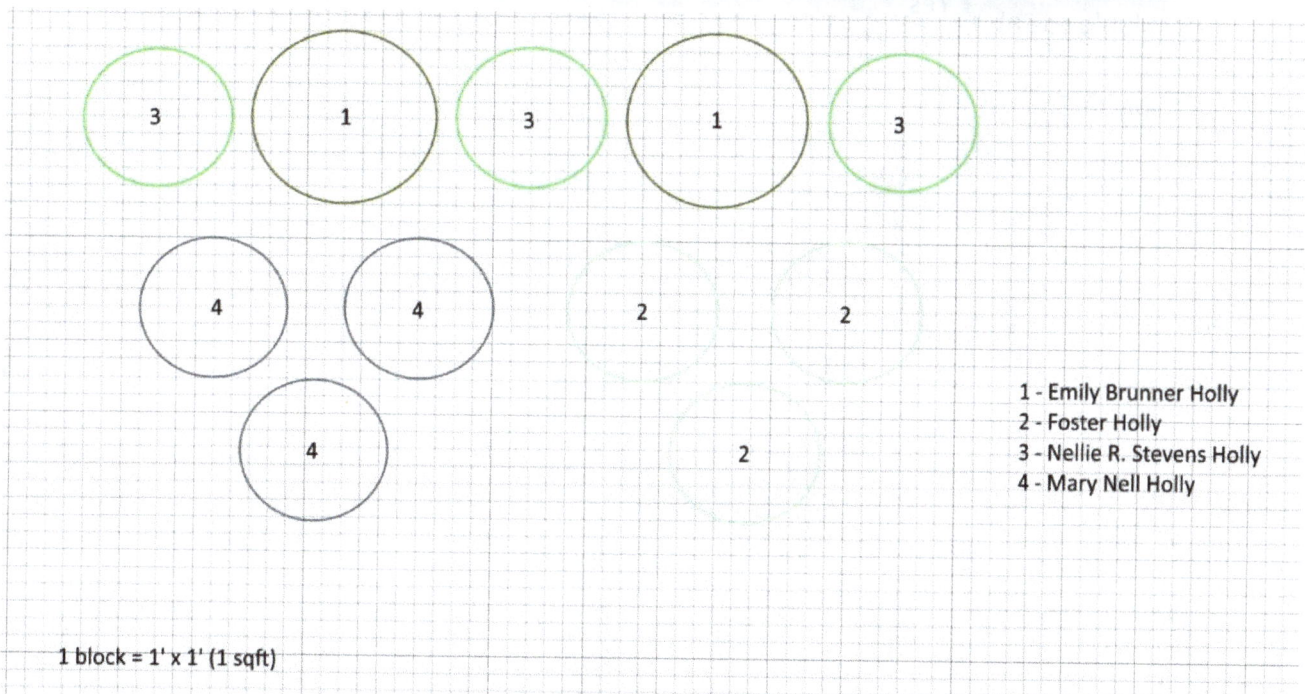

1 - Emily Brunner Holly
2 - Foster Holly
3 - Nellie R. Stevens Holly
4 - Mary Nell Holly

1 block = 1' x 1' (1 sqft)

Assembly Instructions

Garden Size (Approximate):	49'L x 28'W
Pruning Category:	5
Watering Needs:	2
Sun Requirements:	4
Plant Zones:	7-9
Bloom Colors:	None
Bloom Time Range:	N/A
Average Time to Install:	12 hours
Approximate Bedding:	1,372sf
Mulch:	8.5 cuyds
Pine Straw:	33 bales
Rock:	17 tons at 3" thick
Other Cultivars Available to Sub:	Yes
Special Needs:	

Till garden and amend soil with composted material such as mulched leaves or shredded pine.

Using the planting diagram, measure for plant placement and sit each plant in its proper place. Adjust placement based on the shape of the actual bed.

Dig each hole twice as wide as the root ball. Sprinkle in starter fertilizer to the bottom of the hole (follow directions on package for proper application). Set plant in hole. Push soil back around plant, tamping in tight with the handle end of the shovel to remove all air pockets. Tamp soil tight at top of root ball.

Repeat for each plant.

Water in all plants thoroughly.

Top beds with mulch, pine straw or other bedding materials to hold moisture and keep roots warm in winter and cool in summer.

Common Name	Emily Brunner Holly
Scientific Name	Ilex x 'Emily Brunner'
Status	Evergreen
Mature Size (H x W)	25x15
Pruning Category (1-5)	5
Watering Category (1-5)	2
Sun Category (1-5)	4
USDA Hardiness Zone:	7-9
Bloom Season	None-Inconspicuous

Common Name	Foster Holly
Scientific Name	Ilex x attenuata 'Fosteri'
Status	Evergreen
Mature Size (H x W)	20x7
Pruning Category (1-5)	5
Watering Category (1-5)	2
Sun Category (1-5)	4
USDA Hardiness Zone:	7-9
Bloom Season	None-Inconspicuous

Common Name	Nellie R. Stevens Holly
Scientific Name	Ilex x 'Nellie R. Stevens'
Status	Evergreen
Mature Size (H x W)	25x15
Pruning Category (1-5)	5
Watering Category (1-5)	2
Sun Category (1-5)	4
USDA Hardiness Zone:	7-9
Bloom Season	None-Inconspicuous

Common Name	Mary Nell Holly
Scientific Name	Ilex x 'Mary Nell'
Status	Evergreen
Mature Size (H x W)	15x8
Pruning Category (1-5)	5
Watering Category (1-5)	2
Sun Category (1-5)	4
USDA Hardiness Zone:	7-9
Bloom Season	None-Inconspicuous

La Tee Da

Description

Ferns create the perfect setting for a woodland garden. The natural boulder can be used to sit for a time and contemplate life. The delicate pink blooms of the rhododendron and azaleas will follow each other in spring and summer for a long, soft pink bloom. Winter will fill with color as the camellias bloom from December to February. Mulch the bed heavily in the colder months to protect ferns and hostas.

Ingredients

(1) Rhododendron Catawbiense
(3) Big Leaf Hosta
(3) George Tabor Azalea
(3) Camellia Japonica
(7) Autumn Fern
(5) Acorus Grass
(3) Foxtail Fern

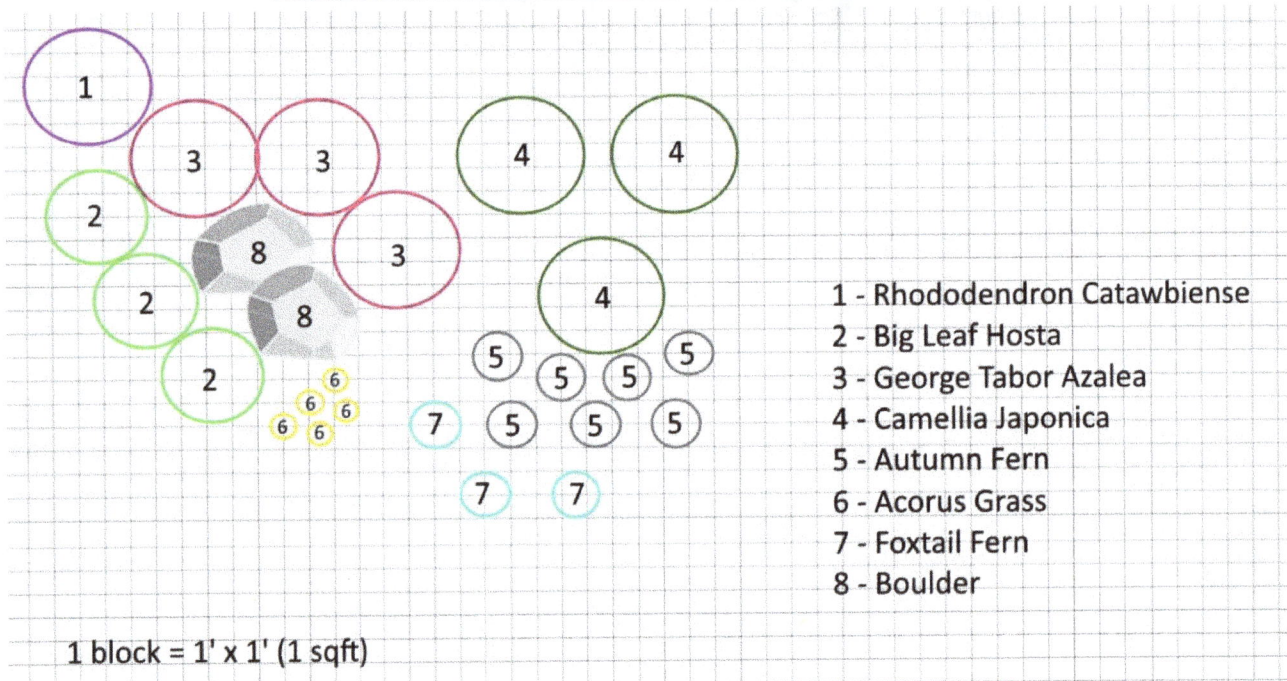

1 - Rhododendron Catawbiense
2 - Big Leaf Hosta
3 - George Tabor Azalea
4 - Camellia Japonica
5 - Autumn Fern
6 - Acorus Grass
7 - Foxtail Fern
8 - Boulder

1 block = 1' x 1' (1 sqft)

La Tee Da

Assembly Instructions

Garden Size (Approximate):	28'L x 21'W
Pruning Category:	1
Watering Needs:	3
Sun Requirements:	2
Plant Zones:	3-10
Bloom Colors:	Pink, White, Red
Bloom Time Range:	Winter, Spring
Average Time to Install:	12 hours
Approximate Bedding:	588sf
Mulch:	3.6 cuyds
Pine Straw:	14 bales
Rock:	7.3 tons at 3" thick
Other Cultivars Available to Sub:	Yes
Special Needs:	Plant rhododendron with ½ existing soil mixed with ½ shredded pine for better drainage.

Till garden and amend soil with composted material such as mulched leaves or shredded pine.

Using the planting diagram, set boulders by digging into the soil several inches to create a foundation slightly below the grade of the garden. Set the boulder on to the foundation then spread the removed soil around the boulders to bring the soil height back up to grade level.

Measure for plant placement and sit each plant in its proper place. Adjust placement based on the shape of the actual bed.

Dig each hole twice as wide as the root ball. Sprinkle in starter fertilizer to the bottom of the hole (follow directions on package for proper application). Set plant in hole. Push soil back around plant, tamping in tight with the handle end of the shovel to remove all air pockets. Tamp soil tight at top of root ball.

Repeat for each plant.

Water in all plants thoroughly.

Top beds with mulch, pine straw or other bedding materials to hold moisture and keep roots warm in winter and cool in summer.

Common Name	Rhododendron Catawbiense
Scientific Name	Rhododendron Catawbiense
Status	Evergreen
Mature Size (H x W)	8x6
Pruning Category (1-5)	1
Watering Category (1-5)	3
Sun Category (1-5)	3
USDA Hardiness Zone:	4-8
Bloom Season	Spring

Common Name	Big Leaf Hosta
Scientific Name	Hosta
Status	Perennial
Mature Size (H x W)	4x4
Pruning Category (1-5)	1
Watering Category (1-5)	2
Sun Category (1-5)	2
USDA Hardiness Zone:	3-8
Bloom Season	Summer

Common Name	George Tabor Azalea
Scientific Name	Rhododendron x 'George Tabor'
Status	Evergreen
Mature Size (H x W)	5x5
Pruning Category (1-5)	2
Watering Category (1-5)	3
Sun Category (1-5)	3
USDA Hardiness Zone:	7-9
Bloom Season	Spring

Common Name	Camellia Japonica
Scientific Name	Camellia japonica
Status	Evergreen
Mature Size (H x W)	12x6
Pruning Category (1-5)	1
Watering Category (1-5)	2
Sun Category (1-5)	3
USDA Hardiness Zone:	7-10
Bloom Season	Winter

Common Name	Autumn Fern
Scientific Name	Dryopteris erythrosora
Status	Perennial
Mature Size (H x W)	2x2
Pruning Category (1-5)	1
Watering Category (1-5)	3
Sun Category (1-5)	2
USDA Hardiness Zone:	4-8
Bloom Season	None

Common Name	Acorus Grass
Scientific Name	Acorus gramineus
Status	Perennial
Mature Size (H x W)	1x1
Pruning Category (1-5)	1
Watering Category (1-5)	1
Sun Category (1-5)	2
USDA Hardiness Zone:	6-9
Bloom Season	None

Common Name	Foxtail Fern
Scientific Name	Asparagus aethiopicus
Status	Perennial
Mature Size (H x W)	2x2
Pruning Category (1-5)	1
Watering Category (1-5)	3
Sun Category (1-5)	2
USDA Hardiness Zone:	4-8
Bloom Season	None

Description

Keep it soft and easy with this delicate spring blooming woodland garden. The boulders and rhododendron add a very natural feel to the landscape like a stroll through a mountain trail. Cast iron plant adds height and texture while the lungwort (ugly name for a pretty plant) adds blooms and interest out front. Keep the blue fescue in check at the end of each season by pulling out unwanted volunteer sprigs.

Ingredients

(3) Rhododendron Catawbiense
(1) Artemisia
(4) Wood Fern
(3) Lungwort
(3) Sea Urchin Blue Fescue
(1) Otto Luyken Laurel
(3) Cast Iron Plant

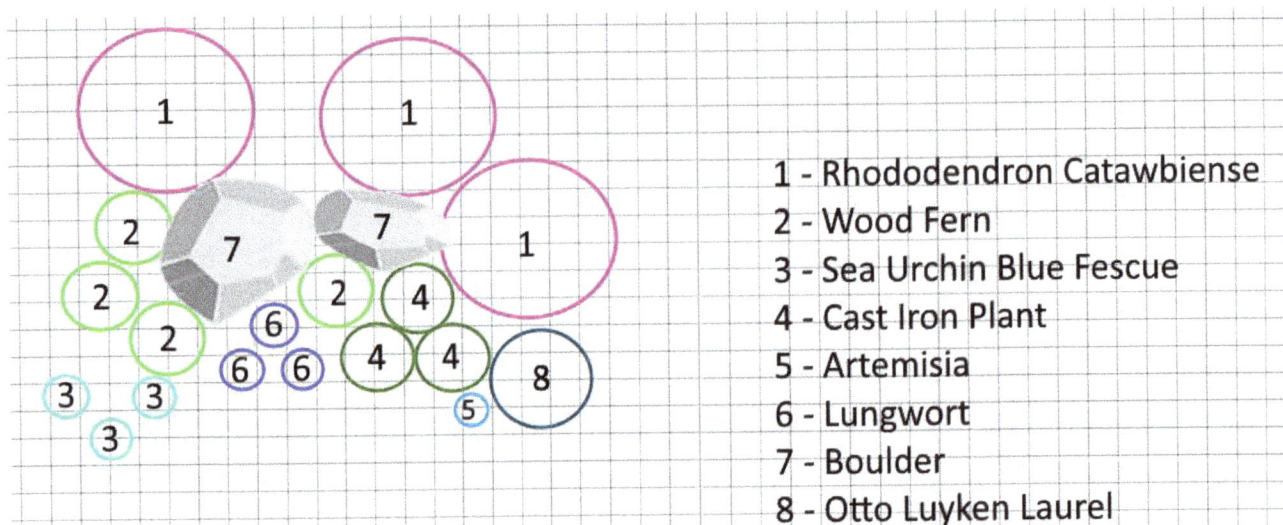

1 - Rhododendron Catawbiense
2 - Wood Fern
3 - Sea Urchin Blue Fescue
4 - Cast Iron Plant
5 - Artemisia
6 - Lungwort
7 - Boulder
8 - Otto Luyken Laurel

1 block = 1' x 1' (1 sqft)

Assembly Instructions

Garden Size (Approximate):	19'L x 16'W
Pruning Category:	1
Watering Needs:	2
Sun Requirements:	3
Plant Zones:	4-11
Bloom Colors:	Pink, White
Bloom Time Range:	Spring, Summer
Average Time to Install:	9 hours
Approximate Bedding:	304sf
Mulch:	2 cuyds
Pine Straw:	8 bales
Rock:	3.8 tons at 3" thick
Other Cultivars Available to Sub:	Yes
Special Needs:	Plant rhododendron with ½ existing soil mixed with ½ shredded pine for better drainage

Till garden and amend soil with composted material such as mulched leaves or shredded pine.

Using the planting diagram, set boulders by digging into the soil several inches to create a foundation slightly below the grade of the garden. Set the boulder on to the foundation then spread the removed soil around the boulders to bring the soil height back up to grade level.

Measure for plant placement and sit each plant in its proper place. Adjust placement based on the shape of the actual bed.

Dig each hole twice as wide as the root ball. Sprinkle in starter fertilizer to the bottom of the hole (follow directions on package for proper application). Set plant in hole. Push soil back around plant, tamping in tight with the handle end of the shovel to remove all air pockets. Tamp soil tight at top of root ball.

Repeat for each plant.

Water in all plants thoroughly.

Top beds with mulch, pine straw or other bedding materials to hold moisture and keep roots warm in winter and cool in summer.

Easy Street

Common Name	Rhododendron Catawbiense
Scientific Name	Rhododendron Catawbiense
Status	Evergreen
Mature Size (H x W)	8x6
Pruning Category (1-5)	1
Watering Category (1-5)	3
Sun Category (1-5)	3
USDA Hardiness Zone:	4-8
Bloom Season	Spring

Common Name	Sea Urchin Blue Fescue
Scientific Name	Festuca glauca 'Sea Urchin'
Status	Perennial
Mature Size (H x W)	1x1
Pruning Category (1-5)	1
Watering Category (1-5)	2
Sun Category (1-5)	3
USDA Hardiness Zone:	4-8
Bloom Season	Summer

Common Name	Artemesia
Scientific Name	Artemisia vulgaris
Status	Perennial
Mature Size (H x W)	3x10
Pruning Category (1-5)	1
Watering Category (1-5)	1
Sun Category (1-5)	3
USDA Hardiness Zone:	4-9
Bloom Season	None

Woodland Gardens

Common Name	Wood Fern
Scientific Name	Dryopteris
Status	Perennial
Mature Size (H x W)	4x3
Pruning Category (1-5)	1
Watering Category (1-5)	3
Sun Category (1-5)	2
USDA Hardiness Zone:	4-8
Bloom Season	None

Common Name	Cast Iron Plant
Scientific Name	Aspidistra elatior
Status	Perennial
Mature Size (H x W)	2x4
Pruning Category (1-5)	1
Watering Category (1-5)	1
Sun Category (1-5)	2
USDA Hardiness Zone:	7-11
Bloom Season	Spring-Inconspicuous

Common Name	Lungwort
Scientific Name	Pulmonaria officinalis
Status	Perennial
Mature Size (H x W)	1x1
Pruning Category (1-5)	1
Watering Category (1-5)	2
Sun Category (1-5)	4
USDA Hardiness Zone:	4-8
Bloom Season	Spring

Common Name	Otto Luyken Laurel
Scientific Name	Prunus laurocerasus
Status	Evergreen
Mature Size (H x W)	3.5x3.5
Pruning Category (1-5)	3
Watering Category (1-5)	2
Sun Category (1-5)	3
USDA Hardiness Zone:	6-8
Bloom Season	Spring

Description

There is plenty of charm to this shaded, woodland garden. Create the backdrop with spring blooming rhododendron and the soft texture of an Eastern hemlock. Front and center is the lovely bulbous bloom of the agapanthus. Create texture and interest with the cast iron plant and ferns for the perfect woodland setting.

Ingredients

(1) Eastern Hemlock
(2) Rhododendron Catawbiense
(1) Gold Dust Aucuba
(5) Wood Fern
(3) Agapanthus
(3) Cast Iron Plant

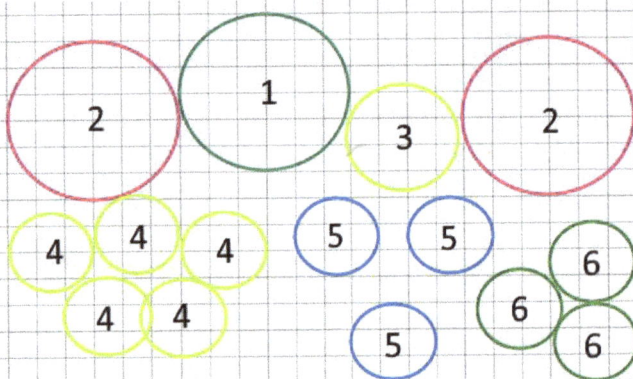

1 - Eastern Hemlock
2 - Rhododendron Catawbiense
3 - Gold Dust Aucuba
4 - Wood Fern
5 - Agapanthus
6 - Cast Iron Plant

1 block = 1' x 1' (1 sqft)

Prince Charming

Woodland Gardens

Assembly Instructions

Garden Size (Approximate):	22'L x 14'W
Pruning Category:	1
Watering Needs:	3
Sun Requirements:	2
Plant Zones:	4-11
Bloom Colors:	Pink, Blue
Bloom Time Range:	Spring
Average Time to Install:	8 hours
Approximate Bedding:	308sf
Mulch:	2 cuyds
Pine Straw:	7 bales
Rock:	3.8 tons at 3" thick
Other Cultivars Available to Sub:	Yes
Special Needs:	Hemlock requires well drained soil. Plant rhododendron with ½ existing soil mixed with ½ shredded pine for better drainage

Till garden and amend soil with composted material such as mulched leaves or shredded pine.

Using the planting diagram, measure for plant placement and sit each plant in its proper place. Adjust placement based on the shape of the actual bed.

Dig each hole twice as wide as the root ball. Sprinkle in starter fertilizer to the bottom of the hole (follow directions on package for proper application). Set plant in hole. Push soil back around plant, tamping in tight with the handle end of the shovel to remove all air pockets. Tamp soil tight at top of root ball.

Repeat for each plant.

Water in all plants thoroughly.

Top beds with mulch, pine straw or other bedding materials to hold moisture and keep roots warm in winter and cool in summer.

Prince Charming

Common Name	Eastern Hemlock
Scientific Name	Tsuga canadensis
Status	Evergreen
Mature Size (H x W)	6x6
Pruning Category (1-5)	1
Watering Category (1-5)	3
Sun Category (1-5)	2
USDA Hardiness Zone:	5-7
Bloom Season	None

Common Name	Gold Dust Aucuba
Scientific Name	Aucuba japonica 'Gold Dust'
Status	Evergreen
Mature Size (H x W)	4x4
Pruning Category (1-5)	2
Watering Category (1-5)	2
Sun Category (1-5)	2
USDA Hardiness Zone:	7b-10
Bloom Season	None

Common Name	Agapanthus
Scientific Name	Agapanthus africanus
Status	Perennial
Mature Size (H x W)	2.5x2.5
Pruning Category (1-5)	1
Watering Category (1-5)	2
Sun Category (1-5)	2
USDA Hardiness Zone:	8-11
Bloom Season	Spring

Woodland Gardens

Common Name	Rhododendron Catawbiense
Scientific Name	Rhododendron Catawbiense
Status	Evergreen
Mature Size (H x W)	8x6
Pruning Category (1-5)	1
Watering Category (1-5)	3
Sun Category (1-5)	3
USDA Hardiness Zone:	4-8
Bloom Season	Spring

Common Name	Wood Fern
Scientific Name	Dryopteris
Status	Perennial
Mature Size (H x W)	4x3
Pruning Category (1-5)	1
Watering Category (1-5)	3
Sun Category (1-5)	2
USDA Hardiness Zone:	4-8
Bloom Season	None

Common Name	Cast Iron Plant
Scientific Name	Aspidistra elatior
Status	Perennial
Mature Size (H x W)	2x4
Pruning Category (1-5)	1
Watering Category (1-5)	1
Sun Category (1-5)	2
USDA Hardiness Zone:	7-11
Bloom Season	Spring-Inconspicuous

Counting Sheep

Woodland Gardens

Description

This garden evokes feelings of cool nights and smores around the campfire. Use it as a back drop to a more elaborate woodland setting or let it stand alone with its bright colors rarely found in wooded areas. Trim back the elderberry at the end of the season to prevent drooping on to other plants over the years. Mulch heuchera and clethra heavily over the winter to protect tender roots.

Ingredients

(1) Elderberry Lemony Lime
(3) Clethra Alnifolia
(3) Soft Caress Mahonia
(5) Heuchera

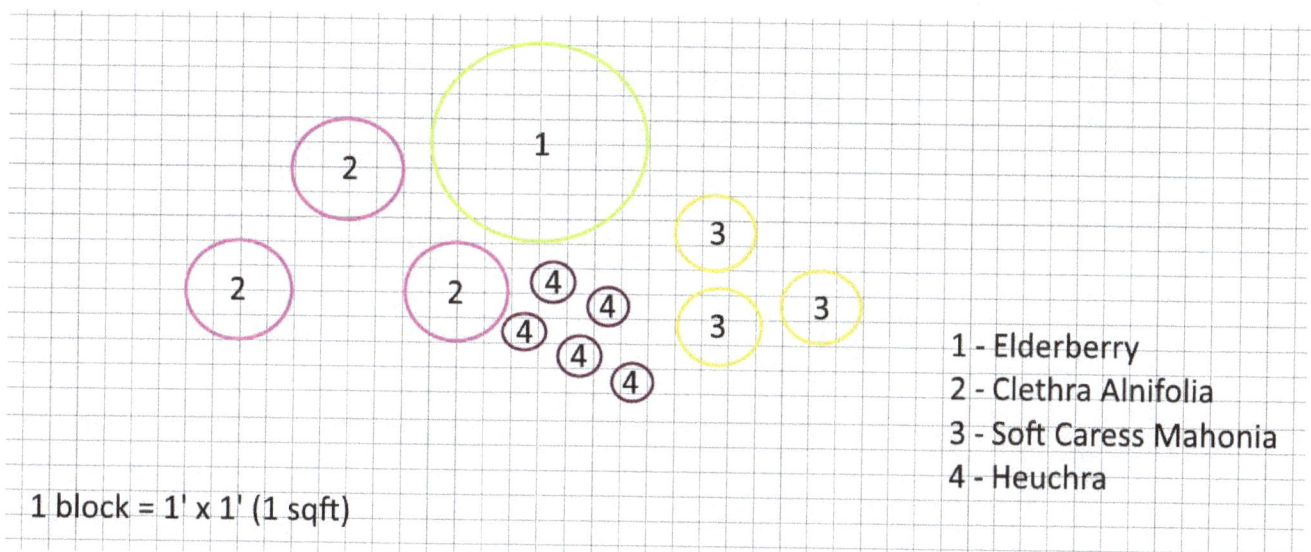

1 block = 1' x 1' (1 sqft)

1 - Elderberry
2 - Clethra Alnifolia
3 - Soft Caress Mahonia
4 - Heuchra

Assembly Instructions

Garden Size (Approximate):	25'L x 14'W
Pruning Category:	1
Watering Needs:	2
Sun Requirements:	2
Plant Zones:	3-9
Bloom Colors:	White
Bloom Time Range:	Spring-Winter
Average Time to Install:	6 hours
Approximate Bedding:	350sf
Mulch:	2 cuyds
Pine Straw:	8 bales
Rock:	4.3 tons
Other Cultivars Available to Sub:	Yes
Special Needs:	Clethra can tolerate salt spray in coastal areas.

Till garden and amend soil with composted material such as mulched leaves or shredded pine.

Using the planting diagram, measure for plant placement and sit each plant in its proper place. Adjust placement based on the shape of the actual bed.

Dig each hole twice as wide as the root ball. Sprinkle in starter fertilizer to the bottom of the hole (follow directions on package for proper application). Set plant in hole. Push soil back around plant, tamping in tight with the handle end of the shovel to remove all air pockets. Tamp soil tight at top of root ball.

Repeat for each plant.

Water in all plants thoroughly.

Top beds with mulch, pine straw or other bedding materials to hold moisture and keep roots warm in winter and cool in summer.

Common Name	Elderberry Lemony Lace
Scientific Name	Sambucus racemosa 'Lemony Lace'
Status	Deciduous
Mature Size (H x W)	5x5
Pruning Category (1-5)	1
Watering Category (1-5)	3
Sun Category (1-5)	2
USDA Hardiness Zone:	3-7
Bloom Season	Spring

Common Name	Clethra Alnifolia
Scientific Name	Clethra Alnifolia
Status	Deciduous
Mature Size (H x W)	5x4
Pruning Category (1-5)	1
Watering Category (1-5)	3
Sun Category (1-5)	2
USDA Hardiness Zone:	3-9
Bloom Season	Summer

Common Name	Soft Caress Mahonia
Scientific Name	Berberis ganpinensis 'Soft Caress'
Status	Evergreen
Mature Size (H x W)	3x3
Pruning Category (1-5)	1
Watering Category (1-5)	2
Sun Category (1-5)	2
USDA Hardiness Zone:	7-9
Bloom Season	Winter

Common Name	Heuchera
Scientific Name	Heuchera
Status	Perennial
Mature Size (H x W)	2x3
Pruning Category (1-5)	1
Watering Category (1-5)	2
Sun Category (1-5)	2
USDA Hardiness Zone:	4-9
Bloom Season	Summer

Description

A stroll in the woods can evoke romantic feelings and this garden woodland bed doesn't disappoint. The variety of textures rarely seen in a woodland setting make it stand out in your landscape. Give the leather leaf mahonia plenty of room to grow and keep it as a stand-alone focal point for best results. Mulch the entire bed heavily in the winter to protect roots. Keep soil evenly moist throughout hotter months.

Ingredients

(1) Leather Leaf Mahonia
(2) Globosa Nana Dwarf Cryptomeria
(1) Aucuba Japonica
(3) Soft Caress Mahonia
(3) Astilbe
(1) Fatsia

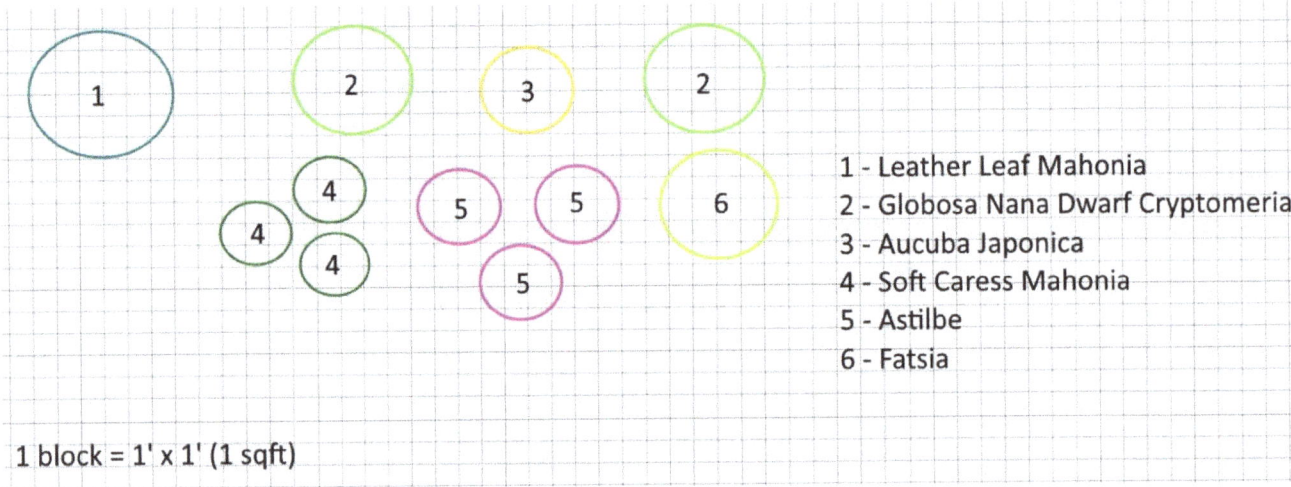

1 - Leather Leaf Mahonia
2 - Globosa Nana Dwarf Cryptomeria
3 - Aucuba Japonica
4 - Soft Caress Mahonia
5 - Astilbe
6 - Fatsia

1 block = 1' x 1' (1 sqft)

Stealing Kisses

Woodland Gardens

Assembly Instructions

Garden Size (Approximate):	32'L x 14'W
Pruning Category:	1
Watering Needs:	2
Sun Requirements:	2
Plant Zones:	3-11
Bloom Colors:	Yellow, White
Bloom Time Range:	Summer-Winter
Average Time to Install:	6 hours
Approximate Bedding:	448sf
Mulch:	2.75 cuyds
Pine Straw:	11 bales
Rock:	5.6 tons
Other Cultivars Available to Sub:	Yes
Special Needs:	

Till garden and amend soil with composted material such as mulched leaves or shredded pine.

Using the planting diagram, measure for plant placement and sit each plant in its proper place. Adjust placement based on the shape of the actual bed.

Dig each hole twice as wide as the root ball. Sprinkle in starter fertilizer to the bottom of the hole (follow directions on package for proper application). Set plant in hole. Push soil back around plant, tamping in tight with the handle end of the shovel to remove all air pockets. Tamp soil tight at top of root ball.

Repeat for each plant.

Water in all plants thoroughly.

Top beds with mulch, pine straw or other bedding materials to hold moisture and keep roots warm in winter and cool in summer.

Common Name	Leather Leaf Mahonia
Scientific Name	Mahonia bealei
Status	Evergreen
Mature Size (H x W)	6x4
Pruning Category (1-5)	1
Watering Category (1-5)	2
Sun Category (1-5)	2
USDA Hardiness Zone:	7-9
Bloom Season	Winter

Common Name	Nana Globosa Dwarf Cryptomeria
Scientific Name	Cryptomeria japonica 'Globosa Nana'
Status	Evergreen
Mature Size (H x W)	4x4
Pruning Category (1-5)	1
Watering Category (1-5)	1
Sun Category (1-5)	3
USDA Hardiness Zone:	6-9
Bloom Season	None

Common Name	Aucuba Japonica
Scientific Name	Aucuba japonica
Status	Evergreen
Mature Size (H x W)	6x4
Pruning Category (1-5)	2
Watering Category (1-5)	2
Sun Category (1-5)	2
USDA Hardiness Zone:	7b-10
Bloom Season	None

Common Name	Soft Caress Mahonia
Scientific Name	Berberis ganpinensis 'Soft Caress'
Status	Evergreen
Mature Size (H x W)	3x3
Pruning Category (1-5)	1
Watering Category (1-5)	2
Sun Category (1-5)	2
USDA Hardiness Zone:	7-9
Bloom Season	Winter

Common Name	Astilbe
Scientific Name	Astilbe chinensis
Status	Perennial
Mature Size (H x W)	2x2
Pruning Category (1-5)	1
Watering Category (1-5)	2
Sun Category (1-5)	2
USDA Hardiness Zone:	3-8
Bloom Season	Summer

Common Name	Fatsia
Scientific Name	Fatsia japonica
Status	Evergreen
Mature Size (H x W)	5x5
Pruning Category (1-5)	1
Watering Category (1-5)	3
Sun Category (1-5)	3
USDA Hardiness Zone:	7-11
Bloom Season	Fall

Scientific Name	Common Name	Status	Size (hxw)	Pruning 1-5	Water 1-5	Sun 1-5	Zone	Bloom Season	Special Needs
Abelia x grandiflora	Glossy Abelia	Semi Deciduous	3x3	1	2	4	6-9	Fall	
Abelia x grandiflora 'Edward Goucher'	Edward Goucher Abelia	Semi Deciduous	3x3	1	2	4	6-9	Fall	
Abelia x grandiflora 'Kaleidoscope'	Kaleidoscope Abelia	Semi Deciduous	3x3	1	2	4	6-9	Fall	
Abelia x grandiflora 'Mardi Gras'	Mardi Gras Abelia	Semi Deciduous	3x3	1	2	4	6-9	Fall	
Acer palmatum 'Bloodgood'	Bloodgood Japanese Maple	Deciduous	15x10	1	2	4	5-8	None	
Acer palmatum 'Emperor I'	Emperor Japanese Maple	Deciduous	15x10	1	2	4	5-8	None	
Acer palmatum var dissectum	Dissectum Japanese Maple	Deciduous	6x9	2	2	3	5-8	None	
Achillea filipendulina	Fernleaf Yarrow	Perennial	2x2	1	1	3	3-7	Spring	
Acorus gramineus	Acorus Grass	Perennial	1x1	1	1	2	6-9	None	
Agapanthus africanus	Agapanthus	Perennial	2.5x2.5	1	2	2	8-11	Spring	
Agave shawii x attenuata 'Blue Flame'	Agave	Succulent	5x5	1	1	5	8-10	None	
Aizoaceae	Ice Plant	Perennial	1x1	1	2	3	6-8	Summer	Annual in zones 4-5
Ajuga reptans 'Chocolate Chip'	Chocolate Chip Ajuga	Evergreen	2x2	1	3	3	4-9	Spring	
Allium schoenoprasum	Chives	Perennial	2x2	1	2	4	3-9	Summer	
Anethum graveolens	Dill	Perennial	3x2	1	1	4	3-11	Summer	
Artemisia vulgaris	Artemisia	Perennial	3x10	1	1	3	4-9	None	
Asparagus aethiopicus	Foxtail Fern	Perennial	2x2	1	3	2	4-8	None	
Aspidistra elatior	Cast Iron Plant	Perennial	2x4	1	1	2	7-11	Spring-Inconspicuous	
Astilbe chinensis	Astilbe	Perennial	2x2	1	2	2	3-8	Summer	Shade in hotter climates
Athyrium niponicum	Japanese Painted Fern	Perennial	2x2	1	3	2	4-8	None	
Aucuba japonica	Aucuba Japonica	Evergreen	6x4	2	2	2	7b-10	None	Needs well drained soil
Aucuba japonica 'Gold Dust'	Gold Dust Aucuba	Evergreen	4x4	2	2	2	7b-10	None	Needs well drained soil
Berberis ganpinensis 'Soft Caress'	Soft Caress Mahonia	Evergreen	3x3	1	2	2	7-9	Winter	
Borago officinalis	Borage	Annual	2x2	1	2	4	NA	Summer	Annual but self-seeding readily
Buddleia	Butterfly Shrub	Deciduous	6x4	2	2	5	5-11	Summer	Use wooly butterfly bush for hotter climates
Buddleia	Dwarf Butterfly Shrub	Deciduous	3x3	2	2	5	5-11	Summer	Use wooly butterfly bush for hotter climates
Buxus microphylla var. japonica 'Green Beauty'	Green Beauty Boxwood	Evergreen	4x4	4	3	4	4-9	None	

Scientific Name	Common Name	Status	Size hxw)	Pruning 1-5	Water 1-5	Sun 1-5	Zone	Bloom Season	Special Needs
Buxus microphylla var. japonica 'Gregem'	Baby Gem Boxwood	Evergreen	2x2	4	3	4	4-9	None	
Buxus microphylla 'Wintergreen'	Wintergreen Boxwood	Evergreen	3x4	4	3	4	4-9	None	
Buxus sempervirens	American Boxwood	Evergreen	5x5	4	3	4	4-9	None	
Camellia japonica	Camellia Japonica	Evergreen	12x6	1	2	3	7-10	Winter	Need 5.5-6.5 pH soil for best results
Camellia sasanqua	Sasanqua Camellia	Evergreen	12x6	1	2	3	7-10	Spring	Need 5.5-6.5 pH soil for best results
Canna indica	Canna Lily	Perennial	6x4	1	3	4	4-9	Summer	
Caryopteris	Caryopteris	Perennial	3x3	1	2	4	5-9	Summer	
Catharanthus roseus	Vinca	Annual	1.5x1.5	1	1	5	4-8	Summer	
Cedrus deodara	Deodar Cedar	Evergreen	50x30	1	2	3	6-7	None	Mulch roots heavily to cool in warmer zones
Cephalotaxus harringtonia 'Prostrata'	Dwarf Plum Yew	Evergreen	3x3	1	2	3	4-8	None	
Chaenomeles	Flowering Quince	Deciduous	6x5	2	2	4	4-10	Spring	Acidic soil pH 7 or less
Chamaecyparis	Gold Mop Cypress	Evergreen	6x6	1	1	4	6-9	None	
Chamaecyparis obtusa	Hinoki Cypress	Evergreen	5x4	1	1	4	6-9	None	
Chamaecyparis pisifera 'Gold Thread'	Gold Thread Cypress	Evergreen	12x10	1	1	4	6-9	None	
Clethra Alnifolia	Clethra Alnifolia	Deciduous	5x4	1	3	2	3-9	Summer	Can tolerate salt spray
Cordyline fruticosa	Cordyline	Tropical	3x2	1	1	5	10-11	Summer	
Coriandum sativum	Cilantro	Perennial	3x3	1	2	4	3-11	Summer	Zone 3-8, plant in spring. 9-11 plant in fall or winter
Cornus florida	White Dogwood	Deciduous	20x15	1	2	2	3-8	Spring	
Cornus florida 'Rubra'	Pink Dogwood	Deciduous	20x15	1	2	3	3-8	Spring	
Cornus Kousa	Kousa Dogwood	Deciduous	20x10	1	2	4	3-8	Spring	
Cryptomeria japonica	Cryptomeria	Evergreen	50x30	1	1	4	6-9	None	
Cryptomeria japonica 'Globosa Nana'	Nana Globosa Dwarf Cryptomeria	Evergreen	4x4	1	1	3	6-9	None	
Daphne Odora	Daphne Odora	Evergreen	4x4	2	2	3	4-9	Spring	Frost hardy
Dianthus gratianopolitanus 'Fire Witch'	Fire Witch Dianthus	Perennial	1.5x1.5	1	2	3	3-9	Summer	
Distylium 'Vintage Jade'	Vintage Jade Distylium	Evergreen	3x2.5	2	2	2	7-9	Spring	
Dryopteris	Wood Fern	Perennial	4x3	1	3	2	4-8	None	
Dryopteris erythrosora	Autumn Fern	Perennial	2x2	1	3	2	4-8	None	
Echinacea	Purple Cone Flower	Perennial	2x2	1	2	4	3-9	Summer	Mulch heavily in cooler climates
Fatsia japonica	Fatsia	Evergreen	5x5	1	3	3	7-11	Fall	
Festuca glauca 'Sea Urchin'	Sea Urchin Blue Fescue	Perennial	1x1	1	2	3	4-8	Summer	

Scientific Name	Common Name	Status	Size hxw)	Pruning 1-5	Water 1-5	Sun 1-5	Zone	Bloom Season	Special Needs
Forsythia	Forsythia	Deciduous	8x8	2	2	4	5-9	Spring	Full sun for best bloom
Fothergilla gardenii	Fothergilla	Deciduous	4x4	1	2	3	4-9	Spring	
Gardenia jasminoides 'August Beauty'	August Beauty Gardenia	Evergreen	5x5	2	3	4	7-11	Summer, Fall	
Gardenia jasminoides 'Kleim's Hardy'	Hardy Daisy Gardenia	Evergreen	4x4	2	3	4	7-11	Summer, Fall	
Gardenia jasminoides 'Radicans Variegata'	Radicans Gardenia	Evergreen	3x3	2	3	4	7-11	Summer, Fall	
Gaura	Whirling Butterflies	Perennial	3x2	1	1	4	5-9	Summer	
Hamamelis	Witch Hazel	Deciduous	6x6	1	1	3	5-9	Fall	
Heliopsis helianthoides	Heliopsis	Perennial	2x2	1	2	4	3-9	Summer	
Hemerocallis 'Red Hot Returns'	Red Daylily	Perennial	2x2	1	2	4	3-9	Summer	
Hemerocallis 'Stella d'Oro'	Stella d'Oro Daylily	Perennial	2x2	1	2	4	3-9	Summer	
Heuchera	Heuchera	Perennial	2x3	1	2	2	4-9	Summer	
Heuchera 'Caramel'	Caramel Heuchera	Perennial	2x3	1	2	2	4-9	Summer	
Hibiscus syriacus	Rose of Sharon	Deciduous	18x12	1	3	5	5-10	Summer	
Hosta	Big Leaf Hosta	Perennial	4x4	1	2	2	3-8	Summer	
Hosta 'Guacamole'	Guacamole Hosta	Perennial	4x4	1	2	2	3-8	Summer	
Hosta 'Patriot'	Patriot Hosta	Perennial	3x3	1	2	2	3-8	Summer	
Hydrangea Arborescens	Hydrangea Arborescens	Deciduous	6x6	1	3	3	4-9	Summer	
Hydrangea macrophylla 'Bailmacfive' PPAF	Endless Summer Hydrangea	Deciduous	3x3	1	3	3	4-9	Summer	
Hydrangea macrophylla 'Nikko Blue'	Nikko Blue Hydrangea	Deciduous	3x3	1	3	2	4-9	Summer	
Hydrangea macrophylla 'PIIHM-I'	Twist and Shout Hydrangea	Deciduous	4x4	1	3	3	4-9	Summer	
Hydrangea paniculala 'Limelight'	Limelight Hydrangea	Deciduous	6x6	1	3	4	4-9	Summer	
Hylotelephium telephium 'Autumn Joy'	Autumn Joy Sedum	Perennial	2x2	1	1	5	3-8	Fall	
Hyssopus officinalis	Hyssop	Perennial	2x2	1	2	4	4-9	Summer	
Ilex cornuta 'Carissa'	Carissa Holly	Evergreen	4x4	4	2	4	7-9	None-Inconspicuous	
Ilex glabra	Nordic Inkberry Holly	Evergreen	3x3	4	2	4	5-8	None-Inconspicuous	
Ilex x attenuata 'Fosteri'	Foster Holly	Evergreen	20x7	5	2	4	7-9	None-Inconspicuous	
Ilex x 'Emily Brunner'	Emily Brunner Holly	Evergreen	25x15	5	2	4	7-9	None-Inconspicuous	
Ilex x 'Mary Nell'	Mary Nell Holly	Evergreen	15x8	5	2	4	7-9	None-Inconspicuous	
Ilex x 'Nellie R. Stevens'	Nellie R. Stevens Holly	Evergreen	25x15	5	2	4	7-9	None-Inconspicuous	
Illicium Parviflorum	Illicium	Evergreen	5x5	2	1	3	7-10	Spring	

Scientific Name	Common Name	Status	Size hxw)	Pruning 1-5	Water 1-5	Sun 1-5	Zone	Bloom Season	Special Needs
Iris germanica	Bearded Iris	Perennial	2x2	1	4	3	3-8	Spring	
Iris pseudacorus	Yellow Flag Iris	Perennial	2x2	1	4	2	3-8	Spring	
Iris sibirica	Siberian Iris	Perennial	2x2	1	4	3	3-8	Spring	
Iris versicolor	Blue Flag Iris	Perennial	2x2	1	4	2	3-8	Spring	
Juniperus chinensis 'Blue Point'	Blue Point Juniper	Evergreen	15x8	1	1	4	6-9	None	
Juniperus chinensis 'Gold Lace'	Gold Lace Juniper	Evergreen	2.5x6	1	1	4	6-9	None	
Juniperus chinensis 'Sea Green'	Sea Green Juniper	Evergreen	2x5	1	1	4	6-9	None	
Juniperus chinensis 'Spartan'	Spartan Juniper	Evergreen	20x6	1	1	4	6-9	None	
Juniperus communis 'Gold Cone'	Gold Cone Juniper	Evergreen	15x8	1	1	4	6-9	None	
Juniperus communis 'Gold Cone'	Spiral Gold Cone Juniper	Evergreen	15x8	1	1	4	6-9	None	
Juniperus squamata 'Blue Star'	Blue Star Juniper Shrub	Evergreen	3x4	1	1	3	6-9	None	
Lagerstroemia 'Gamad I' Razzle Dazzle Cherry	Dwarf Crape Myrtle	Deciduous	6x6	1	2	4	6-11	Summer	
Lagerstroemia indica 'Whit II' Dynamite	Dynamite Crape Myrtle	Deciduous	15x10	1	2	4	6-11	Summer	
Lagerstroemia indica x fauriei 'Natchez'	Natchez Crape Myrtle	Deciduous	30x10	1	2	4	6-11	Summer	
Lagerstroemia indica x fauriei 'Tonto'	Tonto Crape Myrtle	Deciduous	15x10	1	2	4	6-11	Summer	
Lantana	Lantana	Perennial	3x5	1	2	5	7-11	Summer	
Leucanthemum x superbum	Shasta Daisy	Perennial	2.5x2.5	1	2	4	4-10	Summer	
Liatris spicata	Liatris	Perennial	3x2	1	2	4	5-9	Summer	
Ligustrum sinense 'Sunshine'	Sunshine Ligustrum	Evergreen	4x4	4	2	5	7-10	None-Inconspicuous	
Lilium auratum	Asiatic Lily	Perennial	2x1	1	3	3	4-9	Spring	
Liriope muscari	Liriope	Perennial	2x2	1	1	4	6-10	Summer	
Loropetalum chinense 'Beni-Hime'	Mini Loropetalum	Evergreen	3x3	2	2	3	7-10	Spring	
Loropetalum chinense 'Shang-hi' PP18331	Purple Diamond Loropetalum	Evergreen	5x5	2	2	3	7-10	Spring	
Loropetalum chinense var. rubrum 'Crimson Fire'	Crimson Fire Loropetalum	Evergreen	4x4	2	2	3	7-10	Spring	
Magnolia grandiflora 'Southern Charm'	Teddy Bear Magnolia	Evergreen	20x12	1	2	4	7-9	Spring	
Magnolia x soulangeana	Saucer Magnolia	Deciduous	15x10	1	2	4	7-9	Spring	
Mahonia bealei	Leather Leaf Mahonia	Evergreen	6x4	1	2	2	7-9	Winter	
Miscanthus sinensis 'Adagio'	Adagio Miscanthus Grass	Perennial	5x5	1	1	4	6-10	Summer	
Miscanthus sinensis 'Zebrinus'	Zebra Grass	Perennial	3x3	1	1	3	5-9	None	
Monarda	Bee Balm	Perennial	3x3	1	2	4	2-10	Summer	

Scientific Name	Common Name	Status	Size hxw)	Pruning 1-5	Water 1-5	Sun 1-5	Zone	Bloom Season	Special Needs
Nandina domestica 'Harbour Dwarf'	Harbor Dwarf Nandina	Evergreen	3x3	2	2	3	5-10	Summer	
Ocimum basilicum	Basil	Perennial	2x1	1	2	4	2-11	Summer	Zone 10+ to treat as perennial
Origanum vulgare	Oregano	Perennial	3x2	1	2	4	5-10	Summer	
Osmanthus fragrans	Tea Olive	Evergreen	6x6	3	2	3	8-10	Spring	
Osmanthus heterophyllus	False Holly	Evergreen	3x3	2	2	3	6-9	Fall	
Paeonia	Peony	Perennial	2.5x4	1	3	3	3-8	Spring	Need winter cold to bloom
Perovskia atriplicifolia	Russian Sage	Perennial	5x5	1	2	5	5-10	Fall	
Petrosedum rupestre 'Blue Spruce'	Blue Spruce Sedum	Perennial	1x3	1	1	5	3-9	Fall	
Phlox paniculata	Tall Garden Phlox	Perennial	3.5x2	1	2	3	3-8	Fall	
Physostegia virginia	Obedient Plant	Perennial	2x1	1	2	4	3-10	Fall	
Picea abies 'Pendula'	Dwarf Weeping Norway Spruce	Evergreen	5x5	1	2	3	3-8	None	Mulch roots heavily to cool in warmer zones
Picea glauca	Dwarf Alberta Spruce	Evergreen	5x4	1	2	3	3-8	None	Mulch roots heavily to cool in warmer zones
Picea pungens 'Globosa'	Dwarf Blue Spruce	Evergreen	2x2	1	2	3	3-8	None	Mulch roots heavily to cool in warmer zones
Pieris japonica	Pieris	Evergreen	3x3	2	2	2	5-9	Winter	Prefers shade and acidic pH
Pinus mugo	Dwarf Mugo Pine	Evergreen	4x3	1	1	3	3-7	None-Inconspicuous	Use in partial shade in hotter climates
Prunus laurocerasus	Otto Luyken Laurel	Evergreen	3.5x3.5	3	2	3	6-8	Spring	
Prunus pendula	Weeping Cherry	Deciduous	25x15	1	2	4	4-8	Spring	
Pulmonaria officinalis	Lungwort	Perennial	1x1	1	2	4	4-8	Spring	
Rhododendron 'Conleb'	Autumn Embers Encore Azalea	Evergreen	4x4.5	2	3	4	7-10	Spring, Fall	
Rhododendron 'Mootum' PP18416	Autumn Moonlight Encore Azalea	Evergreen	3x3	2	3	4	7-10	Spring, Fall	
Rhododendron 'Roblec' PP15339	Autumn Carnation Encore Azalea	Evergreen	4x4.5	2	3	4	7-10	Spring, Fall	
Rhododendron 'Robled' PP15862	Autumn Chiffon Encore Azalea	Evergreen	3.5x3.5	2	3	4	7-10	Spring, Fall	
Rhododendron Catawbiense	Rhododendron Catawbiense	Evergreen	8x6	1	3	3	4-8	Spring	Plant with organic material such as 1/2 soil, 1/2 shredded pine. Keep soil moist
Rhododendron 'Gumpo'	Gumpo Azalea	Evergreen	3x3	2	3	3	7-9	Spring	
Rhododendron indicum 'GG Gerbing'	G.G. Gerbing Azalea	Evergreen	3x3	2	3	3	7-9	Spring	
Rhododendron indicum 'Satsuki azalea'	Satsuki Azalea	Evergreen	3x3	2	3	3	7-9	Spring	
Rhododendron x 'George Tabor'	George Tabor Azalea	Evergreen	5x5	2	3	3	7-9	Spring	
Rosa 'Meijocos'	Drift Rose	Deciduous	3x3	2	2	5	5-10	Summer	
Rosa Radrazz	Knock Out Rose	Deciduous	4x4	2	2	5	5-10	Summer	

Scientific Name	Common Name	Status	Size hxw)	Pruning 1-5	Water 1-5	Sun 1-5	Zone	Bloom Season	Special Needs
Rosmarinus officinalis	Rosemary	Perennial	3x4	1	2	4	5-10	Summer	
Rudbeckia hirta	Blackeyed Susan	Perennial	2x2	1	2	4	3-9	Summer	
Salvia officinalis	Sage	Perennial	3x3	1	2	4	5-8	Fall	9-11 grown as an annual; doesn't tolerate heat well
Sambucus racemosa 'Lemony Lace'	Elderberry Lemony Lace	Deciduous	5x5	1	3	2	3-7	Spring	
Sedum nuttallianum	Yellow Sedum	Perennial	1x3	1	1	5	3-9	Fall	
Selleophutum Urb. Tuckermannia Nutt.	Coreposis	Perennial	2.5x1	1	2	4	3-9	Summer	
Sempervivum tectorum	Hens and Chicks	Succulent	2x2	1	1	5	3-8	None	Well-drained soil
Solenostemon scutellarioides 'Color Blaze'	Colorblaze Coleus	Semi Tropical	3x2	1	2	4	10-11	Summer	Semi Tropical- annual most zones
Stachys byzantina	Lamb's Ear	Perennial	2x2	1	2	3	4-8	Summer	Very drought hardy
Stokesia laeis	Stokes Aster	Perennial	2x2	1	2	4	8-9a	Summer	
Tagetes	Marigold	Perennial	2x2	1	2	4	2-11	Summer	
Taraxacum	Dandelion Weed	Perennial	1x1	3	1	5	3-10	Summer	Don't allow this to go to seed; readily spreads
Taxus x media	Hicks Yew	Evergreen	6x4	1	2	3	4-8	None	
Ternstroemia gymnanthera	Cleyera	Evergreen	10x8	4	2	3	7-10	Spring	
Thuja occidentalis	Emerald Green Arborvitae	Evergreen	15x5	1	3	4	4-8	None	
Thuja standishii × plicata 'Green Giant'	Green Giant Arborvitae	Evergreen	20x10	1	3	4	4-8	None	
Thuja occidentalis 'Degroot's Spire'	Degroots Spire Arborvitae	Evergreen	20x3	1	3	4	4-8	None	
Thymus vulgaris	Thyme	Perennial	1x2	1	2	4	5-10	Summer	
Tiarella	Tiarella Foam Flower	Perennial	2x2	1	3	3	4-9	Summer	
Trachelospermum jasminoides	Star Jasmine	Perennial	vine	3	2	5	7-10	Summer	
Tropaeolum	Nasturtium	Perennial	2x5	1	2	4	4-8	Summer	Perennial in zone 9-11
Tsuga canadensis	Eastern Hemlock	Evergreen	6x6	1	3	2	5-7	None	Mulch roots heavily to cool in warmer zones
Veronica spicata	Veronica Spicata	Perennial	2.5x2.5	1	2	4	4-8	Summer	
Viburnum opulus 'Roseum'	Snowball Viburnum	Deciduous	10x10	1	2	3	3-8	Spring	
Viola tricolor var hortensis	Pansy	Annual	2x1	1	2	3	NA	Winter	Cold Hardy
Yucca filamentosa 'Color Guard'	Color Guard Yucca	Succulent	2x2	1	1	5	5-11	Summer	
Yucca gigantea	Cane Yucca	Succulent	6x4	1	1	5	5-11	Summer	
Yucca nana	Yucca	Succulent	4x4	1	1	5	5-11	Summer	
Zantedeschia aethiopica	Calla Lily	Perennial	1.5x1.5	1	3	4	4-9	Spring	
Zinnia elegans	Zinnia	Annual	3x1	1	2	5	4-11	Summer	

Common Name	Gardens Where Featured
Glossy Abelia	Exit Stage Left
Edward Goucher Abelia	Always a Bride's Maid
Kaleidoscope Abelia	Look At My Bloomers!; Business Casual; Executive Privilege
Mardi Gras Abelia	Heavenly Hedge; Fabuloso
Bloodgood Japanese Maple	Shady Corners, Not Shady Neighbors; That's Amore; Fall Festival
Emperor Japanese Maple	Fabuloso
Dissectum Japanese Maple	Serenity at Last; Zen Vogue; That's Amore
Fernleaf Yarrow	Flirty Fences; Southern Belle
Acorus Grass	Buffed, Puffed and Fluffed; Rain, No Rain…Whatever; Brand New Do; That's Amore; La Tee Da
Agapanthus	Come Sit a Spell; Serenity at Last; Prince Charming
Agave	Size Matters
Ice Plant	Size Matters; Spectacular Debut
Chocolate Chip Ajuga	Serenity at Last
Chives	Pot Garden; Bee's Knees; Play with Your Food
Dill	Pot Garden; Play with Your Food; Granny's Pantry
Artemisia	Easy Street
Foxtail Fern	Afternoon Tea; Rocky Top Retreat; La Tee Da
Cast Iron Plant	Easy Street, Prince Charming
Astilbe	Stealing Kisses
Japanese Painted Fern	Afternoon Tea; Rocky Top Retreat
Aucuba Japonica	Stealing Kisses
Gold Dust Aucuba	Prince Charming
Soft Caress Mahonia	Counting Sheep; Stealing Kisses
Borage	Pot Garden, Tootie Fruity – Hold the Fruit; Granny's Pantry
Butterfly Shrub	Spectacular Debut
Dwarf Butterfly Shrub	Sassy and Sunny; Rhymes with Emu; Common Scents; Southwest But With Color
Green Beauty Boxwood	Home Sweet Home
Baby Gem Boxwood	Brand New Do; Jacket and Tie
Wintergreen Boxwood	Eye Candy; Jacket and Tie

Common Name	Gardens Where Featured
American Boxwood	That's Amore; Fall Festival
Camellia Japonica	That's Amore; La Tee Da
Sasanqua Camellia	Nook Nook, Who's There?; Eye Candy; Encore Performance
Canna Lily	The New Black; Homecoming Queen; No Apologies
Caryopteris	Flirty Fences
Vinca	Shady Corners, Not Shady Neighbors; Jack and Jill; De-Vine-Ly Simple
Deodar Cedar	Rock and Roll; Rocky Top Retreat
Dwarf Plum Yew	Cheeky Garden; Encore Performance; Size Matters
Flowering Quince	Frankly My Dear
Gold Mop Cypress	Just the Facts; Heavenly Hedge; Spring Fling; Executive Privilege
Hinoki Cypress	Just the Facts; No Peeking
Gold Thread Cypress	No Prune, No Kidding; Business Casual; Rocky Top Retreat
Clethra Alnifolia	Encore Performance; Sugar Daddy; Counting Sheep
Cordyline	Size Matters
Cilantro	Pot Garden; Play with Your Food; Down to Earth; Granny's Pantry
White Dogwood	Nook Nook, Who's There?; Silver Lining
Pink Dogwood	Cheeky Garden
Kousa Dogwood	Just the Facts
Cryptomeria	Rocky Top Retreat; No Peeking
Nana Globosa Dwarf Cryptomeria	Magic Balls and Broomsticks; Executive Privilege; No Prune, No Kidding; Jacket and Tie; Stealing Kisses
Daphne Odora	Silver Lining
Fire Witch Dianthus	Flirty Fences; Size Matters
Vintage Jade Distylium	Cheeky Garden
Wood Fern	Easy Street; Prince Charming
Autumn Fern	Cheeky Garden, Nook Nook, Who's There?; Afternoon Tea; Rocky Top Retreat; Easy Like Sunday Morning; La Tee Da
Purple Cone Flower	Sassy and Sunny
Fatsia	Zen Vogue; Afternoon Tea; Rocky Top Retreat; No Peeking; Stealing Kisses
Sea Urchin Blue Fescue	Easy Street
Forsythia	Sunny Disposition; Common Scents; Bee's Knees
Fothergilla	Bee's Knees; Granny's Pantry

Common Name	Gardens Where Featured
August Beauty Gardenia	Flirty Fences; Moonlight Serenade; Spectacular Debut
Hardy Daisy Gardenia	Spring Fling; Executive Privilege; Gravitas, Beer Thirty
Radicans Gardenia	Moonlight Serenade; Spring Fling; Encore Performance;
Whirling Butterflies	Sassy and Sunny
Witch Hazel	Sunny Disposition; Tootie Fruity – Hold the Fruit
Heliopsis	Southwest But with Color; Homecoming Queen
Red Daylily	Common Scents; No Apologies
Stella d'Oro Daylily	Style for Miles; Sunny Disposition; Spring Fling; Common Scents; Executive Privilege; Beer Thirty; Season's Greetings; Jacket and Tie
Heuchera	Counting Sheep
Caramel Heuchera	Serenity at Last
Rose of Sharon	Frankly My Dear
Big Leaf Hosta	Shady Corners, Not Shady Neighbors; Nook Nook, Who's There? ; Afternoon Tea; La Tee Da
Guacamole Hosta	Come Sit a Spell; Cheeky Garden
Patriot Hosta	Cheeky Garden; Pot Garden
Hydrangea Arborescens	Shady Corners, Not Shady Neighbors
Endless Summer Hydrangea	Style for Miles; Beer Thirty; Homecoming Queen
Nikko Blue Hydrangea	Shady Corners, Not Shady Neighbors; Nook Nook, Who's There?
Twist and Shout Hydrangea	Encore Performance; Rocky Top Retreat
Limelight Hydrangea	Style for Miles; Buffed, Puffed and Fluffed; Spring Fling; Nook Nook, Who's There?; Jack and Jill; Southern Belle
Autumn Joy Sedum	Come Sit a Spell; Bursting at the Seams; Always a Bride's Maid; Rain, No Rain…Whatever; Southern Belle; Spectacular Debut
Hyssop	Rhymes with Emu; Pot Garden; Tootie Fruity – Hold the Fruit; Down to Earth
Carissa Holly	Spring Fling; Nook Nook, Who's There?; Enticing Entrances; Fall Festival
Nordic Inkberry Holly	Beauty Queen; Eye Candy; Zen Vogue; Brand New Do
Foster Holly	Home Sweet Home; Raising the Bar
Emily Brunner Holly	Raising the Bar
Mary Nell Holly	Business in the Front, Party in the Back; Raising the Bar
Nellie R. Stevens Holly	Home Sweet Home; Raising the Bar
Illicium	No Peeking; Belle of the Ball
Bearded Iris	Afternoon Tea
Yellow Flag Iris	Pot Garden; Old Friends

Common Name	Gardens Where Featured
Siberian Iris	Old Friends
Blue Flag Iris	Comfy Cozy; Old Friends
Blue Point Juniper	Spring Fling; Rock and Roll; Brand New Do; Executive Privilege; Rocky Top Retreat
Gold Lace Juniper	Easy Peesy; Southern Belle; No Peeking
Sea Green Juniper	Easy Peesy
Spartan Juniper	No Prune. No Kidding; Fabuloso
Gold Cone Juniper	Exit Stage Left; Enticing Entrances
Spiral Gold Cone Juniper	Business Casual
Blue Star Juniper Shrub	Home Sweet Home; Easy Peesy
Dwarf Crape Myrtle	Gravitas; Sugar Daddy
Dynamite Crape Myrtle	The New Black; Sugar Daddy
Natchez Crape Myrtle	Look at My Bloomers!; Executive Privilege; Easy Like Sunday Morning
Tonto Crape Myrtle	Encore Performance
Lantana	Bursting at the Seams; Jack and Jill; Homecoming Queen
Shasta Daisy	Flirty Fences; Moonlight Serenade; Spring Fling; Jack and Jill; Homecoming Queen; Spectacular Debut
Liatris	Pot Garden; Homecoming Queen
Sunshine Ligustrum	Sunny Disposition; Business in the Front, Party in the Back; Jacket and Tie
Asiatic Lily	Come Sit a Spell; Business in the Front, Party in the Back
Liriope	Come Sit a Spell; Nook Nook, Who's There?; Brand New Do; Jacket and Tie; Beer Thirty
Mini Loropetalum	Come Sit a Spell; Zen Vogue; Eye Candy; Brand New Do; That's Amore; Gravitas; Jack and Jill
Purple Diamond Loropetalum	Heavenly Hedge; Rock and Roll; Home Sweet Home; Fabuloso
Crimson Fire Loropetalum	Just the Facts; Spring Fling; Belle of the Ball
Teddy Bear Magnolia	No Prune. No Kidding.; Rocky Top Retreat
Saucer Magnolia	Prom Date
Leather Leaf Mahonia	Stealing Kisses
Adagio Miscanthus Grass	Come Sit a Spell; Comfy Cozy; Rock and Roll; Afternoon Tea; Rain, No Rain…Whatever; Southwest but with Color; Old Friends
Zebra Grass	Rain, No Rain…Whatever; Brand New Do
Bee Balm	Sassy and Sunny; Always a Bride's Maid; Common Scents; Tootie Fruity – Hold the Fruit; Granny's Pantry; Beer Thirty
Harbor Dwarf Nandina	Always a Bride's Maid; Beer Thirty
Basil	Pot Garden; Bee's Knees; Play with Your Food

Common Name	Gardens Where Featured
Oregano	Pot Garden; Play with Your Food; Down to Earth
Tea Olive	Encore Performance; Common Scents; Business Casual; Rocky Top Retreat
False Holly	Just the Facts; Encore Performance
Peony	Old Friends
Russian Sage	Bursting at the Seams
Blue Spruce Sedum	Eye Candy
Tall Garden Phlox	Sassy and Sunny
Obedient Plant	Play with Your Food; Southern Belle
Dwarf Weeping Norway Spruce	Easy Peesy
Dwarf Alberta Spruce	Shady Corners, Not Shady Neighbors; Enticing Entrances
Dwarf Blue Spruce	Rhymes with Emu; Nook Nook, Who's There?; Rocky Top Retreat
Pieris	Eye Candy
Dwarf Mugo Pine	Afternoon Tea; Rocky Top Retreat
Otto Luyken Laurel	Business in the Front, Party in the Back; Easy Street
Weeping Cherry	Always a Bride's Maid
Lungwort	Easy Street
Autumn Embers Encore Azalea	Look at My Bloomers!; The New Black; Spring Fling; Executive Privilege
Autumn Moonlight Encore Azalea	Moonlight Serenade; Prom Date; Brand New Do; Enticing Entrances
Autumn Carnation Encore Azalea	Prom Date
Autumn Chiffon Encore Azalea	Sassy and Sunny; Always a Bride's Maid; That's Amore; Beer Thirty
Rhododendron Catawbiense	La Tee Da; Easy Street; Prince Charming
Gumpo Azalea	Zen Vogue
G.G. Gerbing Azalea	Shady Corners, Not Shady Neighbors
Satsuki Azalea	Eye Candy
George Tabor Azalea	Serenity at Last; Always a Bride's Maid; Rocky Top Retreat; La Tee Da
Drift Rose	Always a Bride's Maid; Common Scents; Gravitas; Frankly My Dear; Beer Thirty; No Apologies; Southern Belle
Knock Out Rose	Style for Miles; The New Black; Buffed, Puffed and Fluffed; Beauty Queen; Prom Date; Spring Fling; Jack and Jill; Beer Thirty; Season's Greetings
Rosemary	Pot Garden; Rain, No Rain...Whatever; Southwest but with Color; Bee's Knees; Down to Earth; Jack and Jill; Spectacular Debut
Blackeyed Susan	Bursting at the Seams; Sunny Disposition; Common Scents; Jack and Jill; Old Friends; Spectacular Debut
Sage	Come Sit a Spell

Appendix B

Cross Referenced Plant Index

Common Name	Gardens Where Featured
Elderberry Lemony Lace	Counting Sheep
Yellow Sedum	Rain, No Rain...Whatever
Coreposis	Sassy and Sunny; Homecoming Queen
Hens and Chicks	Size Matters
Colorblaze Coleus	Come Sit a Spell
Lamb's Ear	Spring Fling
Stokes Aster	Southern Belle
Marigold	Pot Garden; Bee's Knees; Play with Your Food; Granny's Pantry
Dandelion Weed	Play with Your Food
Hicks Yew	Spring Fling
Cleyera	Brand New Do; Gravitas
Emerald Green Arborvitae	Magic Balls and Broomsticks; Eye Candy; Rock and Roll; Jacket and Tie; Height of Excellence
Green Giant Arborvitae	No Prune. No Kidding.; Height of Excellence
Degroots Spire Arborvitae	Gravitas
Thyme	Come Sit a Spell; Pot Garden; Bee's Knees; Play with Your Food; Down to Earth; Southern Belle
Tiarella Foam Flower	Nook Nook, Who's There?
Star Jasmine	Flirty Fences; De-Vine-Ly Simple
Nasturtium	Tootie Fruity – Hold the Fruit
Eastern Hemlock	Rocky Top Retreat; Prince Charming
Veronica Spicata	Rhymes with Emu; Jack and Jill
Snowball Viburnum	Moonlight Serenade; Spring Fling
Pansy	Pot Garden
Color Guard Yucca	Rain, No Rain...Whatever; That's Amore
Cane Yucca	Southwest but With Color
Yucca	Southwest but With Color
Calla Lily	Sunny Disposition
Zinnia	Bursting at the Seams